D1246011

LEADERSHIP COACHING
IN CHINA

© Fielding Graduate University, 2021
Published in the United States of America.

Fielding University Press is an imprint of Fielding Graduate University. Its objective is to advance the research and scholarship of Fielding faculty, students, alumni and associated scholars around the world, using a variety of publishing platforms. For more information, please contact Fielding University Press, attn. Jean-Pierre Isbouts, 2020 De la Vina Street, Santa Barbara, CA 93105. Email: jisbouts@fielding.edu. On the web: www.fielding.edu/universitypress.

All rights reserved. No part of this publication may be reproduced or transmitted, in any form by any means, without the prior permission of Fielding University Press.

Library of Congress Cataloging-in-Publication data
Leadership Coaching in China by Marjorie Woo et al. (Eds.)

1. Business Studies – Leadership Coaching

LEADERSHIP COACHING IN CHINA

EDITED BY
MARJORIE WOO, TOM PAYNE, JAMES WARNER
AND JEFF HASENFRATZ

Fielding University Press

Katrina S. Rogers
President, Fielding Graduate University

Monique L. Snowden
Provost, Fielding Graduate University

Jean-Pierre Isbouts
Managing Editor, Fielding University Press

Leadership Coaching in China

Editors:
Marjorie Woo, Tom Payne, James Warner and Jeff Hasenfratz

Contributors:
Bryan Adkins
Alan Babington-Smith
Joey W.K. Chan
Joseph Chan
Daniel Denison
Joyce yuan Gong
Jeff Hasenfratz
Axel Kuhlmann
Sabine Menon
Andrew Newmark
Allen Parchem
Tom Payne
Jason Ramey
Frank Rexach
Marcia Reynolds
Amanda Shang
Monique L. Snowden
Cindy J.W. Su
Pam Van Dyke
Gary Wang
Yi Wang
Yimin Wang
James Warner
Marjorie Woo
Jack denfeld Wood
Katherine Xin
Tianran Yin
Alex Eunkyeong Yu
Nancy Zhang
Karen Zong

PRAISE FOR
LEADERSHIP COACHING IN CHINA

"A multi-faceted collection of insights into leadership coaching, Chinese culture, and the relationship between the two! This is a unique resource for anyone interested in any of these three fascinating topics."
   - Robert Kegan, Professor, Harvard University

"This is a must-read book for those interested in coaching in China - whether business leaders, professional coaches, or those thinking of starting careers in the coaching field. The editors have gathered the collective wisdom of experts with years of professional coaching experience in China and other parts of the world."
   - Juan Antonio Fernandez, Professor, CEIBS

"Required reading for all consultants in China, beginners and veterans alike, Marjorie Woo has created a carefully curated collection of insightful articles chronicling the early challenges, initial acceptance and future course of coaching and advisory work in China."
   - Grant W. Levitan, PhD, Senior Partner, RHR International LLP

"Wish this book was available during my assignment as HR Director in China from 2006 to 2015. This book, packed with relevant topics arranged in a logical flow, is easy to read. The case studies, experiences and lessons learnt, the conversations amongst professors, practitioners, coaches and coachees are insightful."
   - Dr. Kuan Thye Sean, FedEx Express Asia Pacific

"Leadership Coaching in China' is the comprehensive, experienced-based guide enabling Chinese and foreign leaders and coaches to fully leverage the benefits of coaching across organizations. Besides learning how to structure coaching practices in a culturally-effective way, readers will gain empowering insights about how to be a better leader and a better coach, and therefore co-create greater value with others."
   - Jean-Francois Cousin, MCC, 2019 Chairman of the ICF Global Board

"This is an insightful book which highlights the need for formal leadership coaching in an interconnected world in which China is playing an increasingly important role. Understanding how Chinese cultural nuances can support the development of China-responsible leaders, vs. simply following tried and tested western approaches, provides valuable perspective and leverage."
   - Jafar Amin, President, Wells Fargo Asia Pacific

"So glad to read this book, which focuses on leadership coaching in China. Coaching is a great tool to develop leaders in China, especially those who have gone through the traditional education system here. The coaching experience I had, with one of the editors of this book, definitely made a positive difference for me."
   - Michael Zhang, General Manager, Albea China

"This highly recommended edited volume is both an academic analysis of the scope and practice of leadership coaching in China and also a practical guide to successful practice. Its introduction into the Chinese context has been particularly important. Western managers have needed to learn to operate in an environment that is less transparent than normally encountered. Chinese managers, who probably understand the local context, nevertheless often have to translate that context to Western accounting, managerial, and negotiating norms. This book is therefore very useful for three reasons: 1) studying the Chinese context of business practices, 2) understanding the methodology of coaching, and 3) developing and evolving an effective coaching business and approach. The volume provides an important understanding of the Western and Chinese ingredients central to operating in a cross-cultural environment."
   - Dr. William Vocke, Fulbright Foundation

"This book offers critical perspectives that explore the complexity of coaching in China, including leadership preparation, the use of data, cultural influences, team coaching, and the importance of understanding human development for evidence based coaching. Useful for any coach or leader working in china or with multinational firms."
   - Dr. Katrina S. Rogers, President, Fielding Graduate University

"As a scholar working in education management for 24 years, I can understand the important value of Leadership Coaching described in this book for managers. This is a brand-new way to build the soul of managers, and it can also be said to be an exploration and innovation of leadership development. Whether it is the excellent global leadership that global business organizations aspire to, or the excellent educational leadership that educational institutions aspire to, you can get useful inspiration from this book. 'Leadership Coaching in China' is another masterpiece of the promoters Professor Mobley and Dr. Marjorie to promote cultural and professional exchanges between China and the United States."
   - Lizhong Yu, Professor, China Eastern Normal University

"I truly believe that the journey for leadership coaching is as challenging as the Journey West in Chinese historical works. I also believe that it will be blooming in China soon and will become a "religion" for the business community. I congratulate the editors, especially Dr. Woo, and the authors for putting so much time and effort to make the book possible. I know the impact will be great and long lasting."
   - Jacky So, VP and Dean, Macau University of Science and Technology

Acknowledgements

We would like to thank the many people involved in taking this book from inception to completion. First, we would like to acknowledge the late Dr. William H. Mobley, who generated the idea for sharing the knowledge and experiences of those working in leadership coaching in China in a book. This seed of an idea has grown and produced a resource that will enhance and strengthen leadership coaching in China into the future.

We offer heartfelt thanks to all of the talented and experienced coaches-authors-professionals who contributed to the book by sharing the experiences, wisdom, and insights gained through shaping the transformation of leadership development China. Their efforts have brought together insights from Eastern and Western coaching approaches which make it possible for future leaders to gain perspectives different from those available only from their own native cultures and environments. A special note of gratitude to Samantha Oates who coordinated and curated the manuscript throughout the process, and to Frank Rexach who contributed his marketing expertise to support the book launch.

We would also like to express our heartfelt appreciation to Fielding Graduate University President, Dr. Katrina S. Rogers, and to Provost, Dr. Monique L. Snowden for their vision of and commitment to an equitable and sustainable world by supporting the publishing of a book about coaching beyond US borders, and for contributions to the book's content.

We would also like to express our deep gratitude to Fielding University Press Executive Editor, Dr. Jean-Pierre Isbouts, for his guidance and direction in making this book a reality. His enthusiasm, publishing expertise and experience were key in moving this endeavor from an idea to a completed publication. We would also like to express our gratitude to the Fielding University Press team, notably Nancy Haight, who so ably copy edited the initial manuscript, to Catherine Labrador, who supervised the FUP team of artists, and to the many artists themselves, whose graphical layout supported the sensitive reflection of Chinese culture.

TABLE OF CONTENTS

Dr. Marjorie J. Woo and Dr. William H. Mobley, Endowment Chair on "Servant Leadership" from Dong-Hai University, Taipei, Taiwan (Keystone Group, Inc.).

In Dedication:
William "Bill" Mobley

November 15, 1941 - March 25, 2020

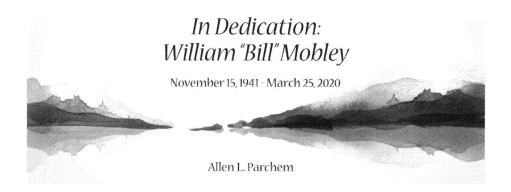

Allen L. Parchem

This volume will allow the reader to explore the evolution of the practice of coaching in China. The evolution is many-faceted and robust. Now that so many practitioners and researchers have embraced and adapted leadership coaching in China and in other Asian countries, it may seem that this evolution was inevitable. But the pioneers of leadership coaching in Asia had a delicate job of balancing research on coaching in the West and the applicability of such knowledge in the East. It took a patient practitioner to plant the ideas, to nurture the practice of coaching in a unique culture, and to encourage the adoption of this new management development tool.

Foremost amongst the pioneers was William H. "Bill" Mobley, PhD. Bill had a distinguished professional journey. The first two-thirds of his career included Texas A&M University, where he served as President (1988-1993) and Chancellor of the Texas A&M University System (1993-1994). His interests during this period began to branch out, and he promoted international educational opportunities for faculty and students. He then moved to China in 1994 for the final third of his career, residing in Hong Kong, then Shanghai and Macau and founding Mobley Group Pacific, a consulting firm specializing in organization and leadership development. He soon became involved in the academic world in Asia, teaching at Hong Kong University of Science and Technology, the China Europe International Business School (CEIBS), and Macau University. At CEIBS he was honored as the first Professor Emeritus.

But all the honors and accomplishments do not really describe why Bill was such a perfect pioneer for coaching in Asia. He was the ultimate patient gardener. He allowed ideas and concepts to take root and flourish. Equally important, he did the same with the people he met, collaborated with, and taught. He knew how to nurture both people and ideas.

This volume is not a series of tributes to this kind and gracious man. He would not want such a book, and his modesty would not allow it. What he wanted was to celebrate the growth of the practice of coaching and gently urge others to move the practice forward. He never doubted that the basic philosophy undergirding coaching was adaptable to the Asian mindset. You will read evidence of the influence of his approach in the chapters of this volume. The authors all had a connection with Bill. Aided by his wife, Marjorie Woo, PhD, Bill knew how to recognize and celebrate the growth and accomplishments of those around them. He would be most proud of the contributors to this volume [1].

[1] For a more complete coverage of Dr. Mobley's life, please visit: https://www. dignitymemorial.com/obituaries/austin-tx/william-mobley-9098909

Foreword

Marcia Reynolds

It is my honor and pleasure to set the stage for this important collection of insights that will tell the story, give the facts, and hopefully inspire the further growth of leadership coaching in China. It is a critical time for the leadership in Chinese and foreign multinational organizations (MNC) to evolve as the country rises in economic stature, while the requirements for building closer relationships with colleagues and employees also increases. This latter requirement includes the need to engage in group dialogue more effectively, both live and remotely.

I have been teaching coaching skills and coaching executives in China for over 10 years. When I started teaching classes for leaders and coaches, hiring coaches was largely reserved to support North American and European executives based in MNCs in China. Over the years, the acceptance of coaching in Chinese organizations has also grown, as China has undertaken four simultaneous changes: marketization, urbanization, privatization, and globalization.

These changes sparked the curiosity of Chinese executives about evolving Western leadership practices. They also gave Chinese top performers a glimpse of different ways they could be managed and developed, creating the demand for their leaders to use new engagement practices. As a result, I witnessed an increase in both teaching leaders how to use a coaching approach in their conversations, as well as requests for well-trained, Chinese-speaking leadership coaches.

Yet coaching is still considered new to many Chinese executives, which continues to pose challenges to the expansion of coaching in the country. Many older executives remain skeptical of the value of having a coach. Concepts such as executive presence, creating psychological safety, using emotions to set the conversational tone, active listening, and authenticity require a shift in mindset, as well as in the behavior of such leaders. Some resist the changes, saying the coach doesn't understand what it takes to be successful in their company. If the coach is not Chinese, the executive often adds a statement about the coach's lack of knowledge of how leadership works "in this part of the world." Coaches need to be adept at transforming such resistance to acceptance if they are to be successful in China.

In addition, given the value Confucianism places on hierarchy, Chinese executives may find it difficult to feel the partnership is necessary for coaching to be effective. The coach is neither a subordinate nor an expert, so the leader might not understand how best to relate to the coach. Yet, if the coach is seen as a peer, the executive might avoid sharing anything that makes him or her look weak. It is critical for the coach to know how to describe the intended coaching relationship, the benefits of that relationship to the executive, and why this approach supports executive development well. There must be an agreement on the expectations of both the executive and the coach. This book offers the information coaches need to handle such challenges well, and for leaders to see the value of leadership coaching.

Given cultural nuances, the successful coaching of Chinese executives may well require a longer rapport-building period than is typical with Western executives. Coaching relationships tend to involve business and leadership mentoring as well as coaching. Understanding how best to use a hybrid approach, while also remaining a thought partner for the executive, will be important in maintaining and increasing the value of coaching in China.

Even taking cultural differences into account, the ROI from using coaching for executive development in China appears to be strong. Such returns include greater productivity and effectiveness, more rapid onboarding of executives, and higher engagement and retention of top performers. Many leaders in my classes have told me that while they don't necessarily like making shifts in how they relate to others, they know they must do so in order to succeed in today's business world.

I therefore applaud the concepts and practices described in this book. It shares the history of leadership coaching in China, outlines current challenges, and mentions benefits specific to Chinese executives. It also describes typical coaching engagements, including stakeholder participation and what coaches need to know to prepare and deliver coaching, and it looks at the impact of leadership coaching on individuals, teams, and organizations. As you can see, the book is a comprehensive guide that will be useful to both leaders and coaches for years to come.

Finally, I especially praise the ongoing and persistent efforts of Marjorie Woo to elevate executive performance in China. When I first met Marjorie, I saw her as a wise and elegant businesswoman. Then I got to know her better. Beyond her mastery of formality is a fiercely-focused, funny, and clever woman committed to bringing quality leadership coaching to China. Her passion is the heart of this book. China is fortunate to have Marjorie's desire to create a lasting and powerful success story.

Preface

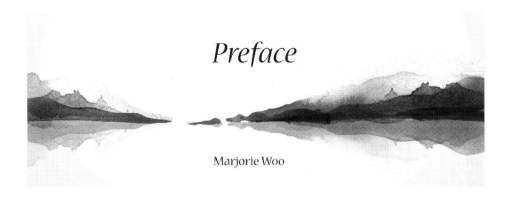

Marjorie Woo

As Dr. William H. (Bill) Mobley stated in the Advances in Global Leadership series, "Leadership and coaching theories are like fingerprints; everyone has them, and no two are alike."

The study of leadership coaching has been bedeviling scholars, practitioners, and business executives since learners in this community first organized themselves. In the past 25 years, the coaching field has been advancing on many fronts. In this book, we would like to focus on what we have learned, are learning, and hope to be co-creating in China in the future. In our exploration of the past, present, and future of leadership coaching in China, we seek to identify ways leadership coaching functions, and to find alternative ways to innovate across a variety of situations. We explore the challenge of applying leadership coaching in the China context, with authors sharing their experience and insights from coaching in multinational corporations, in Chinese enterprises (public and private) and with entrepreneurs.

For the purpose of providing context, I've added below a slide based on data from a recent global study done by the ICF, which I recently used in a presentation made at the 5th Annual China Executive Coaching Conference. It offers a snapshot of where the coaching field is in Asia, including China.

Key Statistics-Asia

From the slide, a few interesting "takeaways" emerge:

• The average hourly coaching fee, globally, at US $240, is a bit lower than it is in Asia.

• The average coaching fee may be a bit higher in China, given a relative shortage of certified coaches in the country.

• There are about 18,000 leadership coaches in the world, with just over 2000 in Asia.

• The level of accreditation (% of coaches in the market) is just about the same in Asia as it is globally.

• The annual revenue per coach, from coaching, is not particularly high; from this we can assume that most coaches do not practice full time, but rather consult, or provide training or other services, as well.

• 73% of potential clients expect the coaches they hire to be credentialed. In terms of obstacles to the growth of coaching in China, 41% of potential clients were concerned about uncredentialed or unprofessional coaches in the market, and 47% didn't know how to judge the value proposition of coaching to their organization. (The value proposition of leadership coaching, as well as credentialing, are topics addressed in this volume.)

The world of business, in the past 30 years, has changed dramatically. Interestingly, we now seem to be trending backward, from global to local, and with a new twist: technology is enabling and connecting people on Zoom and other conferencing applications globally. Everyone is trying to cope and to figure out how to deal with the current situation more effectively. The coaching field is experiencing similar challenges, as we have had to shift from in-person coaching to replicating that feel and safety through Zoom, Webex, Skype and other online media platforms. There is no question that people's adaptive capabilities have been tested. Many people have shared with us that they sometimes feel as if they are trying to navigate in unfamiliar waters. Our intention is to help you all become better navigators on your journeys.

To help us navigate this project, we have brought together a team of scholars, leadership coaches, and business leaders, with diverse interests and experience, to share their observations and insights in dealing with the challenges (including COVID-19) they have faced in China. What we have all realized is that we have to adapt and be resilient, which is what we ask of our coachees. Our aim is to make this sharing of experience and insights helpful to you and to the next generation of leaders and coaches in China and beyond. We have focused on three areas, which we think will appeal to the diverse audience who may read this book in search of answers. We have tried to represent some historical developments and current thinking, in the past, present and future of leadership coaching in China, in a business and societal context.

As organizations and leadership become more global, there are pressing needs for better-developed conceptual models and definitions of what is meant by leadership coaching. More empirical evidence, effective processes, and tools for developing leaders and professional coaches are also needed. In addition, there is a need to integrate models and empirical evidence from multiple cultures and from non-Western authors. The published leadership coaching literature continues to be dominated by Western culture, practitioners, and scholars. Yet, many of the leadership coaching challenges involve emerging markets and the integration of Western and non-Western cultures.

We believe that exploring evidence-based coaching (EBC) will continue to offer some of the greatest returns, as coach and coachee look at and leverage the same reliable and credible data to help them achieve desired outcomes. The EBC approach mitigates doubt and adds clarity. We also believe that, as coaches, the tools we employ and the data we use need to be based on science, so that the data presented is based on reliable and valid evidence. Coaches should be using modern, scientifically-valid and reliable assessments, tools and processes that yield solid results for the coachee and the organization.

There are talented individuals throughout the world working on leadership coaching issues and clarifying market confusion. These individuals need additional outlets for their work, and those interested in leadership coaching need more exposure to authors from cultures other than their own. There is also an art to effective coaching. This art can develop through using evidence-based coaching, years of experience, and cultural agility. Value is added when great coaches share relevant examples, and make informed generalizations, to help the coachee see that he or she is not the first person to face certain challenges.

One of the objectives of *Leadership Coaching in China* is to establish a basis for a series of ongoing writings…

> 1. that include high-quality, insightful, original thinking that advances the science, practice, and art of global leadership coaching within the China context.
> 2. by authors who have been invited to advance the development of leadership coaching from both scholarly and practitioner perspectives. The authors in this volume collaborated on chapter topics, integrating multiple insights and creating resonance.
> 3. by authors from multiple cultures, and work being done in multiple cultures and in multiple organizational settings, which generate an overlapping Western and non-Western "Resonance Code" of best practice.

It is our intention to develop not only this volume, but a series as well as an on-line platform that will be of value to a variety of readers, including those choosing to follow coaching as a profession and those international business executives aspiring to be more effective leaders by incorporating elements of coaching into their leadership style. We also believe that the series will be useful to learning and training professionals, as they teach and facilitate subjects related to leadership and coaching, to international managers wishing to be more culturally adept, and to those designing and conducting coaching and executive education programs. We hope that the series will also prove valuable to practitioners and consultants working in the area of global leadership.

By combining conceptual, empirical, and practitioner perspectives from multiple cultures, we hope to stimulate a healthy cross-pollination of ideas and perspectives. Although every chapter may not be of value to every reader, we trust that there will be a sufficiently rich array of material to offer value to every reader.

It is a pleasure for me to serve as the editor of this series. My interest in leadership coaching began in the 1980s, when I began my career in management at the Xerox Corporation, later serving in International Business Operations for Asia Pacific and China as a managing executive for 11 years. I later founded Leadership Management International Ltd. (LMI-China) and the Keystone Group Shanghai Inc. (Keystone), and I am currently a member of the Board of Directors of LMI-China and Chairman Emeritus of Keystone. My 30+ years in leadership development and coaching includes not only practitioner experience, but also scholarly work, the latter stimulated by the doctoral program in Human and Organizational Development Systems from Fielding Graduate University. Additionally, I hold the qualification of master certified coach (MCC) through the International Coaching Federation (ICF) and currently serve as an ICF director on the Professional Service Global Board.

The first Evidence-Based Coaching Certification Class in Shanghai, China
(Keystone Group, Inc.)

Our plan for the *Leadership Coaching in China* series was to invite guest authors for all chapters, with three authors also serving as co-editors and teaming to organize the chapters into topical sections. These co-editors are Tom Payne, James Warner, and Jeff Hasenfratz, all highly talented individuals with experience working in multinational companies and the private sector, and all dealing with leadership issues on a regular basis. They have served as editorial consultants for the authors and worked closely with Fielding University Press. Their contribution of time and substance to this series, even with already-full schedules, is much appreciated.

The authors contributing chapters to this volume are listed in the Table of Contents, and their biographical summaries are included in the appendices. Special appreciation is expressed to each of these authors for their substantive contributions. Also, we are grateful for their willingness to take a risk on a new series when they could have published their papers in a variety of other sources. Finally, we express gratitude to the authors for their patience during the daunting task of meeting deadlines, as an international cast of co-authors and content and technical editors was coordinated to bring this volume to print.

Even as we go to press with Volume 1, we are planning Volume 2. Already suggested for inclusion in the next volume are the topics of coaching for entrepreneurs, for future generations, for mid-life transition, etc. Your feedback on Volume 1, as well as your suggestions for topics, authors and formats for Volume 2, is encouraged and warmly welcomed.

Introduction

Marjorie Woo, Tom Payne, James Warner, and Jeff Hasenfratz

Welcome to *Leadership Coaching in China*. The topic of leadership coaching is of interest to an increasingly broad array of organizations and individuals, scholars and practitioners alike. We have experienced exponential advances in the integration of the world's economies and telecommunications, with rapid flows of international information, capital and human resources, and multinational organizations of increasingly varied structure and ownership. Chinese state-owned enterprises (SOEs) and private enterprises (POEs) going global, and derailment rates among leaders at international and national levels, are among the forces driving heightened interest in leadership coaching globally, and in China in particular.

In this book, we hope to suggest some structure for coaching practices in China so that, in the future, new coaches can build on what others have provided for them as a foundation.

A word about terms. For ease of understanding, we have, throughout the text used "coachee" to mean the person the coach is working with. "Client" has been reserved for the organization that is paying for the coaching. The "sponsor" is someone within the organization who serves as the primary contact for both coach and coachee, as necessary, and the person who receives and secures confidential communications with the coach, plus serves to afford the coach access to organizational information the coach requires to manage the coaching relationship. Other universal terms used include "MNC," for foreign multinational corporation, usually a significant foreign investor in the China market who brings in quite a number of expatriate leadership team members, either non-Chinese or foreign-born ethnic Chinese. (As you might agree, just because someone looks Chinese and speaks Mandarin doesn't mean that they think or act like a China native!)

This book is presented in three sections. The first and largest section is *Coaching Practices in China Today*. It contains the first 9 chapters and describes how coaching in China has evolved to its current state. It walks the reader through how and why organizations use coaching for leadership development. The section further explores the benefits of coaching, including why it is a good investment in talent development. It goes on to deal with situations that are best suited to coaching, vs. training, and suggests best practice tools and processes. There is a chapter on matching the coach with an individual likely to benefit from a coaching relationship, and the importance of "fit" between coach and coachee. The section also explores the dynamics among the client organization, the sponsor (sometimes the coachee's boss or HR colleague), the coachee, and the coach, and how they need to work separately and together. It describes the qualifications a coach should possess and how a program for preparing professional coaches in China might be structured, based on local learner needs and global advancements in the profession.

Also discussed in this section is a description of tools and processes the coach will likely employ with the coachee, and how these benefit the coaching process. Further on, it discusses what a typical coaching engagement looks like, including the time commitment, expectations, and costs. The authors also explore coaching as a business, for those interested in transitioning into coaching as a career choice. It is interesting, though perhaps not surprising, that a number of executives have decided that they would like to turn to coaching as a profession. Given this interest, their capabilities, and a passion to pursue certification and training, these executives may find coaching to be a valuable choice as a mid-career change. Finally, there is a chapter on the uniqueness of coaching given the influence of Chinese culture. We continue to believe that it is almost always useful in China for coaches to have some "grey hair," as managing people brings skills useful for developing rapport between the coach, sponsor, and coachee.

The second section is focused on the future of coaching in China, where the field is likely to grow, particularly as more Chinese companies begin to use coaching as a development tool. Some of the challenges to the use of coaching are explored in more depth. There is a discussion about the use of educational guidance and career guidance, which are important topics in China and ones we hope to share more about in the next volume of the series. There is also a chapter on the differences between 1-on-1 coaching and team coaching, which is just starting to emerge as a coaching specialty in China. The last authors in this section, Katherine Xin and Jack D. Wood from the China Europe International Business School (CEIBS) and Monique L. Snowden from Fielding Graduate University, provide thoughtful and useful perspectives as to what lies ahead in the practice of leadership coaching, both in China and globally.

The third section of the book, *Reflections*, offers observations from several coaches on where they came from and where they might go in their coaching journey. These authors relate personal stories of how their coaching journey has contributed to meaning in their own life and to the lives of those around them.

While our carefully selected authors brought different perspectives, from both the East and the West, they were able to collaborate and formulate a "resonance" across cultures. We hope that you will begin to formulate your own sense of what is important to the ongoing understanding of leadership coaching, in China and elsewhere. As we have read the various chapters and connected them to our own experience, we've begun to think that there are sets of characteristics and behaviors that differentiate effective leadership coaches and coaching from ineffective ones, especially in the China context.

We find that geopolitical lines get blurred as common interest within organizations is likely to focus on development of executive talent and how leadership coaching can play an important role in this journey. While each of us comes from a unique culture, we are also a lot alike, and perhaps in the future, we should look more closely at the 80% we are alike than 20% we are different, especially as there seems to be more convergence on a global set of leadership competencies driven by stakeholder desires and employee needs. Historically, nations were the arbiters of global interactions and more recently it has been nation-states or consortia of nations. As production, commerce and communication continue to become increasingly driven by individuals, it is critical these individuals be able to work effectively with others who may have different perspectives, beliefs and expectations. Coaching is an effective means for the growth of these individuals.

Because of the challenge on which the global world attempts to balance, leadership coaching needs to be tolerant of differences but not of all differences. Conflicts are inevitable, and processes of responding and resolving conflict need to be more universal. Most of the conflicts are rooted in misunderstanding the "other" and attributing that to some immutable difference. Communication skills will be increasingly critical. Being mindful, listening carefully, not rushing to judgement, and spending the time and energy to understand each other is going to be increasingly important to successful executives. Using language carefully and well is an ongoing challenge. Competence can be built, but we, as the architects of a new vision, must work hard to create accurate blueprints to guide ourselves, our clients, and our coachees into the future.

Section I

Coaching Practices in China Today

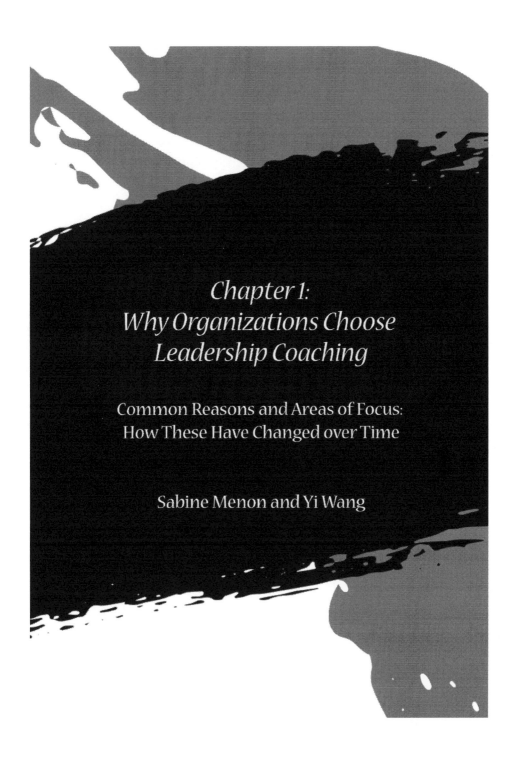

Chapter 1:
Why Organizations Choose Leadership Coaching

Common Reasons and Areas of Focus: How These Have Changed over Time

Sabine Menon and Yi Wang

"There are two ways of spreading light: to be the candle or the mirror that reflects it."

- Edith Wharton

Abstract

This chapter provides an overview of the short history of leadership coaching in China. In addition to this historical perspective, it describes how leadership coaching in China is growing to quickly become a profession incorporating international coaching certification processes and tools, and that more client companies are seeking coaches with these credentials. Despite these advances, leadership coaching is still not well understood and is now being seen more as an effective and accelerated way of developing leaders.

Introduction

It is only very recently that coaching has been introduced to China. MNCs, who provide coaching back in the home country as a part of their ongoing executive development, started extending that to their leaders based in China. For the longest time, it was nearly impossible to find a fully trained (in recognized organizations) coach in China, even less so a local Chinese as a coach. That is until the ICF chapter of Korea came to do its very first training in Beijing, opening the gates of coaching training in China. Beijing and Shanghai were the very first cities to introduce coaching into organizations at a larger scale (including with the development of LMI in Beijing); with it, executive and leadership coaching started to become much more common practice in the China market. As it evolved, so did the profession.

To understand why coaching is an increasingly preferred intervention in talent and leadership development, it is necessary to lay out the landscape of talent market supply. For the past 40 years since China opened its market economy, the market has experienced a constant talent shortage. Businesses can double their growth with capital injections, mergers and acquisitions. People cannot grow overnight to keep up with the business demand. Not only must MNCs cope with talent shortage, but local companies are finding themselves in situations where leaders they considered as talents when the business took off 10 years ago are no longer capable of keeping up with today's demand, let alone leading business and people into the future. Realizing the challenge in developing local leaders, businesses are more open to coaching that aims at transforming talent.

Today many Chinese enterprises are becoming world leaders in their respective industries. They not only need good leaders, but also good leaders in large quantity, capable of competing with their more developed peers in the Western markets. In addition, the concept of VUCA (volatility, uncertainty, complexity and ambiguity) is also redefining the success profiles of future leaders. Generations of 90s and 00s joining the workforce inevitably demand leadership traits that are open, tolerant, and inspirational. This places a particular challenge on traditional Chinese leaders who tend to be more effective in a top-down, autocratic cultural environment.

Leadership coaching describes a specific type of intervention that can be carried out strategically with individuals and/or teams. Its aim is to direct a person or group of people towards a specific mutually determined goal. Given this element of a shared goal, leadership coaching can accelerate progress by providing focus and awareness. It is about helping the people who are being coached to reach a fuller potential—a point at which they not only know themselves better but also feel comfortable with who and what they are (Kets de Vries, 2005).

Leadership coaching should also be viewed as an iterative process by which people can test and evaluate a new behavior in their daily life and adjust until they feel that they have got it right. When done properly, leadership coaching is very dynamic and contributes to creativity and innovation in organizations (Kets de Vries).

In a culture of top-down leadership where the education system expects one to receive and absorb information and not ask questions—and certainly not challenge knowledge—a non-directive approach can be somewhat disturbing.

When coaching local Chinese, the default reaction in a 1:1 meeting between the coachee and the coach is, "Tell me what to do." A non-directive approach allows the coach to operate by asking questions—sometimes challenging ones—with the belief that the coachee will find the answers within. The alternate approach of "tell me what to do" is more comfortable for the coachee than to ask questions that will make one reflect and potentially disturb inner processes (*inner processes* is a psychological term that defines what happens in an individual's mind; it includes memory, perception, and thinking, such as

33

ideation, imagination, belief, reasoning, etc.). Challenging the way a coachee "sees the world" by disturbing inner processes will grow the individual a lot further and deeper.

Within multinationals, coaching is part of executive development to provide tailor-made support to accelerate the development of key talent and leaders in business-critical roles. Fundamentally, it is part of the support available to leaders to be at their best in their complex roles.

Since leadership coaching officially entered China, experienced leadership development professionals have been flocking to leadership coaching as the last hope to achieve breakthroughs in their talent development efforts while many are becoming coaches themselves. These professionals, the majority of whom have an MNC background, have had rich experience in working with different development interventions. They believe coaching is more effective in personal transformation. In recent years, Chinese companies have also invested in coaching to accelerate their leadership development.

Common Coaching Requests and Areas of Focus

We cannot realistically make a complete list of all the reasons why an organization based in China, MNC or SOE, chooses coaching, but here are the general trends, patterns, and requests that we have observed over the years.

Recognition and retention is a good way to keep an employee motivated when at a very senior level or when they have reached a plateau (very few jobs at that level) and there is no clear window of new work opportunity,

Tailor-made development with time efficiency. Beyond a certain level of expertise and seniority, there is not much more a leader can still learn in a business school setting, but more importantly, very few want to take 2 to 4 weeks off their busy schedule to join a program in Europe or in the US. Coaching provides a mechanism to deliver a tailor-made solution for their leadership challenges, especially if they are **leading change or addressing specific business needs.**

Transition ensures a good foundation in a new or enlarged role, a new business, a new organization, or to smooth the transition from a managerial role to a leadership role.

Preparing leaders for the next role and helping them step up, for example, from manager to leader, becoming a board member or enlarging scope and span of control, from a country (China) to a region (APAC).

Cultural differences and cultural aspects specific to China (this part will be developed in the case studies below), which might happen during an expatriation to China, a joint venture, M&A, and dealing with Chinese partners once the deal is made. Moving a leader of Chinese origin, one who even speaks Mandarin, who has grown up in Singapore, Malaysia or anywhere other than China can be just as challenging an adaptation for the new leader. Also moving a PRC citizen to another market requires helping the newly appointed leader to adapt to their new environment.

General leadership development, including specific leadership skills development, involves listening, delegating, empowering, personal and/or team resilience, effective communication, influencing, and emotional intelligence (also developed in the case studies below).

Coaching can help accelerate a leader's transition into a new role, whether they join new companies, are promoted, or are relocated to lead different markets.

The ideal coach is familiar with the environments where the leaders are coming from and leaving for. Coaches are more effective as they hold up mirrors in front of leaders, letting them not only see themselves clearly, but also revealing their new and challenging environments in ways of key stakeholders' expectations and feedback. They help leaders reflect how their capabilities and expertise can be adapted to new requirements, so they create confidence in their teams. In the meantime, coaches remind leaders to not lose sight of relationship, as building trust with people is critical in tough and new situations.

It is important to understand that a move in geographic distance, culture, language, business, markets, etc. puts a lot of pressure on the new leader, and they will most likely benefit from having a coach or mentor for the first 6 -12 months. A failed new senior leader can be a disaster to a company. On the contrary, integrating a leader into a new team quickly creates multiple wins, e.g., for the company, for the leader, and for the search firm if hired from outside. Through smart investment in coaching new leaders, companies increase their positive leadership momentum.

Coaching is also effective in challenging women's unconscious biases, which interfere with female leaders' effectiveness. What makes it harder for Chinese females to succeed, compared with their Western counterparts, is the pressures put on them by families and society. Chinese traditional values suppress women's roles outside their homes and refer to women as inferior to men. While there have been efforts to lift women's social status, the old traditions are embedded in the fabric of everyday life. To achieve success, women must always overcome unconscious biases and question their own limiting assumptions. Who is more helpful than a coach in this regard? In fact, many coaches working with Chinese expressed their preference for female coachees as they are more agile and motivated to change once the coach finds the right way to help.

While most companies engage coaches to develop their leaders, coaches are sometimes hired specifically to deal with performance issues. The key to success of coaching for performance is that the coachees are willing and ready to change and their supervisors are supportive along the way. To minimize defensiveness, input such as a high quality Big 5-Based Personality Assessment can be useful at the onset of coaching. With increased self-awareness and motivation to improve, a coaching relationship is likely to make an impact.

When a team is faced with tough challenges, such as a crisis or a merger and acquisition, team coaching can be introduced as an effective means of support for sustaining a high-performing team spirit. To deal with complex and challenging issues during an intense period, leaders are heavily emerged in fighting fires, coping with uncertainties, and dealing with emotions. A team of individuals may not be the sum of its total, as people tend to focus on their own battles or even wins at others' expense. Tension and misunderstanding can destroy team spirit impacting not only the team itself but also others who interact with the team. Coaching offers teams time to focus on reflection, soul searching, and self-discovery. Through coaching conversations, team members listen to each other intently, seek understanding, and challenge each other's beliefs and assumptions. Through harnessing team members' energy and strengths, coaches help teams bond while the members tackle tough issues, learn, and grow together.

Collaboration, teamwork, and communication are critical skills an effective leader must have to succeed in a VUCA world. Career success demands more emotional intelligence when a person progresses in their career. Being self-aware, being able to listen mindfully to others, and having enough drive to change are critical factors in personal transformation. While ambition and drive can be a strength for Chinese managers, the education system, one emphasizing all but knowledge acquisition and retention, ill prepares managers to be proficient in interpersonal skills, self-awareness, and emotional intelligence.

In addition, Chinese culture values harmony, so people do everything possible to avoid conflict. When conflict becomes eventually unavoidable, people and organizations tend to be paralyzed. Coaches can help as they play the role of thinking partners, offering different perspectives of approaching an issue or of fixing a relationship. Through coaching, managers develop more self-awareness, regulate their emotions, read people and situations, and improve their emotional intelligence.

Coaching in China has become a useful and helpful tool to develop executive talent, explore, and develop the potential of managers and directors. Something specific to China, however, is the difference between an MNC (multinational company) whose HQ is usually based outside China and is usually led by an expatriate (in order to ensure that value and culture of the organization are preserved) versus a SOE (state-owned enterprise) that is 100% owned by local Chinese. While the coaching needs presented above are generic to most companies requesting coaching in China, we have identified coaching needs and requests specific to MNCs and SOEs, as illustrated in the two case studies presented below.

Case Study: SOE

One of the prevailing practices is to embed coaching in talent management and development programs, especially in senior leadership programs. If it is done right, with time, coaching can be transformational to a company's culture through the leadership team. A world-leading chemical company with a strong Confucius heritage has grown significantly over the decades and more rapidly in the last few years due to international market expansion. Because of its remote location, it is more difficult to compete for talent, and because of its fast growth, it lacks strong leaders. Campus recruitment is increasingly an important talent source, and young graduates demand a different leadership style that is open and flexible. After some failed senior appointments, leadership and HR began soul searching for more effective means of talent assessment and development.

After personally attending a one-week coaching training, the HR head was convinced coaching was what they needed to accelerate the talent pipeline. The HR head not only got the investment, but also handpicked coaches he knew and believed in. As coaching is relatively new to many leaders, people in the leadership program were given the option of working with coaches based upon their knowledge of coaching and their desire to change. Now coaching is part of the senior leaders' programs, complementing years of talent development efforts that have focused on training, assessment, action learning, etc.

In the case of this chemical company, we see coaching not only effective in individuals' transformation, but we also anticipate a significant company culture shift. Being located in the heart of Confucius's home base, the company's dominate culture is described as a "big brother" culture, where senior leaders and authorities are regarded as big brothers who are revered and always right. In this environment, loyalty and execution are competitive advantages while individual creativity is downplayed. As leaders increase their self-awareness through coaching, they also reflect on their leadership effectiveness and company culture. Today, senior leaders aspire to develop a coaching culture in the long run in tandem with the next chapter of the company's growth and its globalization strategy.

Case Study: MNC

Klaas is a Dutch gentleman, working for a multinational in oil and gas. He has been working for the company for 20 years, growing in various management roles. He became director of global operations four years ago, which implied a move to Singapore, his very first expatriation, with a primary objective: to ensure the success of an upcoming joint venture with a leading Chinese group that would give his company a much-needed step into APAC. As a result of the joint venture, a third company was created, and Klaas was appointed CEO of this newly created company, owned 55% by the Chinese, reporting both to the CEO of his company back at HQ and to the board of the Chinese firm, an SOE. To take over this new and challenging role, Klaas recently moved to China while his family moved back to Holland. At the same time that Klaas was transitioning, a colleague and long-time friend of his who was working with him in Singapore was appointed to the parent company's board and relocated to HQ. To help with this onboarding process and complex situation, Klaas was offered a leadership coaching process. With it came the tacit agreement that he had no right to fail.

A 55-year-old, pleasant gentleman, Klaas is a moderate extravert. He has a direct style of "saying things as they are," and he is used to picking up the phone and convincing people that his idea is the right one. He is used to getting his way. With his extensive network in the company, he is used to dropping in on colleagues to influence and sell his point of view. He worked briefly for another company right after engineering school but learnt everything he knows in terms of leadership and management from his current company, including its company culture. Though it's an MNC with international employees, a Dutch management style prevails—a consensus-driven, healthy direct conversation, with no fear for confrontation but happy to have a beer together at the end of the day. That culture suits Klaas very well. In addition to that, the company CEO used to play golf with Klaas on a regular basis, making it easier for Klaas to express his opinions and to get access to the CEO on points otherwise difficult to get through "normal lines of communication."

In summary, while very competent and fully deserving of his successful career, Klaas has worked most of his life in one company, accustomed to one company culture, and used to getting things done his way, either through legitimate channels or by going around them, thanks to his EQ and social networking skills.

At the chemistry meeting, Klaas admits that he is not fully convinced that coaching is needed, but since he has never experienced it before, he welcomes the opportunity to fulfil his curiosity. "It can't hurt," he says. He is very enthusiastic about his new role—a major promotion, which, if everything goes well, will ensure his next career move. He is fully aware of the pressure to succeed and how key to his career and ability it is to step up to being a board member. As mentioned, while he agrees to coaching, he does not see it as very relevant for the moment, except for the fact that he just moved to China and does not speak Chinese. He is starting to realize that there are many differences between Singapore and Shanghai, starting with the realization that not everybody speaks English here.

Often, with professionals who are used to travelling to and working in Malaysia, Singapore, Hong Kong, etc., there is a misconception that China is similar. While cities like Beijing and Shanghai have everything that international cities of that size can offer, they are still grounded in a traditional Chinese culture, language and traditions one cannot ignore or do without.

The first few sessions are therefore mostly dedicated to cultural differences and approaches, including in day-to-day life, as an expatriate and as a leader, especially to engage with local Chinese team members. However, it becomes quickly evident that Klaas is struggling to find his place in the upper management at HQ, including finding the right boundaries with his board member friend and more specifically, his difficulties to effectively interact and successfully get his point across with the joint venture Chinese chairman. Also, as trust was being built, Klaas also shared his concern that for him to take the role of the CEO of the joint venture, he had in practice to officially leave the previous company. He is fully aware that, should he fail, the Chinese law would make it quick and easy to fire him. He trusts his parent company but feels quite vulnerable.

We had an opportunity to interview the CEO of the Chinese company in question, let's call him Mr. Yang, right at the beginning of the coaching process, as part of the main stakeholders interview. Mr. Yang is a 54-year-old gentleman from Beijing who made his entire career in that company and who is very close to retirement. Highly educated by the top Xinhua University in Beijing, he was appointed CEO a few years ago. He doesn't speak English and works with a translator. He relies a lot on his executive secretary (who speaks English) to make appointments and type letters and memos, including with his local employees. One could define Mr. Yang as "old school" in his leadership style, but he brings to the table a rich experience of the business in China, and most importantly, his Guanxi (network, crucial in this country). Mr. Yang sees this joint venture has a way to "finish his career on a good note" and to give face to his organization by acquiring a foreign company. While very pleasant to engage with, his leadership style is much more top-down—"Do as you are told and don't ask questions" —which doesn't go too well with Klaas. As the Chinese company is the main shareholder in the joint venture, Mr. Yang has the key to financing most projects that Klaas is supposed to implement and lead, and most decisions must be approved by him, something Klaas has a difficult time with.

Two years later, the joint venture proved to be a success. Klaas learnt to compromise, take a lot of perspectives before acting and, most importantly, before speaking.

While still is not able to speak Mandarin, coaching helped him to see various situations through Chinese lenses, especially in communicating and interacting with Mr. Yang but also with everyone at the plant. The unexpected side effect and benefit for Klaas was how he self-developed by challenging his behaviour and coming back to his basic values and motivations. Year after year, promotion after promotion, Klaas never had to question the next move. He did not really pause to reflect and address why he would say yes to the promotion that was being offered. It was natural and taken for granted. This role forced him, almost daily, to remind himself why he was doing what he was doing, for which purpose, and with what objective versus fulfilling his sense of legitimacy and his own career aspirations and professional identity.

This was also the first time in a long time that he was being constantly challenged and critiqued by his HQ back at home and, more subtly, by the SOE locally.

He was clearly affected by the change of tone in his friendship with the now board member who had a different sense of boundaries, but he was eventually able to see it from his friend's perspective.

Coaching helped at various levels: fine tuning his leadership skills, interacting with the local Chinese community, and being able to find common ground and agreements. While Klaas and the local CEO differ tremendously in their leadership style, through coaching, Klaas was able to find a way to connect with his counterpart, speaking the same language—the language of vision, objectives and goals. As it turned out, they both shared a passion for golf as well, thus providing another communication channel that offered a more neutral, less non-judgmental sounding board.

It's lonely at the top, and even more so for someone in a different country far away from friends and family. Klaas was also able to accept the fact that while local Chinese are more fact-oriented and fact-based, they too have emotions, even though they don't show them. Klaas used to express easily his opinion, not always listening actively, and this experience forced him to do just that. He reassessed his own set of values and motivations to better step back and understand what he was reacting to when he was reacting.

There is something very specific to expatriates living in China: a 24/7 pressure. They do their 9 to 5 jobs (more like 6/7 am to 8pm), then Europe wakes up and the evening calls start up to midnight, if not later, and if they are (un) lucky to work for an MNC with operations also in the US, which have usually tight ties with China, the US wakes up when China goes to sleep and vice versa. If the expatriate leader doesn't pay attention, it's easy to get into the 24/7 vicious cycle with no limits, even more so for an expatriate whose family stays in their home country, with no incentive to manage the work-life balance. That round-the-clock pressure is a sure recipe for burnout.

Our role as coaches is to teach coachees where to put boundaries in their work-life balance. Coaching helped Klaas to stop saying yes to all the meetings, especially to those beyond reasonable working hours and to be ok with that (not feeling the guilt or work pressure).

Evolution

Looking at the Chinese coaching market in 2009, when first moving to China, coaching was still a very limited practice. There were very few ICF PCC graduates, and very few coaches were actually local Chinese. Requests for coaching were very specific in terms of coaching for cultural differences, onboarding or coaching specifically a returnee Chinese.

Fast forward 10 years and it's a very different environment. A survey led by the Asian Coaching Association reports that in China, coaching often takes the form of a mixture of advice, mentoring, and actual coaching. Less than a third of coaching interventions are limited to this practice, and almost half of the interventions combine coaching and mentoring. Seen as a modern management tool, with no guarantee of return on investment, any recourse to coaching is conceived with the blessing of CEOs at the highest level. One of the major concerns is therefore the non-respect of the ethical rules of confidentiality specific to the profession since less coaching-educated clients (mostly in HR roles) ask all conversations with the coachee to be reported to them. Another major concern of coaching in China is that of the reliability of coaches. The survey shows that while two-thirds of coaches employed in China are certified by a coaching school, only one-third are certified by a recognized professional body and only a third of the companies that employ coaches in China verify these certifications. Finally, culturally, China continues to be more sensitive to the seniority and industrial and commercial experience of coaches rather than to their professional skills as a coach.

We also interviewed our clients, specifically HR professionals working for an MNC more conversed with coaching, asking them how they see the evolution of coaching over the last 10 years. Their answers were very aligned with what we observed. At the beginning of the coaching movement, coaching was an asset to support the executives to self-develop and increase their awareness, specifically supporting transformational leadership—a highly developed ability to articulate a vision for the future and to inspire followers to make the vision happen that can be a challenging and even lonely task. To be effective, leaders often feel that they must be all things to all people, taking responsibility for the charismatic and architectural leadership roles in their organization (Kets de Vries). Coaching for performance focus has become more important, as well as a move towards a more targeted use of leadership coaching on specific leadership skills development.

Specific Effects of COVID-19

As we write this chapter, over the last few months, China has managed to control the outspread of COVID-19 internally, but the borders are still closed to foreigners and a two-week mandatory quarantine in special centers is still in place. The immediate consequences have included expatriates not returning, expatriates leaving, and local leaders being groomed to step up within a very short period of time in an especially challenging market and economy. Furthermore, we can observe a shift worldwide, with a stronger inner-focus centered nationally (not just in China, but globally).

While China has one of the largest populations in the world, leadership talents are scarce. China cannot be equated to the cities of Shanghai and Beijing, and it's difficult to attract high-profile leaders to second- and third-tier cities, making the development of local talents in those cities even more crucial, which is something coaching can definitely achieve.

Conclusion

Leadership coaching in China is a new asset, which, for the longest time, was carried by the booming Chinese market and economy and seen almost as an accessory. As mentioned above, we have seen a shift from coaching for development to coaching for performance. Now in a more difficult market, environment, and worldwide affected economy, ROI and KPIs will become crucial. The question will be asked, should China become more isolated from the rest of the world? How will coaching play out in a VUCA environment and with younger and less experienced people taking the lead of multinationals?

The demand for leadership coaching will only go up despite geopolitics, the pandemic, or whatever challenges China may face. In the past 40 years, Chinese people have tasted the fruits of economic reform and open market economy. As a competitive and hardworking nation, people will strive to make their lives better at all costs, including personal transformation if required. For the Chinese economy and society to keep developing people's pursuit of individual growth and development, it must keep pace with what is required. In recent years, with the internet and technological advances, Chinese have better access to the advanced management and human resources theories and practices in the US and in Western societies. Development interventions such as coaching will only become more in demand as people see and experience their profound impact. Coaching in China is still very much an evolving profession, but it is one that needs to mature and self-regulate. There is no doubt that coaching will have a role to play in the success of SOEs or MNCs in China in the next few years.

Chapter 2
Benefits of Leadership Coaching to the Individual and the Organization

Reasons why Organizations support Coaching
Engagements for their Executives and Managers

Frank Rexach and Jason Ramey

"When the best leader's work is done, people say, 'We did it ourselves.'"

- Lao Tzu

Abstract

The first chapter addressed the evolution and development of leadership coaching in China. Coaching is still in its infancy, but like everything in China, it is quickly catching up and adapting. Coaching is becoming more professional with the growth of international coaching certifications with accepted processes and tools for coaches to use and follow. Along with the professionalism comes accountability for the ROI to justify the investment in coaching. Coaching was perhaps originally often misapplied to "fixing" managers and executives, whereas now, the focus has moved to the development of leaders. In Chapter 2, you will hear from two expatriated executives in China that have benefited from working with professional coaches and how their resulting transformation has made them better developers of local talent. You will discover how they learned to manage in a culture that was not their own and how they learned to adapt to that. They were responsible for implanting their corporate culture and values in their teams in China. They also had to identify, recruit, and develop the next generation talent to sustain their organizations. Many foreign MNCs and some new market entrants face this challenge today. The authors share their experiences, their lessons learned, and how they developed future leaders and how that helped them in their personal development.

Introduction

Although leadership coaching in China is still in its infancy, there is noticeable momentum in its application given the inherent benefits in the investment of both the C-suite and next generation talent that are going to be responsible for driving some of the largest companies in the world. Once largely the domain of multinational companies, local businesses are also recognizing the value in having external coaches support their leadership teams, particularly as former HR and business leaders from within China have become certified in leadership coaching with global tools and processes under their belts.

With the primary goal to develop an executive holistically, these leadership coaches have multi-faceted roles depending on the specific requirements of the leader but also their own personal experiences, which come many times from being coached themselves in their career journey. This enables the leadership coach to be a trusted mirror to the business leader in a safe environment with the guard rails to ensure their development is sustainable. Ultimately, it is not about them as an individual; it is about how they can inspire those around them to maximize the performance of their organization in an increasingly competitive environment.

For those companies investing in leadership coaching in China, the benefits are plentiful with a positive return on long-term performance of the business given the ripple effects of a good leader. Here are a few that are worth highlighting with examples through a lens of leaders in China who have put them to good use in building great teams and businesses.

1. Self-Awareness

Effective leadership begins with being self-aware, which is also the most challenging trait to build as one moves up the corporate ladder in what is widely accepted as the loneliest job. This becomes even more complex in a country like China where the notion of "saving face" or ensuring that one does not lose respect from others is critically important to defining who they are as a person. An effective and trusted leadership coach is therefore paramount to a leader having the ability to get real-time feedback around how they may be perceived so that they can quickly address any issue and make the necessary improvements to be organizationally effective. This reinforces the benefits of evidence-based coaching (EBC). Using reliable, credible data to support guidance and insights helps the coachees' acceptance of the feedback. This also includes having the objective and fair organizational performance assessments of those they manage where not having an accurate pulse could result in losing key members of their team or, conversely, retaining those who may not be up to the challenge, which can damage the credibility with those who are shouldering the larger burden.

By proactively addressing self-awareness, they also have the opportunity to focus on emotional intelligence, emotional literacy, the role of vulnerability, authenticity in leadership, well-defined accountability and responsibility, impactful communication, dealing with difficult exchanges and individuals, vision, self-awareness and self-management through meditative practices, realizing blind spots and leadership shadows among other important leadership competencies. This ties back to the insights from using the Johari window as a tool for expanding self-awareness in leaders. Feedback is the breakfast of champions.

Overseas leadership roles for executives can come earlier in a career than domestic roles, where there tends to be more of an established structure and a defined process to career advancement within a corporation. This is particularly true in China where multinational companies in many cases entered the country within the past 20 years and ramped up at a speed unlike other parts of the world because of the tremendous scale inherent in the domestic economy, as well as its growing importance in supporting a global agenda in sourcing and innovation.

Frank's Story

Frank had just turned 42 when he relocated from Australia to Shanghai to assume the role of Vice President and General Manager for Asia Pacific, which included overseeing operations for the company in the region. Although Frank had previously worked in Hong Kong in a senior role and spoke Mandarin, this would be the first time that he had a large organization under his oversight in a market that he was less familiar with.

Frank was fortunate to have had a personal tie to William Mobley, who became a mentor to him when he first met Bill in Hong Kong. Frank describes the situation: "At the time, I was a managing director for a newly acquired business in Australia by global self-adhesive giant Avery Dennison. I was selected to go through a new executive development program for the company, and Bill was the Asia regional CEO of PDI that Avery Dennison worked with for this initiative in Asia Pacific. I was very fortunate that Bill personally delivered my feedback from the intensive 2-day simulations, and his candor and constructive comments shaped my subsequent path of leadership."

Dr. Mobley was recruited by CEIBS to lead a new program focusing on executive development. This is where Frank and Bill's paths would next cross a year later when Frank relocated from Sydney to Shanghai. When Frank stepped into his new position, the company, like many others, was emerging from a very deep global recession with a need to turnaround their regional business. As Dr. Mobley was in the process of identifying companies to write cases studies for the CEIBS M.B.A. program, he offered Frank a deep-dive analysis and engagement with the business. Dr. Mobley provided Frank with an experienced leadership coach. The coach participated in Frank's leadership meetings where he could observe (shadow) firsthand Frank's management style with his new team.

After each meeting, the coach provided Frank with real-time, direct feedback, which was like having a mirror in front of him where he was able to understand for the first time what perception others had of Frank. He was able to help Frank determine how he could alter that perception where necessary to create a more positive and engaged team. In a China context, this was even more nuanced as a direct communication style typically used by Americans to reflect to the leaders the transparency of what they may be thinking could actually have the opposite effect with his new mainly Chinese team. Singling out someone in a group and challenging their point of view could potentially embarrass that manager in front of their peers, or worse, it could be perceived as reflecting the new leader's lack of support for them. The coach helped Frank strategically in several key interactions to not step on this hidden landmine for what would otherwise have been culturally acceptable back in Australia or in the United States.

Jason's Story

Throughout his life, Jason had a lot of help and coaching along the way from family, teachers, and sports coaches, but professionally it really started with Charles Tracy who was a senior partner with a boutique accounting firm and took a genuine interest in developing Jason as a new partner and then teaching and experiencing doing business in China with Jason two decades ago. After several years of doing business in China, Jason joined Grant Thornton, as they had an aggressive expansion plan in China; the timing matched up very well with his previously learned skills and relationships in China. Jason immediately hit the ground running, and at the age of 35, he had a significant amount of responsibilities to recruit new talent, set up new service lines, and grow the business. Ultimately, he managed the Shanghai office and subsequently had increased responsibilities across mainland China and Hong Kong.

Jason's next coach and mentor was Stephen Chipman who was CEO and recruited him to Grant Thornton and facilitated his and his family's move to Shanghai. Stephen was based in Hong Kong, so both were expatriates in China. They had much in common and much to learn from each other. While Jason had traveled extensively and spent a significant amount of time on the ground in China, he realized that it was very different living there, and he needed to figure out a different approach than the typical "fly in fly out" of China. Stephen had previously completed an assignment to China in the early 90s and was very instrumental and helped Jason learn and develop even deeper relationships. Through observation and coaching, he learned many of the "soft skills" needed to interact in China and ultimately to be successful with the relationships formed. An example of what he learned was how to get to the outcome or answer without it having to be so direct as most Americans initially approach situations in China. Rather than let him struggle with trying to figure out the dynamics of the situations, Stephen carefully walked him through each relationship and explained the history and his understanding of the situation. He also left room for Jason to learn and grow the relationships from his own perspectives, and they had many "one on one" informal coaching discussions on these relationships and how to best develop and retain key people and future leaders. During Jason's first year or so in China, he was learning from a great mentor, and in hindsight, it was obvious that Stephen knew that he was setting him up for success and greater responsibilities, not just in China but for broader global roles later in his career.

While in China, Jason was very fortunate to meet Bill Mobley in Shanghai who mentored him and introduced him to many contacts and friends and encouraged him to become the President of the Shanghai Texas A&M Club and invited him to speak to his students at China Europe International Business School. Together, they organized and hosted a "Doing Business in China" seminar for the Governor of Texas and his delegation of Texas government officials who were visiting China. Bill was the best global networker Jason had met. His style was infectious, and it inspired Jason to try and do the same. Bill was often a leadership coach by example through his actions. Jason learned from these various leadership styles, which helped him to become more self-aware, shaping him as a leader to influence and coach leaders he developed later.

2. Acceptance as a Leader

Because becoming an impactful leader does not just come from on-the-job experience, it is important for emerging local leaders and those new to China to have access early in their positions to other established executives in the market and to well-seasoned coaches. They can help you to understand the intricacies of the culture both within your organization and that of your clients and suppliers with the goal of building credibility as an accepted leader.

I was fortunate to have been introduced early into my new assignment to a German business unit leader at Siemens who had been successfully operating in China for a number of years. I asked him what advice he would give to a new leader coming into the market in order to garner the support necessary for mobilizing the organization behind you. He shared with me the best advice that I would ever receive. To gain the support of an organization in China required that you win them through their hearts rather than their minds. This was the antithesis of what I had expected, as I had always assumed Chinese and Asian business culture would be more receptive of leaders who led by their intellect rather than looking to establish an emotive connection.

With this in mind, Frank pivoted his approach to bring a more personal focus with his engagements that was underpinned by trust and authenticity. This included consistently doing morning walks through the factory, stopping and speaking to each of the team members on the line, asking how they were doing and about their children, and having more personal conversations rather than business only. What Frank found over time was that this form of sincere engagement enabled him to not only attract the best talent but to retain them even in the most challenging times, including when he could not match compensation when his people were approached from time to time by recruiters or competitors.

While an expatriate CEO provided Jason with a lot of instant credibility through his sponsorship and by endorsing Jason's previous experiences in China, it was so important that he also receive some strong mentoring from local leaders in China and in Hong Kong. The Hong Kong leadership initially had a very strong influence over the mainland China operations, but it became apparent for future business that the firm needed to move headquarters and top leadership to mainland China. This was not an easy thing to do due to much established history of how things worked. This would require transformational and cultural change, and much local wisdom and advice was needed while not taking Western approaches.

After a couple of years, Stephen relocated back to the US, and Jason remained in Shanghai and assumed much of Stephen's previous responsibilities in China. He then started working very closely with two key senior China leadership partners. Mark Fong was based in Hong Kong and had merged his firm into Grant Thornton in 2007, and Xia Zhidong was vice-chair, based in Beijing and merged his firm in 2009. Jason had been in Shanghai where the firm had initially moved the headquarters, and he had a chance to understand the situation there as well as in Hong Kong. The firm had recruited much of the new leadership, but it needed to integrate the firm into a very large firm in Beijing and move the headquarters there.

Jason's new roles and increased responsibilities in China as Senior Adviser to the China Executive Committee, Head of International Business and leading the Shanghai office required him to need even more acceptance as a leader. Jason spent many hours with Mark and Zhidong learning from them and listening to their advice. He needed to win the hearts and minds of many people, including the new top China leadership in Beijing and also in Guangzhou and other large offices. There were many trips taken to get to know the teams and to work hand in hand to ensure there was a smooth transition. It was always exciting to work with the local leadership to inspire the local Chinese employees with the new strategy for the future, both domestically and for the China team's very important role within the global organization.

3. The Importance of Active Listening

Closely tied to acceptance as a leader in China is the importance in applying active listening skills to the workplace, inquiring intently to understand and uncover existing perceptions or thoughts of the team members around the business strategies or goals before the leaders shares their own. Not doing so could lead to an assumption that the leader's positions are fixed. Challenging the leader with alternative points of view, particularly if the leader and the team are new to each other, is likely to be difficult in most Chinese organizations, where longer-term relationships and trust are important. This is even more dangerous in managing a business in China where the team may not tell the leader that they are about to step on a landmine until it is too late.

Although useful within any culture, active listening skills are even more critical to operate effectively in China. Effective listening, however, requires first creating a safe space for richer conversations, so the leaders have to make an extra effort to schedule quality 1:1 meeting time. The Chinese culture prefers this format to speaking in a larger group. Once in these sessions, it is important to ask more questions and to listen without interruption, avoiding going directly to solutions or trying to defend a position. Through this approach, the leader will be unfiltered and provide high-quality insights that could have a dramatic impact on how they approach common problems or opportunities for the business. The leaders can also learn more about the individual and their potential, as there is a tendency in the culture to not self-promote, and the leader could otherwise miss future talent they should be investing in without these personal engagements.

Two decades ago, when Jason first traveled to China for business, he did not realize it at the time, but he was not an active listener at all and could only see things through his Western lens. He had been going to mainland China and Hong Kong for almost six years before living there. He did not really understand active listening until he was on the ground living in China and responsible for hiring and managing people. Working with Chinese leaders and employees helped shape him as a leader to become a much better listener. He had many one on one conversations and learned this style worked very well when he needed to really understand what someone was wanting to tell him. This created many mentor/mentee relationships where Jason could provide the appropriate coaching to the up-and-coming leaders in China. He always felt it was a two-way street though, as in each situation, he may have provided some leadership coaching, but he also felt that he was receiving the benefit of their coaching back to him through active listening. Again, the insights were gained by applying the active listening as well as by sharing more of his personal thoughts, which he could more easily do in 1-on-1 sessions. These are techniques that expand the Johari window and allow for more trust to develop.

4. Empowering Your Team through Trust

Scaling a business in a high-potential market like China can only happen by empowering self-directed team members so they can make key decisions with minimal oversight. This is culturally more challenging in China where managers tend to be more risk averse than the west but also where delegation may not come as naturally for local leadership. Leadership coaches can effectively provide tools for this process, including using situational leadership methods, so that leaders can effectively move from a tactical to a strategic view that only comes by letting go. By building trust first, letting go becomes a less risky strategy.

When dealing with a new team, and in some cases a less experienced one, it is easy to step into a leadership role and try to take ownership of key initiatives as well as continue to drive the process for longer than necessary. Although it may appear to be the right thing to do at the outset for expediency, there are many adverse consequences with this approach. This can include attaining less buy-in from your team but also potentially creating a culture where direct reports may become dependent on approval to move even basic decisions forward. Worse, the leader can bottleneck their business and stunt their own growth in a market that remains one of the fastest growing in the world where it is all about speed and being nimble.

Many leaders have used situational leadership as a tool quite effectively where they focus on a specific task with a direct report rather than making general assumptions about their abilities overall. By managing around the task using the situational leadership model, they can then determine if they still require close direction, coaching, and support or if they can let go and delegate because they have demonstrated their ability to successfully perform the task.

In China, many managers have found that they may not always disclose their lack of readiness around a specific task or project. This could lead to them being stretched too far, headed for burnout or losing confidence in their abilities. One of the key reasons for losing key talent to another opportunity is not providing the room for them to develop because of an overbearing manager or the inability to put their own mark on an initiative where they could get recognition.

When Jason arrived in China, an immediate priority was to aggressively recruit talent and future leaders from competitors. They needed to strengthen the audit and tax capabilities and also develop specialty advisory services. One of the specialty advisory services that was not an immediate priority at the time was transfer pricing. The firm had the transfer pricing service capability in Hong Kong to cover mainland China, but after receiving Rose Zhou's CV in Shanghai, Jason was open to interviewing her. Rose was in her early 30s, and Jason was initially very skeptical of even having the interview as she was seeking a partner role and to be the new transfer pricing practice leader (which was not an open or planned position in the immediate term). During the interview, Rose impressed Jason with her very meticulous business plan, and Jason listened to how Rose would execute the plan. Jason felt strongly that this was an opportunistic hire the firm could not pass up, and after getting her through the process, Jason and the China leadership were able to bring her on board. Jason had no idea about the technical aspects of transfer pricing services, but he and the China team were able to get behind her and trust that with the right resources, she would deliver on her plan. As part of the plan, the firm invested and hired other key resources Rose had recommended to successfully build this practice area.

Rose realized the genuine trust and confidence the firm's leadership had in her by bringing her in as a partner and letting her have the reins to build and grow a team. She was allowed to make mistakes, learn, and grow. The leadership recognized how loyal the team was that followed Rose to the firm and how loyal she was to her team. It became obvious that she would not let them or the clients down. Today, Rose has become an inspirational leader, mentor, and coach to many. She has built a very successful transfer pricing practice and was advanced to Shanghai tax practice leader after just a few years and then to Shanghai managing partner; she now sits on the National Management Committee of the entire firm of 6,000 people.

5. Leveraging Diversity of Culture and Thought

China has been unusually open in their acceptance of international leadership, operating many businesses out of the country. This has enabled many companies to use the country as a hub for regional and global operations where cross-cultural leadership teams have been assembled, representing world-class talent. Emerging Chinese business leaders have benefited greatly in this exposure to the differences in operating across borders and cultures with an experienced international leader who understands how to ensure all points of view are effectively integrated.

There is no better experience as a regional executive than assembling a leadership team representing multiple cultures and harnessing the power of diversity. Each region in the world has its own inherent rivalries between countries, and Asia Pacific is no exception where historical conflicts have shaped perceptions across generations. For this reason, having a neutral leader from outside the region in many cases is of benefit to developing an effective overarching strategy and culture. This is often appreciated because of the opportunity to also glean new insights from Western leaders is valued as part of career development and advancement.

Being an unbiased regional leader provides the ability to facilitate the team to ensure a balanced point of view rather than favoring one individual or market.

This approach has opened the door for direct reports to get exposure to other perspectives within Asia Pacific that can only come with a deeper immersion by interacting with their peers including home country engagements. This exposure accelerated the development of what otherwise would have been highly capable domestic managers who now could advance comfortably to regional leaders, and in some instances, to global leaders.

The accounting profession in China is not as established as the West, and Chinese regulators and local accounting firms have always embraced the US and other countries where it has been more advanced. This includes learning from diverse and experienced leaders in the profession and applying it in China. One of Jason's most rewarding experiences in China was leading recruiting efforts to bring in a very diverse team from a variety of backgrounds. There were existing leaders and many employees in mainland China from Hong Kong. The firm then brought in people from Big 4 competitors locally: US, Japan, UK, Singapore, Malaysia, and Canada. This diversity made the firm more attractive in the market, including on university campuses, and the China team was very proud of having so many international colleagues. There were also opportunities created to send members of the China team on short- or long-term assignments to the US, UK, and Canada, which provided further development and enhanced training opportunities. Many meetings were held between the US and China leadership teams for information exchange. There were coaching relationships developed because of these meetings. Overall, there were ripple effects throughout China and global organizations as a result of incubating and then leveraging a diverse environment, which was strongly embraced by the China team.

6. Enabling Inclusion and Voice

Asian cultures, including Chinese, tend to be more reserved than their Western counterparts in expressing their opinions on matters that may define the difference between success or failure of a business if not explicitly understood. This can lead to a false sense of buy-in for the strategies or policies being proposed by an executive without having access to the insights of all leadership team members and key managers in an organization.

Frank describes an example:

I recall my first few regional leadership meetings, where I quickly noticed a pattern in terms of active participation. Whereas the American, Australian, and Indian direct reports were highly engaged and largely dominated the conversation, the other Asian and in particular Chinese leaders were noticeably silent. This is where Bill Mobley's coaching once again proved invaluable as he shared the importance of proactively soliciting input from these members in the meeting to ensure inclusion rather than assuming this would happen organically. With this in mind, I consciously pivoted how my meetings were facilitated. Although I would continue to allow for the natural flow of conversation among my leadership team on a particular topic, I would ask each person who had not spoken for their own view before I would move to the next issue. I was amazed at both the new information that surfaced but also the quality of the insights that I would have otherwise never uncovered by enabling each voice to be heard.

Jason learned a very good lesson in China through experiencing a failed merger. There was a new merger in Shanghai, and it felt like all the right pieces were in place. Two key missing elements were the following: 1) even though both firms were based in Shanghai, they were not culturally aligned; 2) there was insufficient leadership coaching for either firm pre- and post-merger. There was a lot of discussion and significant due diligence performed, but it did not become obvious until later that many of the partners of both firms did not really want to merge. It was driven by just a few without having enough input from the partners. There were key differences that were not fully understood, such as location of the headquarter offices, service line methodologies, risk management, and go-to-market strategies. If there had been more in-depth leadership coaching, either some of the pitfalls would have been discovered early on or there might have been an opportunity to spend more time listening and coaching to try and resolve the differences and to ensure a successful merger.

7. Differentiation as a Culture

In the growing war for next-generation talent as we enter the next phase of the Industrial Revolution, understanding the culture of an organization has risen to the top of priorities for prospective hires who have more choices than ever before. The tone for a company's culture is largely set at the top, and word travels fast particularly through social media in the posts of employees who either celebrate the environment and friends they work with or remain silent at best.

Being able to differentiate your brand through the power of a positive culture is a strategic lever. A leadership coach can work with the leader to help them create a change management blueprint. Consistent engagement across the organization is one of the primary opportunities for executives to create a culture of openness and transparency. This can be further strengthened by offering both access and by mentoring opportunities, which are valued in China even more so than pure monetary incentives for aspiring managers.

As China continues on its path to becoming the world's largest economy and a source of global innovation, international executives operating businesses in the market need to find new ways to attract and retain the best talent for as long as possible before they move on to new opportunities to advance their careers. Culture was one of those strategic levers that Frank learned to harness to his advantage particularly as one of the businesses he managed lacked the same brand recognition of more visible global companies.

Creating a culture takes time in China, however, and is less connected to brand recognition but more with the reputation of the leader who has been appointed to represent this brand in the market. One of the best ways Frank found to elevate the importance of culture in his business was to ensure accessibility across the organization. In a more hierarchical context of structure particularly found in Chinese SOEs, this would mean your access as a leader would be primarily limited to your direct reports only. Frank quickly established in his in-house town hall sessions that he wanted to be available to meet and engage with all levels of the organization. Frank noted, "This approach enabled me to have critical insights by going layers deeper into the business, and it also provided visibility to high-potential talent who could become future leaders as the organization continued to evolve." More importantly in China, this ability to be approachable as a senior leader was a key tool in retaining the most critical managers. In addition to having healthy exchanges with these employees, they also valued the mentoring opportunity, which might be harder to come by in a less familiar organization.

When Jason first joined his new firm in the US, one of the primary reasons he joined was because of the culture of the firm and its very strong focus on quality. This did not just mean providing quality deliverables as a professional services firm. Quality was always the highest priority, and it was ingrained in the culture, starting with the tone at the top. It meant hiring high-quality people and also having a really strong emphasis on accepting high-quality clients. When Jason relocated to China, one of his key goals was to implement the same culture and values that focus on quality as a top priority. The tone was set with hiring practice leaders who had a shared vision for quality and who wanted to ensure it was obvious in the market that the firm was known for quality and for having a great reputation for talent. Jason tried to be as consistent as possible with this approach. At the time, the middle market cross-border activity was booming and there were many new opportunities coming into or originating in China. Everyone was excited about the growth, but at the same time, the partners and staff wanted to ensure quality was maintained. Jason was very proud to see how the firm had embraced quality. There had been many situations where the firm had to make tough decisions, and the tone that was set from the beginning. The ongoing leadership coaching has continued to pay off in a variety of ways in the market and in ongoing talent recruitment.

8. Building Confidence in New Leaders

As the baton is passed to a new leader in China, it is important that they have access to real-time mentoring to build confidence as they encounter first-time challenges to their leadership both organizationally and commercially. As an expatriate, Frank knew his day would come when he needed to return to the U.S. and that the timing was never predictable. With that in mind, building a strong pipeline of talent with a succession strategy for all key roles was part of his focus from day 1. Frank had always said that a successful leader needed to work towards having a self-directed team in place in the event "you were hit by a bus." This also meant to him that each of these direct reports could potentially elevate from their function to the leader's role as a viable candidate.

Frank found that many of his peers in other corporations would have a special relationship with one or two of their direct reports, usually with the CFO function being one of them. He intentionally avoided this dynamic and would not cultivate these exclusive relationships as he knew the importance of creating fairness across the team to maximize the contribution of everyone to the common goals.

Shannon Tan was originally from Guangdong Province in a small town near Guangzhou. She had attended Texas A&M University in the US and started her professional career in Grant Thornton's Dallas office. When Jason joined Grant Thornton and Shannon heard he was going to lead the execution of the firm's new China strategy, she contacted him immediately and expressed her interest to do an expatriate assignment back to China. Her initial plan was not to remain in China but to go there for a couple of years and then come back to the US. After working as a senior auditor for a couple of years in Shanghai, she was promoted to manager. The firm had consummated a merger around that time in Guangzhou, and there was a significant challenge as the new leadership was strong in the domestic market, but they had no international experience. The previous partners who did have the experience serving international clients exited as part of the merger. There were many staff remaining who had been serving international clients and needed leadership and support. Jason asked Shannon to extend her assignment for one year, help facilitate the integration, and lead the staff there.

Her initial reaction was that she did not believe she could do it, and she did not feel very confident. Jason spent a lot of time with Shannon to convince her that she was the best person with the right background, international experience, language skills, personality, and leadership skills to handle the job. He asked her to accompany him to Guangzhou for a visit with Ken Chen, the new managing partner. After Shannon could see the need, how confident Jason and Ken were in her abilities, and that she was needed to fill this position for at least a couple of years, she agreed to take the assignment. She ended up staying in Guangzhou and was promoted to partner (probably 4-5 years faster than if she had remained in the US or Shanghai), leading the international audit team and ultimately becoming audit team leader for all the international business in mainland China and Hong Kong.

Shannon had strong leadership capabilities, but she did not realize it. She just needed coaching and mentoring and to be put into a position that would stretch and challenge her. She gained strong confidence after exceeding her own expectation as well as those of the firm's leadership, and she became recognized around the world for her leadership skills. Today she has gained well-deserved recognition for her leadership capabilities within the Grant Thornton network.

James C. Warner and Amanda Shang

Chapter 3.
Preparing Leadership
Coaches in China

Education, Qualifications,
Certification, and Ongoing Development

"The only metrics that will truly matter to my life are the individuals whom I have been able to help, one by one."
- Clayton M. Christensen

Abstract

In the previous chapter, you heard how two expatriated executives benefited from working with professional coaches, including how to manage in a culture very different from their home culture. In this chapter, you gain insight into how individual leadership coaches in China are prepared to be effective in their role as professional, certified coaches. You will also learn how Western coach training programs have influenced the development of education for coaches in China to meet the requirements of coachees in MNCs. This section discusses the background of Chinese nationals who have undertaken the coach certification process, and it introduces one effective approach for preparing individuals in an environment that requires different content and learning approaches that reflect the Chinese culture and business environment. It explores an approach that combines leadership training and coaching to gain increased acceptance of leadership coaching in Chinese companies that are not familiar with the benefits of leadership coaching.

For the purposes of this chapter, we consider the term "coaching" to be defined as "unlocking a person's potential to maximize their own performance. It is "helping them to learn rather than teaching them" (Whitmore, J. 1992). Coaching is based on many disciplines, methods, approaches, and foundational theories. Most suggest that coaching is a partnership, not an authoritarian relationship. The coach uses a variety of "facilitative" approaches to help the coachee develop, rather than telling him or her the answer. In this chapter, coaching is distinguished from advising (e.g., as a content expert), training, psychotherapy, and consulting, all of which help participants—but which use very different approaches and have different goals and purposes than coaching. The focus here is on learning approaches used successfully in China to prepare professional leadership coaches.

Motivation to Become a Coach

When asking students in a professional coaching certification program why they decided to pursue coaching, the answer most frequently given is, "I want to do something that is meaningful with my life that will help others grow and develop." There are many career paths that can help people achieve this purpose. For some, it is seeking a new career as a full-time professional coach. For others, it is a desire to stay in their current leadership role and connect more closely with their employees. They want these employees to succeed by learning about their strengths and areas for improvement, and they use coaching skills to accelerate the employee's development.

A large number of individuals who pursue coach training in China have been successful in their current career and are planning to transition from full-time employment to something that provides greater work-life balance in the next phase of their career. Some already work in another profession related to human development, as trainers or psychotherapists, for example, but they want to improve their skills in helping people in one-on-one settings, or helping individuals grow but not have to deal with the dysfunctional aspects of their lives. Some simply want to engage in life-long learning and pursue their own personal development over time. Others want to follow an accelerated path to becoming a coach.

Becoming a professional leadership coach is hard work. It requires a person to gain additional perspective into who they are and how they relate to others. It requires being willing to make the coachee the "focus" of the conversation, rather than looking at what the coach feels should be the focus. It requires sensitivity, empathy, and humility. Effective coaches learn and use many theories of human and organizational development, as well as various coaching models and skills. They build the capacity and agility to apply this learning in a variety of ways so as to quickly become familiar with the coachee's context, situation, and goals. Those who complete professional coaching certification programs have successfully addressed these challenges and are able to help coachees in an efficient and effective way.

Professional Leadership Coach Development in China

The purpose of this chapter is to provide information about approaches that have been effective in preparing leadership coaches in China. It will provide some detail on the structure, content, and learning approaches used in successful programs that prepare leadership coaches and provide opportunities for these new coaches to apply their skills. It is not the purpose of this chapter to provide a deep review and comparison of the many prominent and successful coach certification programs operating in China.

The last ten years has seen the growth of a significant number of organizations within China that provide professional coach training, or support improvements in a participant's current level of leadership skills based on coaching principles. Some of the earlier programs are based on US, European, and Australian coaching programs. These include Erickson, Co-Active Training Institute (CTI), IECL and Keystone Group's Evidence-Based Coaching (EBC), for example. All these programs are accredited by the International Coaching Federation (ICF) at the ACTP level. In some cases, they are franchises of and managed by the parent organization, while others are partnerships or joint ventures with academic institutions or other coach training companies.

Other coach development and certification programs in China are operated by Chinese entrepreneurs who have completed one or more of the Western coaching training programs, or worked as a coach in a MNC or local Chinese company, then started their own coach training organization. These organizations took advantage of the rapid growth of coaching in China from 2010 and subsequent years, leveraging their own knowledge of the China market. MindSpan, Progress U, the Enrichment Coaching Organization, Zhao Qian Organizational Coach, and WXT Coach are some examples. While several of these programs are accredited at the ACTP level, most are accredited by the ICF at the lower ACSTH level.

There are a few predominant coaching approaches taught by these programs. Both Erickson and CTI have well researched, proprietary coaching models, and their certification programs provide instruction on how to use these models and related skills in delivering coaching. At the conclusion of these programs, learners are well prepared to use these models in their coaching work.

Other successful coach development programs in China introduce multiple coaching models and a more comprehensive series of foundational human development theories. These programs introduce basic coaching skills, including the ICF competency model, and they overlay these skills with relevant foundational coaching and human development theories to help coaches develop and grow their own unique style and approach to coaching. This approach provides both theory and practical application of coaching models, plus an introduction to a broad array of foundational theories. It is beneficial for coaches to apply these theories in an introspective way to better understand themselves as a human being and how they relate to coachees. These programs also provide opportunities to apply critical thinking, to determine which theories are most applicable in a given situation, and to practice using these theories in sample situations.

Another set of theories and tools provided by some of these programs are those which prepare a leadership coach to help their coachees in China understand leadership challenges and organizational implications for operating in an ever-more competitive global business environment. These theories provide leadership coachees a deeper understanding of the context facing coachees, and to help these coachees deal with organizational challenges.

In addition to the development of coaching skills and increased understanding of human development theories and opportunities for application, a leadership coach development program in China must also consider the nature of the student and be delivered using appropriate instructional approaches.

For a number of contextual reasons, instructional approaches in China require tailoring to ensure that learning occurs within the time and resources of Chinese adult learners. Some key differences between Chinese and Western adult learners are a result of the significant and rapid changes in the work, cultural, social and economic environment of China in recent years and the instructional approach used in most of China's educational institutions.

Because market-based labor pools and economic competition are relatively new in China, few students in leadership coaching programs have the broad or lengthy work experiences of their Western counterparts. As a result, it is sometimes difficult for learners in leadership coaching certification programs to understand the complexity of their coachees' leadership environment, to comprehend systemic dilemmas the coachee faces, or the challenges the coachees face in aligning people at the team or organizational level. To address this need, leadership coaching programs in China find it necessary to provide context within the instructional program to help learners not only understand the individual executive coachee, but also understand their work environment.

In recent years, there has been a gradual cultural shift away from the influence of Confucianism and hierarchical social structures that focus on societal harmony and power distance. This is especially true in the younger generations, who grew up in the one-child era and whose attitudes and social structures and norms have become more individualistic. In this changing and emerging environment, there is a lack of clarity of the "social task" for which learners are engaging in learning. Rather than learning a new profession because it is a family or societal expectation, individuals have more freedom to choose their own career path—often a career for which they are the creators. Uncertainty, caused by economic slowdowns or global events, can reduce a potential coach's motivation and make it difficult to clarify why they should engage in learning a profession that is not widely understood in China at present. As a result, instruction that focuses on content must be accompanied by activities that help learners visualize and reflect on their future as a professional coach.

An additional factor is the historical approach used in education in China. The requirement for learners to assimilate content knowledge, understand that knowledge, and apply it in specific situations are key components of Chinese education. Students at all levels compete for limited slots in education programs, based on their ability to "memorize and display" understanding of factual knowledge. However, during class sessions, when students are asked to apply knowledge in new or novel situations that are not clearly delineated, they sometimes feel they have not mastered the content—creating anxiety generated by a fear of failure. This requirement leads learners who are expecting to be taught concrete facts and how to apply them in a given situation, to feel that they have not received adequate instruction on how the coaching models and approaches can be applied in new and unique situations. Based on the authors' experiences delivering coaching and coaching training, successful coach training requires coaches to engage in higher-level learning, such as analyzing, evaluating, and creating new solutions based on information gained in the coaching session. As a result, successful programs must be based on instructional methods that help learners engage in critical thinking. This will prepare them to analyze a new situation, evaluate the situation, use relevant underlying principles, and create new solutions with the coachee, rather than using a coaching model by rote or simply providing answers or advice.

Research shows that learners engaged in learning to be coaches feel much better-prepared when attending coaching certification programs, which provide opportunities for using these higher-level cognitive processes. Using the principles of Bloom's taxonomy (2001 version, by Anderson and Krathwohl (Wilson, L. 2016)), some locally available courses have been designed to provide Chinese learners with an opportunity to learn these higher-level skills.

Because of these differences, the use of more cases and examples, which make learning relevant, are required in successful programs. Also, feedback on progress, while desirable, must be delivered in a way that honors cultural norms, e.g., the "face" of the learner.

A Suggested Approach to Coaching Certification in China

To accelerate the launch of a professional leadership coaching program in China, Dr. Marjorie Woo recognized the benefit of building on solid theoretical and instructional principles and practices already in use in other countries. In her search for a relevant program, she investigated and saw the relevance, quality, and benefits for China in the Fielding Graduate University's Evidence-Based Coaching (EBC) Program.

Fielding Graduate University (FGU) focuses on the advanced study of a number of disciplines in the fields of human and organization development. Founded in 1974 and headquartered in Santa Barbara, California, FGU's technology-based instructional approach, accompanied by face-to-face sessions at a variety of global locations, along with its high-quality faculty delivering programs in many countries, make it a truly global institution.

Dr. Woo worked with FGU's administration and faculty to transport and localize their EBC program for China in 2009. The EBC program, although modified for the unique coaching environment and learners of China, and periodically updated to include new foundational theories and instructional approaches, has maintained the high quality of the original EBC program.

Introduction to Evidence-Based Coaching

EBC is based on the notion, borrowed from the medical field, that treatment should be based on relevant evidence, taking into account the expertise of the physician and the specifics of the needs of the patient. According to Grant (2016), "the term 'evidenced-based coaching' was coined at the Coaching Psychology Unit at the University of Sydney in 2003 as a way of distinguishing between coaching that is explicitly grounded in the broader empirical and theoretical knowledge base, and coaching that was developed from the pop-psychology, personal development genre."

In this chapter, we consider the definition of EBC to be "the intelligent and conscientious use of the best current knowledge in making decisions about how to deliver coaching to coachees, and in designing and teaching coach-training programs." (Sackett, Haynes, Guyatt, & Tugwell, 1996 in Grant, A. 2005). Stober et al. (2005) state that "as an emerging profession, it is vital for coaches to begin integrating evidence from coaching-specific research and related disciplines, their own expertise, and an understanding of the uniqueness of each coachee." These three elements make up the foundation of an EBC program used to train professional leadership coaches.

Stober and Grant (2006) further expand on this core premise to state that EBC is based on humanistic psychology and focuses on self-actualization and positive change. As such, it is a philosophy of development, rather than a specific technique, approach, or model. Stober goes on to say that EBC takes into account the coachee as a whole person, even though much of the work is focused on small steps of finding solutions, developing specific skills, or goal attainment. For this reason, EBC programs introduce a number of theories and models.

Based on these premises, it is recommended that effective leadership coaching programs in China include not only instruction about one or two coaching models, skills and approaches, as they are practiced today. They should also include significant instruction and practice in applying foundational and related theories. In other words, it must include instruction about, and deepen the understanding of, new developments in the coaching field. This ensures that coaches are well-prepared to understand the uniqueness of each coachee, and how the coach can continue to enhance his/her own expertise in delivering coaching that meets the coachee's needs.

To ensure the relevancy of any evidence-based program, it must be regularly updated to incorporate new theories, adult learning approaches, and coaching practices relevant for coaching professionals in China. For example, some theories that have entered the literature, and should be incorporated as foundational theories, include advances in positive psychology, very brief cognitive behavioral coaching, neuroscience, embodiment and mindfulness, appreciative inquiry, scenario planning, team coaching, and psychological assessment.

Programs should not only provide instruction on how to use existing models and theories, but also introduce coaches to sources of new research about coaching models. Such sources include publications, such as the *International Journal of Evidence Based Coaching and Mentoring,* dedicated to the research and practice of EBC. In addition to professional journals, a number of books, such as the *Evidence Based Coaching Handbook*, and *Innovations in Leadership Coaching: Research and Practice,* have been published and provide seminal research on the practice of using EBC. There are also a number of international conferences and forums focused on EBC advancement as a subset of the broader coaching theory and practice arena.

As China's government has set policies focused on expanding the number and role of privately-owned enterprises (POEs) and on countering corruption, coach development programs must provide opportunities for coaches to become aware of the challenges facing leadership coachees because of such policies. Examples of content that should be included as part of a robust EBC program include coaching executives who are facing challenges of business financial management, ethical principles and legal requirements when working with distributors and customers, managing a global supply chain, dealing with unplanned shocks such as COVID-19, and working with younger generations of talent. Inclusion of such content will help leadership coaches prepare to work with coachees to align their organization and create a competitive strategy.

One further content area unique to developing leadership coaches in China is that of enabling coaches to help leaders reflect on principles of Confucian philosophy and its embeddedness in cultural norms while engaging in a global strategy. When Chinese organizations start managing operations outside China, Chinese executives often struggle with leading Western team members whom they expect to adhere to Confucian principles, similar to their followers in China. Leadership coaches in China must learn to help their coachees recognize and address this difference. It is important to not just repackage a Western program based on Western culture for delivery in China. It is necessary to take into consideration the cultural norms of leadership and coaching application from a Chinese perspective.

In addition to structuring a leadership coaching program in China to include relevant skills and theories, a successful program should incorporate the development and inclusion of EBC faculty who are Chinese scholar-practitioners. Program faculty must include those who are familiar with the cultural and educational norms of China, who are engaged in practicing coaching, and who are teaching and conducting research into coaching in China. Sources of these faculty can include individuals with experience running or working in a business in China, preferably a global business, and those who have studied coaching and human development at any of a number of European, U.S., and Chinese universities. Examples of faculty who meet these requirements and who are in strong demand—whom students prefer to learn from—include those from FGU, INSEAD, CEIBS, Shanghai Jiaotong University, Eastern China Normal University, Beijing Normal University, United Business Institutes, and Xiamen University, to name a few.

To ensure opportunities for continuous learning for leadership coaches, another resource is the creation of an association, organization, or process to help alumni of coach-development programs continue their growth. For example, to ensure that alumni can continue to develop, Keystone Group EBC established the Keystone Group Alumni Association. The purpose of this organization is to support the sharing of professional learning and practices for coaching, to identify interests for future alumni offerings, to socialize with others in the field, to establish a community for finding and sharing coaching opportunities for alumni, and to advance the coaching field in China.

Dr. Christina Showalter, first Keystone EBC faculty in China (Keystone Group, Inc.)

Suggested China EBC Program Components

In the previous section, we offered a suggested set of "program components" to advance the professional level of leadership coaches in China. These are based on experiences that contributed to the success of the Keystone Group's EBC program becoming known as a source of high-quality, well-prepared leadership coaches. The suggestions are also based on research into improvements in coach training. The following provides insights into the structure, content, and instructional approach needed to make a high-quality program effective and respected. Many of these components are also included in other successful coach development programs in China. While it does not exist today, it would be appropriate to create a China Association of Coaching Training Organizations (CACTO), modeled after the North American Association of Coaching Training Organizations (ACTO). This would be a big step toward developing and promoting common standards and advancing coach development in China.

1. Foundational ICF Coaching Competencies

For students to obtain an ICF coaching certificate, they must learn and apply the ICF core coaching competencies which include demonstrating ethical practice, embodying a coaching mindset, cultivating trust and safety, and 4 others (ICF 2019), to demonstrate mastery in the delivery of effective coaching.

As coaching continues to move toward becoming a mature profession, the coaching-specific literature reflecting new models, theories, and approaches for leadership coaching grows as well.

Each year, new models are available to coaches that help them address novel situations with their coachees. These include TGROW, for foundational coaching; ABCDEF, for cognitive behavioral coaching; and the TENOR model for emotional intelligence coaching. There are also new principles of human development in related fields such as psychology, counseling, and neuroscience. It is important that leadership coaches learn examples of how these theories can be applied to best deal with the uniqueness of each coachee and her/his situation.

To prepare coaches to be successful in the diverse and rapidly-changing China business environment, another approach to accelerating their development would be to learn a foundational model and apply that model to become proficient in the use of essential coaching skills as described in the ICF competencies. Currently, a number of coaching certification programs in China are limited to teaching one coaching model and basic coaching skills. While necessary as an initial approach to learning to coach, over-reliance on one approach can restrict coaches from developing their own models or approaches as they advance.

The use of a foundational model and essential coaching skills will only prepare a coach to be a good coach. To become a "great coach," it is necessary to understand the broader context in which the coachee operates, to formulate courageous and innovative approaches to help the coachee to develop and grow, and to advance one's own expertise and experience by using current science in the field of coaching (Peterson 2010).

As the coach becomes more experienced in applying coaching skills within a foundational model, the coach must extend this ability by adding additional coaching models and deepening coaching skills to help resolve specific coachee situations and challenges. An effective coaching development program should also provide instruction and practice in using additional models and theories to better understand the coachee.

2. Foundational Theories of Human Development Theories for Coaching

Developing leadership coaches should include opportunities for them to learn foundational theories of human development related to coaching. Because new theories of human development and coaching are continuously being discovered, and because the environment in which executives work is also changing rapidly, new research and evidence about approaches to helping people develop, and models for coaching, should be provided in the development of leadership coaches.

Examples include research by the University of Sydney, by FGU's EBC faculty, and by the China-based EBC faculty. Relevant research areas include theories of psychology, adult development and learning, organizational systems, motivation, assessment, culture, leadership foundations, change management, and team/group dynamics. Program content in these areas should be updated regularly as new models and theories emerge in the research.

3. Application of Human Development Theories in Leadership Coaching Situations

While it is necessary to learn about foundational theories of human development related to coaching, only having knowledge of the theory is insufficient if one is to become a successful leadership coach. A successful program must include opportunities for the learner to engage in extended application of these theories in leadership coaching situations. For example, in a recent coaching certification program session, one learner mentioned an example in which one of her coachees, an executive who was promoted to a higher-level, more complex role, was struggling. In this case, having learned about Kegan's brain complexity theory of adult development, the coach knew that this might be a "lens" through which to examine the coachee's struggles more deeply. By using this situation as a case in the application session, the coach went beyond knowing the theory to preparing to use it in working with the coachee. Others in the session had an opportunity to see how the theory could be used and thereby elevate their coaching capability.

In summary, an effective leadership coaching development program requires not only learning such theories, but also providing opportunities to reflect on when the theories might apply, how to apply them, and opportunities to practice with real situations. While not all learners will immediately face opportunities to use all the theories, we know from learning theory that transfer and social learning, through observation, will help others prepare to handle situations when they also need to apply a particular theory.

4. Coaching in Organizations—Increasing Organizational Resilience by Coaching Leaders, Teams, and the Organization

Leadership coaching is different from a number of other types of coaching. It requires the coach to understand the business and organizational context of the coachee, the environment in which s/he operates. While all of us have life and career experiences that help us prepare to coach people who are facing life and career challenges, in China, not everyone has sufficient experience to understand the dynamic and systemic challenges faced by executives in business organizations. To become effective as a leadership coach, coaches must be able to go beyond coaching the individual leader, gaining personal insight, and developing interpersonal skills. The effective leadership coach must also learn coaching skills to help the leader address such larger organizational issues and challenges as increasing team performance, or aligning the organization to face new competitive challenges.

Examples of concepts/tools useful for coaching leaders who are facing challenges in aligning their team, or even the broader organization, include team dynamics and group processes, systems theory, change theory, appreciative inquiry, and scenario planning. While the specific tool used when coaching leaders facing such challenges can include any of these tools, learning how to coach executives (including helping them prepare effectively to analyze strategy, formulate a vision, diagnose critical barriers, work with others to create a plan, and influence and align their team and organization) requires first becoming aware of the tools during the coach training, and then becoming competent with one or more of these tools over a period of time.

Instructional Approach for Developing Leadership Coaches—Ongoing Application and Guided Practice with Feedback

For the most part, the Chinese adult learner is similar to adult learners elsewhere in the world; adult learning principles readily apply. Knowles (1984 in Smith, M. 2002) states that the principles of adult learning—or "andragogy"—include:

• Self-concept – Adults are self-directed and take responsibility for their learning.
• Experience – Adults have a great reservoir of experience they can bring to learning.
• Readiness to learn – The adult is oriented to fulfilling his or her social roles.
• Orientation to learning – A preference for applying the learning by focusing on problems rather than just learning theory.
• Motivation to learn – The level of internal desire to learn.

A successful instructional approach for developing coaches in China should incorporate the following principles to meet the needs of today's Chinese adult learner:
• Workshops that include a combination of theory, the opportunity for discussion in small groups, and relevant case examples to deepen understanding of how the theory can be applied.
• Flexible scheduling of programs, and delivery through an effective combination of online and off-line instruction, using appropriate technology platforms, to accommodate those who work full-time.
• Personal goal-setting, and clarification using a mentoring approach throughout the learning program, including the learner's own self-assessment and career

planning for coaching and coach development.

• Incorporation of a significant number of opportunities for practical, guided experience within the program, including:

    • Coaching practice in the workshops with feedback from peer learners and from faculty and alumni who have experience as leadership coaches

    • Faculty-led coaching practice, and supervision throughout the program, facilitated by faculty with experience as leadership coaches

    • Group mentoring using coaching approaches

    • Certification preparation via one-to-one mentoring by certified, experienced coaches

    • Feedback on and support for progress toward personal coaching goals

    • Prework assignments where learners review real-life cases which then serve as the basis for critical thinking exercises during the workshop

• Opportunities for alumni to contribute, within the courses, by providing coaching and feedback, and gaining practical experience by doing so.

• Provide support to alumni who desire to become certified coaches through periodic group sessions and one-to-one support to assist completion of certification documentation.

5. Continuous Coach Development

Becoming a successful leadership coach requires continuous learning. For this reason, a quality program for developing leadership coaches must go beyond offering a core curriculum which meets the needs described thus far and meet ICF ACTP accreditation requirements to prepare learners for certification at the PCC level. It should also provide offerings to help leadership coaches in China advance their professional capabilities. Based on research with alumni and others seeking ongoing coach development, the following offerings are suggested:

• Team and Group Coaching
• Coaching for Strategy and Strategic Thinking
• Immunity to Change and Self-Development
• Applying Neuroscience in Coaching
• Cognitive Behavioral Therapy and Coaching
• Coaching for Emotional Management
• Using Psychometric and Behavioral Assessments in Coaching

• Coaching for Transformational Leadership
• Developing One's Leadership Coaching Business
• Coaching Supervision

Providing Opportunities for Leadership Coaching in Business

In the previous section, we described an approach that can prepare coaches to be successful in practicing as leadership coaches working with individuals, whether in the coach's own business or as part of a network or coaching consultancy. Since becoming a more effective business leader through coaching support is a relatively new paradigm in China, another opportunity for leadership coaches is to partner with organizations that provide leadership skills training and use coaching as a means of accelerating the development of these skills. In this section, we describe an approach used to provide opportunities to apply coaching in the development of business leaders within a highly acclaimed leadership development program that has met the needs of China business leaders for the last 20 years.

Coaching Application Background in Chinese Local Enterprises

Forty years of "reform and opening" have generated rapid economic development in China. Chinese enterprises have experienced being thrust into a market economy with scarce resources to lead. Chinese enterprises are facing a competitive business environment where they encounter Western enterprises with a long history of leadership development investment, and where they are encouraged in the use of innovation and technology to rapidly advance leadership skills. While still generally behind the West, after 40 years, Chinese enterprises have begun to appreciate the importance of leadership development. While many Chinese enterprises provide access to leadership development for senior leaders, including enrollment in EMBA, MBA, and proprietary leadership development programs, many enterprises overlook the benefit of developing basic leadership skills in their first-line and middle-level leaders.

For some progressive enterprises, there has been a recognition of and a focus on people cultivation or development, shifting from simple knowledge transmission to stimulation of an individual's potential through using effective leadership practices. For these businesses to become truly empowering and innovative, they must develop leaders throughout the organization. In fact, these enterprises now recognize that the organization of the future is an organization where everyone is a leader.

One example of a system that has proven very effective in China in supporting leadership development at lower management levels comes from Leadership Management International (LMI) in the U.S. LMI, founded in Texas in 1966 by Paul J. Mayer, was introduced to China in 1998. In its first decade in China, LMI primarily served multinational companies, including IBM and GE. In the most recent decade, the focus has been on Chinese companies, including Neusoft, Inner Mongolia Yili Industrial Group, China Resource Holdings, Haier, and Hisense, all of which are very large companies with many layers of management. The LMI system includes a series of leadership trainings presented and supported with a coaching approach. The components of this system include a copyrighted textbook, classroom instruction, individual learning exercises, and group and individual coaching.

To enhance the development of leaders, the focus is on learning foundational leadership skills, and then deepening the application of these skills through daily practice. Some of the more successful leadership development programs include coaching as part of the learning system. Rather than focusing on random leadership challenges the coachee brings to the coaching session, the coaching in these programs is focused on application of leadership as taught in the program, strengthening the understanding of these leadership principles.

Some of the tenets of the LMI program include the belief that for leadership development to be effective, it must utilize a complete, integrated, total leadership development process. It is only when people are able to lead themselves that they are actually empowered to be creative and innovative and to lead others. Too many organizations have attempted to develop leaders with a fragmented, piecemeal approach. They focus on one area or attribute of leadership and believe that this is all they need. Leadership is much more complex than that. Leaders must also possess the confidence and mental strength to perform in the heat of competition.

The following describes in more detail the components of the LMI system. It should be noted that there are many other effective leadership development programs in China. Few, however, offer such a robust system, one which embeds coaching to accelerate application via coaching and feedback.

1. Personal Productivity

Personal productivity is the foundation of leadership, our ability to manage ourselves, our time, and our priorities in order to achieve optimal performance. When you have the ability to improve your own performance, you have the real potential to improve the performance of others.

2. Personal Leadership

Personal leadership is the ability to lead oneself. And everyone is a leader in his/her own life. Most people let themselves go and suffer the consequences. Great personal leaders, on the other hand, decide what kind of life they want to live, then plan and act to achieve that goal.

Effective personal leaders continue to grow and improve in six areas of life: family, and the natural bonds and ethical relationships between family members; career and finance; mind and education; body and health; society and culture; spirit and morality. Personal leadership is the core of a leader's personal qualities and the foundation for the development of trusting relationships that are essential to leading others.

3. Motivational Leadership

Motivational leadership is the ability to lead through inspiring others. Effective motivational leaders recognize that "talent" is the source of all progress and innovation and the key to an organization's continued success in the 21st century. Igniting people's internal motivation is essential to building an effective and loyal team. Motivational leaders help others develop and use more of their potential.

4. Strategic Leadership

Strategic leadership is the ability to lead an organization. For an organization to succeed, strategic leaders must have the ability to define and develop organizational goals, core strategies and processes, an optimal organizational structure, and the right staffing strategies. Strategic leadership is not only the ability to set the strategic path, but also the ability to track the strategy and ensure its implementation.

In Western companies, there is often a pool of leaders who possess the necessary skills in each of the 4 areas and who can be promoted. Because commercial and structured business is relatively new in China, many leaders have not had these opportunities for personal and leadership growth. They are thrown into situations where they are not well-prepared, and then they become frustrated because they haven't had the opportunity to develop in all four areas.

This four-part structure focuses on leadership. It stimulates internal motivation of program participants and shapes their abilities as leaders because of opportunity to immediately apply the learning, and to get feedback from a coach/faculty. Many enterprises in China use this system with a cohort of leaders at the same level. The organization, in partnership with the coach, selects one of the component areas as the focus of learning, according to the specific challenges of the coachee. Coaching is incorporated in that module and structured to help the coachee improve the behavior and reach the goal of the module by providing feedback and support. This approach accelerates how the coachee learns to apply standard approaches based on the leadership principles covered in that module. Specific forms of instruction and coaching include:

1) Advance preparation, reading, and reflection. The coachee reads weekly and reflects on each knowledge point through interval repetition.

2) One-to-one coaching. Before, during and after the program, the coach provides one-on-one coaching for each coachee, jointly sets behavioral goals, and tracks these regularly.

3) Weekly group coaching. The program requires half-a-day of group coaching each week. These sessions include group discussion of leadership-related challenges the members are facing, reflections on how to address these challenges, and guidance and feedback from the coach.

The structure and approach of this program ensures that the resulting changes in thinking and behavior are achieved through spaced repetition, listening and reading, and self-reflection. Individual accountability is tracked and guided by the coach. By focusing on individual and organizational change, this approach to leadership development truly changes organizational performance.

Leadership Coaching Experience in China

Chinese enterprises come in various forms, e.g., state-owned enterprises (SOEs), privately-owned enterprises (POEs), and foreign-funded enterprises (often referred to as multinational corporations or MNCs). Each has a different corporate culture and management style. To be effective as a leadership coach in China, it is necessary to understand the differences in enterprise structure and culture for the type of organization one is coaching in. This understanding will enable the coach to determine what leadership problems a client company may be facing, to propose a solution that is applicable to that organization, and to ensure that the right combination of training and coaching is proposed.

While Chinese corporations are somewhat familiar with the benefits of leadership training programs, many SOE and POE executive leaders and HR directors are unfamiliar with leadership coaching. As a result, convincing executives in these organizations to offer individual leadership coaching as an approach for leadership development is often the biggest challenge. These executives lack understanding of how leadership coaching services work and are unfamiliar with the value brought to individual leaders when they are provided with leadership coaching.

Often, even the coachee does not understand the value and operational process of leadership coaching. Questions can arise, such as, "Am I being offered coaching because I'm seen as a low performer?" "Have I made some leader angry?" "Why should I spend time with a coach when I am being asked to deliver significant results?" With such uncertainty, the coachee can be fearful and hesitant, unable to build a trusting relationship with the organization and the coach.

As a result, many leadership coaches spend a lot of time explaining the value of coaching to coachees at the beginning of an engagement. Both the coaches themselves and the firms offering coaching programs need to spend more time winning the trust of their clients.

While more than 70% of local Chinese enterprises have not applied, or are even familiar with, individual leadership coaching, there is still an opportunity for leadership coaching to grow over time. As most local Chinese enterprises are in the period of second-generation entrepreneurship, leadership coaches can play an important role in accelerating leadership development in these companies.

From the experience of the past 10 years, leadership coaching can bring significant value to the development of an organization through the transformation of its people. The road to leadership growth in individuals will likely occur through the use of cohort-based leadership development programs in the short term. As for the development of leadership coaches in China, they will need to constantly adapt, strive for excellence, and participate in offering coaching services that meet the needs of local enterprises. This is part of the mission of leadership coaches in China.

References

Fielding Graduate University (2019). *Fielding Graduate University Vision, Mission and Values.* Retrieved Oct 1, 2020: https://www.fielding.edu/news/fielding-gets-community-engagement-mark-from-carnegie-foundation/

Grant, A. (2005). *What is evidence-based executive, work-place and life coaching?* Retrieved Oct 13, 2020: https://www.researchgate.net/publication/312914530_What_is_evidence-based_executive_workplace_and_life_coaching.

International Coaching Federation (ICF) (2019). *Updated ICF Core Competency Model: October 2019.* Retrieved May 4, 2020. https://coachingfederation.org/core-competencies.

Peterson, D. (2010). "Good to Great Coaching: Advancing the Journey." *Advancing Executive Coaching: Setting the course for successful leadership coaching.* Hernez-Broome, G. and Boyce, L. Editors. Wiley & Sons. New York.

Smith, M. K. (2002) 'Malcolm Knowles, informal adult education, self-direction and andragogy', *The encyclopedia of pedagogy and informal education.* Retrieved October 13, 2020: www.infed.org/thinkers/et-knowl.htm.

Stober, D. & Grant, A. (2006). *Evidence Based Coaching Handbook: Putting best practices to work for your clients.* Wiley & Sons. New York.

Whitmore, J. (1992). *Coaching for performance.* Nicholas Brealey: London.

Stober, D., Wildflower, L. and Drake, D. (2006). "Evidence-Based Practice: A potential approach for effective coaching." *International Journal of Evidence Based Coaching and Mentoring.* Vol. 4, No.1, Spring 2006. Retrieved October 13, 2020: http://www.laurierosenfeld.com/wp-content/uploads/2010/09/vol-4-1-stober-et-al_Evidence-BasedPractice.pdf.

Wilson, L. (2016). *Anderson and Krathwohl Bloom's Taxonomy Revised: Understanding the New Version of Bloom's Taxonomy.* Retrieved October 13, 2020: https://quincycollege.edu/content/uploads/Anderson-and-Krathwohl_Revised-Blooms-Taxonomy.pdf.

Jeff Hasenfratz and Andrew Newmark

Chapter 4.
Lifecycle of a typical One-on-One Leadership Coaching Engagement

Client and Coach Perspectives

A serious but lighthearted
conversation between Jeff (a Coach)
and Andrew (a Human Resources Leader)

"The quality of conversation governs the rate of value creation."
- Mickey Connolly and Richard Rianoshek, *Communication Catalyst*

Abstract

The previous chapter addressed the certification, education, and ongoing development of executive coaches in China. This chapter delves into the "nuts and bolts" of a 1:1 coaching engagement, from two perspectives: that of an executive coach and that of an organizational sponsor. Key elements of the chapter include coach "vetting," coach/coachee matching, contracting, data gathering and goal setting, coaching, and closure of the engagement.

The Engagement Begins

"Hi Jeff, how are you? I'm Susan, a leadership coach based in Ohio. We met at the ICF Conference in California last year. One of my client companies wants to hire a coach to work with their managing director in China. Interested?"

So starts an email or text message from a fellow coach, one of the most common ways a leadership coaching engagement in China begins. To be clear, when I say "leadership coaching engagement in China," I'm referring to an engagement with a foreign multinational firm (MNC) operating in China.

There are also two other common catalysts of leadership coaching engagements with MNCs. One is a request made directly to the coach by a CEO or HR VP, usually sparked by a conversation one of these leaders has had with the coach at a business gathering, such as a foreign Chamber of Commerce event. The request could also arise from a recommendation made to the leader by a trusted source, or as the result of an online search.

A coaching engagement might also be generated through outreach from a coaching firm with whom the coach has a relationship. The firm may have received a query from one of its MNC clients, searched its database for experienced coaches based in China, then contacted the coach.

Many times, the coaching engagement is initiated from an MNC that needs an experienced leadership coach to work with one of its senior executives in China, and the search for a "best fit" coach begins.

Andrew: Thanks Jeff. I am an HR business partner and my experience as a sponsor of coaching engagements began about 10 years ago. From my experience, the idea of engaging a coach typically arises during talent development discussions where coaching has been identified as a means of helping individuals meet their development objectives. Often this is a situation where it is felt that internal resources may not be sufficient and that the opportunity to work with a coach who is external from the business will add value.

Examples of development objectives where I have seen coaching used include preparing talent for a new job assignment, a promotion, or a career transition (like retirement). Another objective may be to help the person build, or strengthen, a leadership competency or behavior that is identified as being essential for their continued growth—for example executive presence, communication, or collaboration.

I have also had experience bringing coaching into leadership development programs, where a group of promising people are provided coaching as part of their participation in the program. In this case, the coaching is integrated with other development activities, such as a 360-degree assessment and educational and experiential content. While this type of engagement may start off with a broad focus, I have seen it narrow into a meaningful experience for the participants, with coaching as an integral part of the overall program.

Coach "Vetting"

Jeff: O.K., onward we go with our exploration of the coaching engagement lifecycle. The cycle typically includes coach contact and "vetting," a chemistry meeting or two, contracting with the coaching sponsor and with the coachee, the coaching process itself, and completion of the engagement. Let's look at how this unfolds in more detail. To make things more personal and interesting, let's assume that you, dear reader, are the coach involved in the engagement.

You, the coach, have been contacted in one of the ways mentioned, and you have agreed to participate in the next step, a "vetting" conversation. In this conversation, which is normally held with someone in the organization who contacted you initially, your prospective fit for, and interest in, the engagement is assessed.

Your conversation partner, often a current or former HR professional, will ask about your coach training, the process you use to coach, your experience coaching at senior leadership levels, and your China cultural knowledge. The partner may also ask about your experience coaching in the organization's industry sector and whether you've coached leaders in their specific organization. If the coachee is Chinese (a most likely possibility), you may also be asked about your level of fluency in spoken Chinese.

Inevitably, you'll also be asked about your fees, often accompanied by an apologetic tone and slightly embarrassed laugh. I normally find this part of the conversation quite amusing, as sharing my fee range normally prompts one of two reactions.

"Oh! Are you willing to be flexible?" To which I will respond, in a smiling voice, "Certainly! I'd be happy to charge you more!" Having lightened the mood, we then talk about the sponsor's budget limits and work to accommodate each other's needs.

Or there is another, similar reaction. Hearing the fee range, there is a brief silence, suddenly broken by, "You're expensive!" After which I then laugh and often respond, "Yes, I'm not the cheapest, but you do get what you pay for!" After a few chuckles, the conversation moves toward a discussion of fee structure differences for China-based coaching vs. coaching provided elsewhere in the world.

We'll come back to fee differences, and the flow of the coaching engagement, shortly. Before that, it might be helpful to offer a bit of context on the growth of coaching in China over the last 20 years.

Coaching and Coaches in China – Some Historical Context

Coaching, viewed as a practice useful to leadership development, began to gain traction in organizations in the U.S. only about 40 years ago. It then spread to Europe, then Asia, where I encountered it in Hong Kong in 2000. A year later, the slumping economy in Hong Kong presented me with the opportunity to jump-start my new coaching practice by supporting executives in career transition.

After moving to Shanghai in 2004, I held similar impressions of coaching as an emerging field as I had felt in Hong Kong. Those impressions involved the relevance, value, and optimal use of coaching within Chinese culture.

By *relevance* I mean that there seemed to be no clear link between coaching and any similar field found historically in China. For example, while Chinese history is replete with accounts of famous philosophers, teachers, and military advisors, there appear to be no references to a field similar to coaching as Western practitioners tend to understand it.

So, as coaching began to take root, 20 years ago, with organizations in China, those organizations were (and mainly remain) MNCs—foreign companies that had experienced the benefits of coaching in the U.S., Europe, and elsewhere, and decided to use it for leadership development in China.

Value is a shorthand way of suggesting that many local organizations (not only in China but also in other countries) still lack a clear understanding of the benefits of executive leadership coaching. Relatedly, many organizations seem unaware that both effective coaching processes, and experienced coaches able to facilitate them, exist to support the emergence of those benefits.

Optimization refers to the conditions within which coaching can be used to optimal effect. From what I've seen in China, and heard from colleagues elsewhere, coaching is often applied, in its early days in a new geography, as a last-ditch effort to "fix" colleagues judged as under-performers.

In my experience, the "fix 'em" rationale for coaching use, grounded in a foundation of threat, is highly unlikely to produce substantial benefits for the sponsor or the coachee. The coachee tends to resent the coaching (and sometimes the coach), and does the minimum necessary to be able to show engagement in the process. The coach, who aspires to work in a positive partnership with the coachee, is forced into the role of enforcer.

Having encountered, and been frustrated by, two such engagements in my early years as a coach, I've become more adept, during vetting conversations at sensing the possible presence of a "fix 'em" rationale. I will then, if offered the engagement, either politely decline it or take it on as a learning opportunity.

Thankfully, I've since found a way to work much more positively and effectively with coachees who are perceived as sub-performers, rather than stars, by their sponsors. Starting from the chemistry meeting, I adopt the mindset that the coachee is indeed a star (just one yet unrecognized as such by the sponsor). I share that view with the coachee and behave accordingly. As one might expect, the coaching relationship and results tend to be much more positive.

Since its early days, the development of leadership coaching in China has seen a shift in focus, a focus on supporting current or potential "stars"—already successful, motivated leaders who have stepped, or could step, into roles of increasing responsibility. Sponsors have increasingly seen coaching as a valuable means of supporting these leaders to become more confident and to perform at a higher level, and to support and inspire such confidence and performance in subordinates.

Returning briefly to the topic of coaching fees, many sponsors, particularly if they live outside China, are surprised to find that fees for coaching senior executives here tend to be higher than for coaching at this level in the U.S. or Europe.

One reason for this difference is supply and demand. While there are many experienced leadership coaches in Western countries, there simply aren't that many in China, particularly coaches who not only have strong coaching skills but who also possess deep cultural awareness and Chinese-language skills.

Relatedly, a clear majority of executives, especially Chinese executives, strongly prefer face-to-face coaching. While the arrival of COVID-19 has shifted this dynamic for the moment, my guess is that, as the virus subsides in China, we'll see a return to face-to-face sessions, and there will be more work for the growing but still relatively limited number of experienced leadership coaches in the country.

To end our reflection on historical context, a brief word about changing coachee profiles. When I first began coaching in China, nearly every leadership coachee was a Caucasian man. Over time, the dominant profile became Chinese men. This changed again, about 2 years ago, so that today, about 70% of my coachees are Chinese women.

Frankly, this change comes as no surprise. Since Deng Xiao Ping, China's leader in the late 70s, opened the country's economic doors to the West, MNCs, followed by Chinese organizations, have been developing local managers using Western leadership concepts. It only makes sense that this "localization" has included offering coaching to Chinese leaders for their continued development.

Andrew: As a sponsor, I see the "vetting" step as an important aspect of the lifecycle and in identifying potential coaches for the coachee. When I first started utilizing coaching as a development tool, I did not have coaching contacts, and I needed to tap into my network to identify potential sources of coaches. This included direct referrals to individual coaches or coaching organizations. I was fortunate to take some sound advice and gain introductions through some of my valued contacts. I soon realized that having a diverse pool of coaches was going to be important and that just finding one or two competent coaches was unlikely to fit the needs of a variety of coachees and their needs.

I particularly learnt this from one of the earliest coaching engagements I needed to organize. It was for a coachee who had recently relocated to the region, having worked in a variety of international locations. It was agreed that providing her with a coach would be a valuable step to support her transition and development. I had worked with a couple of coaches by this time, both of whom I thought were strong and had positive results and reviews with other coachees. I thought they would be good candidates for this new engagement. However, the coachee was very specific about the background and personality of the coach whom she felt would best fit her development and needs. While I needed to do more groundwork to identify a more diverse list of coach profiles, this experience taught me that time taken at this step is critical for each individual coachee.

Professional background, educational qualifications, and life experience are all key elements I learned to review as part of the vetting process before proceeding to the essential step of talking to each coach on the shortlist. As Jeff shared, as a sponsor this is my opportunity to probe further on the profile of the coach, understanding more about their coaching approach and the types of coachees they have worked with in the past. Also, given my knowledge of the coachee, I try to get a sense of how the coach may align with the coachee's needs and what type of chemistry may happen between the two. While ultimately the selection of the coach will be the coachee's decision, gaining an insight into these factors has helped me guide the coachee on how to compare and consider the coaches who are available for the engagement.

I recall another coachee who was preparing for retirement after a long and respected career with the company and in the industry. The coachee was a celebrated member of the team, but it was time to plan for this transition. While the coachee was ready to retire, we identified that taking the steps to retirement was likely to be a sensitive and possibly an emotional journey. The vetting process again was a critical step in identifying the background, style and approaches of the coaches to be put forward for the coachee's consideration. Ultimately, we landed on a coach who had a deep understanding of the culture and sensitivities that needed to be navigated to support a smooth and successful transition for the coachee.

Let me address the "fix 'em" coaching scenario that Jeff touched on. I too have had these requests as a sponsor and I am very wary of proceeding with coaching under these circumstances and for the reasons Jeff mentions. A coaching engagement is a significant investment made by all the parties. If it does not get started with alignment on the objectives and needs, it can be fraught with challenges. Unless there is solid alignment, including with the coachee, on the objective of the engagement, it would be best to look for other solutions.

Speaking of investment, Jeff raised that important topic of fees! Take it from my learning—the vetting stage is definitely the time to be talking about fees with potential coaches. From the organization and sponsor's perspective, it is critical to understand the fees of the coach and the specific services you will be getting for those fees. Sharing from experience, it can be very challenging to have your coachee identify a coach whom they would like to work with, only to find out later that the coach's fees are clearly outside your budget. The vetting stage is the best time to gain this information and to eliminate from consideration any coaches who are truly outside what your budget will permit. Sorry, Jeff, I know you get what you pay for, but a budget is important too!

Jeff: Point well noted, Andrew! All joking aside, it can be quite uncomfortable for all parties if the coach is selected, then feels compelled to withdraw from consideration. Having experienced this "bad karma" situation in the past, I now routinely bring up the topic of fees in the chemistry conversation. While doing so can feel a bit presumptuous, I've found that my conversation partner almost always appreciates my raising the topic. Shall we now return to our consideration of the coaching engagement lifecycle?

The Chemistry Meeting

You've been successfully "vetted"; great! Your conversation partner feels there is a solid fit between your coaching capabilities and the needs of the sponsor and coachee. Now it's time for the "chemistry check" Andrew alluded to.

The purpose of the chemistry check is just as it sounds; it is an opportunity for the coachee and coach to get to know each other enough to decide if there is sufficient rapport to make a successful working relationship likely. In my experience, chemistry sessions in China normally last about an hour and are held face-to-face, or on Zoom, in a quiet place.

There are a number of ways the chemistry session can proceed. If, like me, your Western ethnicity is obvious at a glance, you might like to begin to build rapport by establishing your credibility not only as a coach, but also as a person with some connection with and respect for Chinese culture. You might ask if the coachee would value you speaking first, to share a little of your personal and coaching history. Many Chinese coachees welcome this.

In my case, I briefly introduce myself as an American who has spent the last 30 years in East Asia, first in Hong Kong, then in Shanghai. I mention my family connection to China (spouse) and my coaching experience and training.

As most of my prospective coachees are Chinese, I will offer all or part of this information in Mandarin, to show this capability and to help the coachee feel more comfortable. In reality, nearly all the coachees I meet speak very good English, given the multi-cultural environments of the MNCs they lead. (This reality often leads us to joke that the coachee wants a "2 for 1" —coaching and English lessons.)

I then listen carefully to the background and other information the coachee offers, trying to assess the person's level of motivation to be coached and to do the work required for significant progress. At some point, we will speak about the coachee's potential coaching goals, after which I will ask if s/he wishes to be coached for 20-30 minutes.

Many coachees accept this offer, especially if they've never worked with a coach, in order to gain a visceral sense of how coaching works and of its potential value to them. The chemistry session normally ends with the coachee agreeing to make a coach selection decision within a short time (most organizations will put forward 2-3 coach candidates for the coachee's consideration), after which an HR colleague will contact the selected coach.

Andrew: Once your coaches are shortlisted, the chemistry sessions are critical for the coachee to make their selection of the coach best suited to work with them. As Jeff mentions, normally this will entail meeting 2 to 3 coaches in the first round and potentially expanding this group if your coachee feels they need to meet other coaches as part of their "best fit" decision making process.

Remember my coachee who had recently moved to the region and was transitioning to her new role? This was a situation where we needed to have more chemistry sessions with more coaches to help her decide. This was a coachee who wanted to debrief with me, as her sponsor, after the sessions to talk through the pros and cons of the coaches and how they matched her needs. Keeping in mind that *she* would make the selection decision, I needed to be careful not to unduly influence that decision. I played the role of sounding board, summarizing back her thinking and assessment, to help her gain clarity before she made her decision.

Once the coachee has made a decision, it is my role as sponsor to communicate back to the selected coach. I've found it best to first communicate with the selected coach rather than with those who have not been selected. The reason for this is that there may be a chance that the selected coach chooses to decline the engagement. I have experienced this situation, where a coach may feel they did not have the right chemistry with the coachee, or feel they are not best placed to help the coachee with their development objective.

I recall a specific situation where a coach let me know that they were not sure they could help the coachee even though the coachee was comfortable to proceed. In this particular case, both agreed to hold a 2nd chemistry session to explore the coaching objectives further and enable the coach to share their doubts about whether they would be the right coach for the coachee. Through this 2nd meeting they were able to achieve further clarity on the objectives, and the coach developed a stronger sense that they could support the coachee. The coaching engagement went ahead.

Once the coach is selected and agrees to the assignment, it is time to let the other coaches know they have not been selected. The coaches I have dealt with have been understanding about these decisions. Based on their professional experience, they know that the chemistry and matching of coachee and coach is not always going to result in their being selected.

Jeff: Thanks Andrew, and good work, Coach! You've been selected as the leader's leadership coach!

Contracting with the Sponsor and Coachee
Now that you've been selected, you'll need to contract with the sponsor on a range of matters. These include logistics, e.g., coaching timeframe (normally 6-12 months), session frequency, length and location (normally every 2-3 weeks, for 1.5 -2 hours, in the same city as the coachee) and the content, frequency, and format of progress reports. And, of course, the amount of your fee and desired payment terms.

In nearly every case, you'll also want to ask the sponsor to agree to the use of a quality assessment tool, most likely a high-quality, Big 5-based assessment, available in Mandarin, which they may already use within the organization, and to a certain number of stakeholder interviews.

Critically, you'll also want to gain the sponsor's agreement that the content of your conversations with the coachee will remain *strictly confidential* (absent legal requirements or a highly unusual situation) and that such content will be made available to the sponsor only with the coachee's prior approval.

I'm occasionally asked why the coaching process takes so long, and why I recommend a relatively-close scheduling of coaching conversations.

Regarding the length of engagements, the short answer is, "Change takes time." The sponsor is expecting, and the coachee is experimenting with, valuable changes in mindset and behavior, and it takes time to soften ingrained habits and to develop new ones.

As for the frequency of coaching conversations, I've noticed that 2-3 week intervals are normally long enough to give the coachee sufficient time to try out new behaviors, and short enough to enable the coachee and coach to maintain momentum in the process.

After contracting with the sponsor, you'll also want to contract with the coachee. This is often done verbally; ideally, it will be done in writing as well. While many of the items to be initially agreed (especially confidentiality) will be similar to those in the coach's contract with the sponsor, some items will be additional, such as the coaching language to be used, permission for "shadow coaching," and mutual responsibilities. You'll also find it useful, as well as ethically responsible, to contract and re-contract frequently with the coachee as you proceed through the coaching sessions.

In my early days as a coach, I thought that "continuous contracting" would be an awkward, even burdensome process. As I proceeded in the work, however, I found that "asking permission" to touch on a potentially sensitive topic or to use a certain coaching "tool" became an easy, respectful, and useful practice.

Coaching Phases

With the initial contracting now complete (whew!), you can officially begin the coaching process. There are typically 2 basic "phases" that run in parallel. The initial phase primarily focuses on data gathering, after which the data is used to help the coachee, then the coachee and sponsor together, clearly identify the coaching purpose and goals. The second phase primarily focuses on coaching the leader to reach or exceed the chosen goals.

Phase I

In the first phase, which I call "triangulation," data is gathered from three sources: assessment tool results, stakeholder interviews, and conversations with the coachee. Many of the organizations I've worked with use a well-proven tool like the Hogan Assessment or the Strengths Deployment Inventory (SDI). The coachee responds to questions from the assessment, the results are shared with the coach, and the coach debriefs the results with the coachee.

An extremely useful second source of data for coaching goal formulation is the "qualitative 360" feedback provided by the coachee's key stakeholders. These stakeholders are typically nominated by the coachee and include the coachee's manager, several peers, and often a number of direct reports.

These colleagues are polled individually and in confidence for their views on the coachee's leadership strengths and potential improvement areas. Patterns (similar views by at least 2 colleagues on particular strength or improvement areas) are noted and later shared, without attribution, with the coachee.

It can be useful, in the stakeholder selection process, to ask the coachee to draw an organization chart, including her or himself, so that I can better understand how they see their "world." I can then ask about their interactions with each key colleague, thereby gaining better insight into who they might want me to solicit feedback from. As a key stakeholder by definition, the coachee's manager will always be included among those I gather feedback from.

During the earlier years of coaching development in China, I was often asked by HR leaders if it was worth interviewing direct reports, on the assumption that no subordinate, given Confucianism's strong norms of showing respect to those more senior, would ever say something "negative" about the boss. While I have found this to be true in some cases, I've found it more likely that, when assured of confidentiality, the subordinate will readily offer development feedback.

The third source of data for prospective leadership improvement comes directly from the coachee, of course, usually during the initial coaching conversations. Such data can also come from "shadow coaching," in which the coach silently observes the coachee, from the side or back of the meeting room, while s/he interacts with colleagues.

In my experience, coaching at the executive level almost always includes a goal of improving influencing skills or other communication skills. Shadow coaching, which enables the coach to watch and listen to the coachee interact directly with colleagues, is extremely useful for gaining a sense of how the coachee affects, and is affected by, those colleagues; these energetic forces are often outside the coachee's awareness in the moment of interaction.

Without such observation, it can be very difficult for the coach to gain a hands-on sense of the coachee's communication style and their colleagues' reactions. Fortunately, the great majority of coachees give permission for me to join a meeting, even if they feel a bit uncomfortable at first about being observed or having colleagues know that they have a coach. (Though infrequently encountered, some organizational cultures still view coaching from a "fix 'em" lens.) Having observed coachees in action, I am able, in nearly every case, to offer feedback that enables positive shifts in their communication style.

There is often a fair amount of "overlap" in the perceptions offered by the three sets of data. This overlap normally makes it readily apparent to the coachee, and the coach, which leadership competencies could be valuable areas of improvement focus, and which competencies are already relatively strong and can be leveraged to support improvement.

The coachee then chooses coaching goals based on this information, reflects on how improvement might be measured, then discusses and refines the goals and measures with their manager. I find it quite helpful, after these steps have occurred, to ask the coachee to schedule a 20-minute "alignment call", among ourselves and the manager, to ensure that we're all as clear as we can be on the goals and measures of success, and to allow for any refinements that might arise during our conversation.

Congratulations! Phase I is now complete, and you're heading into Phase II, focusing on coaching leaders to reach or exceed their chosen goals.

Phase II

You may find that coaching tends to be most effective not only when the coachee is motivated by the coaching goals, but also when a certain level of momentum is maintained. Meeting every 2-3 weeks is about the right amount of time, in my experience, to support such momentum. Less time, and the coachee may not have sufficient time to experiment with the new thinking and behaviors that can lead to improvement. More time, and the coachee may easily become caught up in the broader busyness of work and non-work life.

A typical coaching session tends to follow a certain rhythm, and it may well start with a centering exercise to help establish a baseline presence in, and a clear mental space for, the work of the session. The coach will then normally ask how the coachee's life has been going since they last met, and what s/he wants to work on during the session (more contracting!). While the topic will often relate to one of the coachee's coaching goals, sometimes an immediate concern, unrelated to a coaching goal, will take priority.

In my work as an integral coach, I approach the engagement from a wholistic perspective, supporting coachees not only with their "horizontal development," e.g., skills building, but also, if the coachee permits, with their "vertical development," their growth as human beings. The integral approach includes models that help the coach and coachee better understand which coachee capabilities might strongly support, and which might need to be strengthened to support, achievement of the coaching goals. The approach also includes noticing exercises and specific practices that support coachees in moving toward their leadership and personal development goals.

The coach may then wish to explore with the coachee specific actions taken since the previous session, along with the results of those actions. What worked well? What didn't? Any reflections for improvement? In the event the coachee didn't take action as earlier agreed, not to worry! The coach can explore the challenges that precluded the coachee from taking action.

Near the end of the session, the coach will normally ask the coachee to reflect on, and choose among, new options for action, and reflect on potential challenges to action and how these might be resolved. The coach will then ask the coachee to draft and send a brief summary of intended actions to the coach; this summary can be used as a springboard for discussion at the next session.

And so the sessions proceed until the end of the engagement, in an iterative process highly-focused on supporting the coachee's improvement as a leader. The process normally includes a mid-point review with the coachee, manager, and coach to formally assess progress and to make any adjustments useful to the goals or process. There are also, if permitted by the coachee, periodic "spot checks on progress" with stakeholders, and a final review. There may also be follow-up contacts, for example, at the 3 and 12-month points, post-engagement, to assess how much of the coaching value "stuck."

Andrew: From the sponsor's perspective, it is important to formalize the parameters of the coaching engagement in an agreement. Such parameters include clear timelines and deliverables for all stakeholders, including the coachee. For the engagements I have organized, the timeframe on engagements has typically been 3 to 6 months—in some cases longer—based upon the needs of the coachee.

A 360-degree assessment plus stakeholder interviews are staple components to include in the early stages to help the coach and coachee align on development focus areas. As much as possible, I leave the selection of the stakeholders to the coachee. However, I also see it as the role of the coach, and of myself as the sponsor, to help ensure that the coachee is selecting from a large cross section of stakeholders. Coaches I have worked with proactively facilitate this with the coachee, sometimes asking for my input to help arrive at the best selection.

While the engagement is primarily between coach and coachee, from my perspective as sponsor it is also essential to have agreed check-ins with both the coach and coachee to assess progress at different stages of the engagement. While the nature of the meetings between coachee and coach remain confidential, check-ins with both parties are beneficial as they offer an opportunity to spot any challenges and to offer any necessary support. I also see check-ins as another way of demonstrating that the organization is sponsoring and supporting this engagement for the coachee.

Depending on the scope of the coaching assignment, one approach could be to check in at the mid-point, then at the end of the assignment. However, this approach could be adapted based on the length of the assignment and in consultation with coachee and coach. Coaches I have worked with have sought permission from the coachee on the information they would share with me as the sponsor. When the coachee has been comfortable sharing specific information on their progress, this has opened opportunities to provide organizational context to the coach or helped uncover different ideas to guide further steps.

In my role as sponsor, I must honor the integrity of the coaching engagement and find the right balance in checking on progress but not over-inserting myself. This can be a delicate balance, and I have asked coaches to "keep me honest" and let me know if my role oversteps my involvement at any time.

In addition to sponsor check-ins, having similar check-ins with the coachee's supervisor can also be a good step along the way. The same rules and guidance applies. The supervisor needs to be updated on progress and be engaged enough to support the coaching process along the way—but not insert themselves in a way that may impede or inhibit that process. A rule of thumb would be to talk about and agree on these aspects with the coach, coachee, and supervisor before the engagement begins. This helps to ensure, upfront, that all concerned are aware of the touchpoints and the ground rules for handling them.

The wrap-up and follow-up steps in the coaching engagement are also critical as they support the sustainability of the outcomes for the coachee. Keeping in mind that there has been a considerable investment made in this development activity, the engagement should be finished with these important steps.

The coach will facilitate a wrap-up meeting directly with the coachee. This would include a discussion about arranging a debriefing with the supervisor and myself, the sponsor. While this wrap-up meeting is not one that I have been directly involved in, I recognize it as a critical opportunity for the coachee to reflect on and be clear about the outcomes from the coaching engagement and to plan next steps in their development plan, including support they may need from their supervisor and myself.

When it comes to the debriefing, I have experienced this process as separate meetings, for example, one with me as the sponsor and another with the supervisor. Alternatively, I have seen this as a combined group meeting amongst us all. Ultimately, I see this as something the coach and coachee can discuss and agree on what works best. Where there may be sensitivities in this step, the coach would typically discuss such with me, and I could provide my input, as the sponsor, on the best approach.

While the coachee will be sharing their takeaways in the debriefing, it is also vital that the stage be set for what happens after the coaching engagement. As the coachee's development will be ongoing, critical elements for discussion and agreement include next steps, necessary support and resources, and future "progress check" touchpoints. As a sponsor, I have found it helpful to remind the supervisor of this before the debriefing takes place, and to also be available to provide reminders and follow-ups on the agreed next steps in order to support sustainable outcomes from the coaching assignment.

Jeff: Thanks Andrew! As expected, I've learned from our conversation, and I trust that our reader has as well. Shall we do this again?

Tom Payne and Nancy Zhang

Chapter 5.
Data Used to Support Feedback in Evidence-Based Coaching

"It is a capital mistake to theorize before one has data. Insensibly one begins to twist facts to suit theories, instead of theories to suit facts."
 - Sherlock Holmes by Sir Arthur Conan Doyle

Abstract

In Chapter 4, Jeff and Andrew share their perspectives on the life cycle of a coaching engagement. They talk about how to improve the effectiveness of coaching feedback by engaging the coachee in the coaching goals to build momentum. For feedback to be effective, it has to be both balanced and credible. The coachee has to be involved in selecting or at least agreeing on the coaching engagements goals. They suggest as part of the coaching process to have an "alignment call" between the coachee, manager, and coach to assure alignment and therefore buy-in on the coaching goals. In Chapter 5, Tom and Nancy will provide a look at some of the EBC tools that are available to the coach. Tom provides a psychology practitioner's perspective of what makes for reliable and valid assessments and how they can and should be used professionally. Data shared with the coachee can come from the organizations HRIS system, external assessments, 360 surveys (personality, cognitive ability), or interviews with key internal stakeholders. In all cases, the coach should be trained and certified to use whatever tools they employ. Nancy shares some examples of how she has used personality assessment in her work with coachees and the value these bring to the feedback process based her considerable China coaching experience with Chinese coachees and clients

Introduction

At the beginning of a coaching engagement, certain information needs to be shared between the coach, coachee, organization sponsor, and/or boss. This is likely to vary depending on the nature of the engagement, whether it is requested by the organization or the coachee, or if it is part of an overall talent management or group coaching engagement.

It is important that the data provide evidence to support the coaching path the coachee will embark on. The coachee needs to trust the coach and that the coach will only put forward useful and accurate information that will help the coachee discover important insights about themselves. One useful model here is the Johari window concept where through the coaching engagement, the coach can help the coachee get to know more about themselves and how they are seen and perceived by others. Armed with these evidence-based insights, the coach can help the coachee see themselves as others do and begin to make conscientious decisions about their behavior in certain settings to improve their overall effectiveness as a leader.

"Most of the world will make decisions by either guessing or using their gut. They will either be lucky or wrong." - Suhail Doshi

Model of the Johari Window by Joseph Luft and Harrington Ingram (1955)

This photo is licensed under CC BY-SA-NC

In general, the coach would be granted confidential access to certain coachee data, including career progression up to current, performance ratings, notes on behaviors that contributed to more or less successful outcomes, behavioral data from 360 surveys or 360 feedback gathered as part of their performance evaluation, cognitive ability assessments along with a Big 5 based personality assessment.

Testing has a long history in China. Since 607, China has used the Imperial Examination to understand a candidate's suitability for certain civil service jobs. During the Cultural Revolution, in China, the practice of using tests was frowned upon. It has only been in the last 20 years that assessments have been more broadly used. There are many universities in China now that offer programs in psychometric assessment, and the professionalism of these has grown along with research that supports the contributed validity of their use in both selection and coaching.

Limitations of Some Measures under the China Context

Although the above measures are quite commonly used, there are some unique challenges when applied in the China context. 360 results, for example, is a widely used tool as a pre-coaching assessment; however, the quality of the results in a coaching session is much dependent on the organization's culture and the coachee's style. Overall, the results of a 360 survey would reflect the Power Distance Index effect (Hofstede 1980, 2001) as the ratings from subordinates' groups are often the highest among all rating groups including supervisor, peer, and other groups. In general, 360 results collected from multinationals are more objective than those collected from SOEs (state-owned enterprises) in China; there are also some Chinese local companies where employees' careers are based on their supervisors' impressions alone. It is important to be aware that in some Chinese organizations, 360s have been used as a rationale to hand out promotions. This is also a common practice in most SOEs. Thus, 360 results in China may have limited use in coaching due to the occasional misuse of such data.

The other problem that is encountered in 360 ratings is that globally, there has been a disparity in the ratings of the boss and the subordinate. Generally, the ratings of the boss tend to be lower than all other raters in certain areas. The highest correlation of competency ratings is between the individual and others (subordinates and peers). The boss ratings tends to be the outlier. This is also why there is mistrust in most organizations' performance management process and results, which extends to 360 surveys even when they are used for development purposes. This distrust of 360 surveys adds complexity in the use of 360 feedback in coaching.

However, even though there are obstacles, 360 surveys have proven to be incredibly useful and impactful in the hands of a well-qualified coach who is certified to interpret the meaning of the results and to help the coachee gain insight about the perspectives of others, as evidenced in the results. The 360 survey reveals perceptions of others, a view into the "others" portion in the

Johari window that the coachee cannot otherwise see about themselves. The discussion with the coachee should not degenerate into trying to figure out who rated them low, but rather, to focus on why their perception of the coachee is at the level reported. While these views are not necessarily more accurate, they do reveal perceptions that can be valuable and may limit the coachee's performance and career progress. The coachee and the coach can take the time to explore why there are differences in perception. Unattended, perceptions reflected by low ratings can become reality.

Personality assessments are a good addition for the coach to gain an objective understanding of the coachee's overall style and behavioral tendencies. Research on the accuracy and validity of personality assessment has shown that personality traits become more valuable in explaining or predicting managerial and executive success with more complex jobs. High-complexity jobs show a higher threshold of the Big 5 personality traits. In other words, personality assessment gains in importance in evaluating the potential of an individual to be successful at higher levels of responsibility. These assessments can also serve the purpose of helping coachees understand explanations for their behaviors and provide context for the behaviors being due to their values and motives or to general behavioral tendencies.

Personality assessments are used to provide additional information in hiring or promotion decisions and they are also extremely valuable evidence in coaching engagements where they add insights for the coach and coachee to explore. It is important to note personality questionnaires are self-reported, and the personality assessment research shows that about 10-20% of people will demonstrate some degree of "faking" when asked to rate themselves for two reasons. This is corroborated by research on the accuracy of resumes or applications where about 1/3 of applicant provided information is inaccurate (E.g. dates of employment are over-stated, degrees are overclaimed, positions overstated, accomplishments claimed are not 100% the applicant's doing but a team result.)

The first reason for faking on Personality Questionnaires is that there is a small but significant percentage of people will rate themselves higher because they believe that they are better than others. Dr. Delroy Paulus describes this as self-deceptive enhancement (SDE). Then there are some who want others to see them more favorably. Paulus describes this as impression management (IM).

Paulus describes socially desirable responding (SDR) in the development of his Balanced Inventory of Desirable Responding (BIDR) (University of British Columbia. 1984, 1988), all of which can cloud the validity of the assessment. Generally, the higher the stakes the results of the assessment are to the person completing the questionnaire, the more likely they are to demonstrate some degree of response distortion. Except in extreme cases, the results of the personality assessment can still be used with an experienced leadership coach who has been certified in the use of the specific personality assessment by an assessment professional. Most well-researched personality assessments have an internal measure that suggests the assessed candidate's level of "faking." Dr. Jinyan Fan has published his research on people faking in self-report personality questionnaires in China. He has replicated Paulus's work in China. Impression management and self-deceptive enhancement are prevalent at about the same rate in China as they are in other cultures (Fan, J. et al. 2012)

Often, test publishers who provide assessments that are ipsative type (comparing your responses against your responses) like the Meyers Briggs Type Indicator (MBTI) or DiSC, tout the fact that ipsative assessment forms aren't subject to applicant faking as they are not normative. All Big 5 personality assessments are normative tests that allow people who take the same personality assessment to be compared with others. Ipsative tests are non-normative and so are not subject to the risk of faking. While this is true, most organizations who are using personality assessments want to be able to compare the results of person A with person B. Normative assessments allow candidates' results to be compared against other candidates who have taken the same assessment. Ipsative assessments cannot be used to compare one candidate with another. One widely used personality assessment is the MBTI. While a number of leadership coaches use it in their coaching practice, the MBTI manual states that the results of an individual's MBTI type report cannot and should not be used as support in selection settings due to the fact that results of an individual cannot be compared to another. Another reason is that ipsative type tests like the MBTI are very likely to change within a 6-week window. It would not be valuable in evidence-based coaching for the coach and coachee to use data that no longer represents the coachee's personality as reflected by the assessment.

Case Study of a Chinese Leader Being Considered for Further Development and Opportunity

This leader was in competition with two other senior leaders for an opportunity to be selected as the successor to his boss. When he was not the person selected, he self-sponsored a coaching program with the sole purpose of finding out why he was not chosen. During this session, he took a Big 5 personality assessment. With limited feedback and input from other stakeholders, the objective data from a personality assessment helped him better understand the probable reasons preventing him from being selected that were not clearly evident to him on his own. The information the assessment provided about his own tendencies gave him an objective way to confirm his behavior with others and direct a clear path to where he should focus development that would allow him to change his behavior in certain circumstances to become more effective.

The use of personality assessment in coaching is an experienced process, and over the past fifteen years, increasingly more organizations in China are considering them to be a viable addition to their talent development and selection processes. It is important to note that any personality assessment should be given in the coachee's natural language to avoid mistakes in comprehension. Thus, organizations are using high-quality Big 5 personality assessments more regularly for both selection applications and in pre-coaching assessments. This being the case, it is imperative that personality assessments are well validated measurements with scientific foundations, and that there are quality norm bases for the assessments. Additionally, when considering using a personality assessment in business, it would also be helpful to consider personality assessments that have been validated in a business context for the purpose of predicting job success.

"The capacity to learn is a gift, the ability to learn is a skill, the willingness to learn is a choice." – Brian Herbert

Personality Differences under the China Context and Implications on Leadership Style

Personality, values, and cognitive abilities define one's leadership style (Benson & Campbell, 2007; Judge, Bono, Ilies, & Gerhardt, 2002). These factors affect one's behaviors, decision-making tendencies, and the leadership environment one cultivates, all of which subsequently affect organizational performance (Barrick, Day, Lord, & Alexander, 1991; Day & Lord, 1988; Kaiser, Hogan, & Craig, 2008; Peterson, Smith, Martorana, & Owens, 2003; Thomas, 1988). Quality personality data provides key information on where to focus on coaching. However, it is important to check with the boss, sponsor, and coachee to assure that the areas selected for development are aligned with everyone's understandings and expectations.

While many different types of personality assessments exist, assessments that measure personality under normal, day-to-day circumstances are commonly used tools. These types of assessments are mostly based on the five factor traits of extraversion, neuroticism, agreeableness, openness to experience, and conscientiousness. These assessments provide a baseline for understanding someone's natural strengths and weaknesses under normal circumstances. Big 5 assessments can measure negative personality characteristics that occur especially under stress and pressure, during times of boredom or disengagement, or when the person is relaxed and not self-monitoring. Certain publishers produce results that can help a person understand risk behaviors and potential threats that may get in the way of their career success, for example, someone like the coachee who was unaware of why he or she was not chosen to succeed their boss. Personality assessment provides some measure of an individual's values and motives—the characteristics that cause someone to be motivated on their job, to prefer certain types of work environments, or to create a certain type of company culture as a leader. If a coachee can understand this aspect of their personality, then they can understand how to better lead, how to create a culture or environment most conducive to success, or how to provide direction in a career path.

Included under the general heading of individual assessments are cognitive ability or intelligence assessments, skills assessments (typically relate to demonstrating a body of skills associated with a specific job or family of jobs) and personality assessments. For managerial and executive positions, personality assessments have proven to be insightful in both selection and development. A good reliable and valid personality assessment can contribute up to 40% of the predicted behavior of a manager or executive.

There are a number of reliable psychometric personality assessment vendors in the China market whose questionnaires are translated both linguistically and culturally into Mandarin. Saville Holdsworth Limited (SHL), DDI, Korn Ferry, Hogan Assessment Systems, Talent Assessments International, and the NEO PI all offer well-researched personality assessments that have been widely recognized in the scientific community and broadly used commercially.

As an example of how personality assessment data can be used to understand a coachee's tendencies compared to others in the same population, we will use the Hogan Leadership Suite, which has three key inventories: HPI (Hogan Personality Inventory), HDS (Hogan Development Survey) and MVPI (Motivation Values and Preference Inventory). HPI measures personality in a day-to-day circumstance; HDS measures personality displayed under pressure or when someone is too relaxed; MVPI measures a person's underneath values and motivation. In one of Hogan's published papers on personality across cultures, "Understanding Leadership in China" (Shalhoop and Sanger, 2012), there are clear patterns identified when comparing Chinese managers with those from Western countries, as shown in Figure 1 (next page).

1. Compared to managers in several Western countries, Chinese managers tend to be more comfortable following an organization's structure and processes instead of proactively taking active leadership roles. Chinese managers tend to score lower on the Hogan ambition scale; those who score lower on the ambition scale tend to be less competitive and proactive in leadership positions on a day-to-day basis. Thus, Chinese managers may appear to be more passive/less willing to take charge, especially in situations where responsibilities are not clearly defined, or leadership roles are not clearly assigned. Another related impact is they may view themselves as representing the group instead of just representing themselves as an individual; therefore, they would be less comfortable in sharing their own personal views in public situations.

2. Under pressure, however, Chinese leaders are more likely to demonstrate behaviors of being overly confident, dominant, and authoritative; it may be hard to receive input and opinions from others, and they may be difficult to influence. Chinese managers score higher on the bold scale, which means they tend to be overly confident and dominant, ignoring their own mistakes and unwilling to admit when they are wrong when under stress, when disengaged, or when not self-monitoring. The resulting contrast of lower ambition scale scores in normal day-to-day situations with higher bold scale scores when under pressure or not

Figure 1. Differences between Chinese Mainland, German, US, and Australian managers on the HPI, HDS and MVPI assessments. Data from a subset of Mainland Chinese (N=992), U.S. (N=4,184), German (N=1,779), and Australian (N=4,864) managers.

self-monitoring often leads to confusion for people from other countries.

3.   Other significant personality differences are the tendencies of Chinese managers to show greater care about process, details, and risk management. This often leads to great execution, but also a lack of courage in taking risks and learning from mistakes, and a lack of flexibility or willingness to deviate from originally set plans. Chinese managers score higher on the Hogan prudence scale, which suggests they are concerned about impression management, looking good in front of others, rules, processes, and procedures on a day-to-day basis.

4.   Under pressure or when disengaged or bored, Chinese managers tend to rely on authority to make the final call or to defer to authority when making decisions. Higher dutiful scale scores under stress/when not self-monitoring suggests they are less likely to push back even when they do not concur with their superior.

5.   Shaloop and Sanger (2012), as shown in Figure 2, found the within-group differences between Chinese leaders from MNCs and SOEs to be much smaller than the between-group differences of Chinese leaders and leaders from other countries. This implies national differences are more stark and have more impact than the differences in organizational culture of companies within China. Specifically, Shaloop and Sanger found Chinese leaders of both MNCs and SOEs tend to have lower ambition scale scores and higher prudence scale scores, whereas a leader from a US organization tends to have a higher ambition scale score and a lower prudence scale score than their Chinese counterpart. Even though a Chinese leader may work for a US MNC, the personality of that leader will likely be more similar to their SOE counterpart than their US counterpart in the US MNC. Some common themes that came across as for both SOE and MNC Chinese managers is their lack of proactiveness in competing beyond their scope of responsibility and ability to empower and delegate.

Coaching Implications

Over the past 16 years, Nancy has had the opportunity to coach and support over a hundred leaders with various cultural backgrounds. Among them, about 50% are local mainland Chinese, and the other 50% are expatriates working in China. The following are some of the most common coaching themes summarized based on her coaching experiences, which also resonate with the key findings above.

Figure 2. Differences between Chinese Mainland SOE and MNC managers on the HPI, HDS and MVPI assessments. Data set contains MNC=584 (HPI), 402 (HDS), and 520 (MVPI); SOE=334 (HPI), 323 (HDS), and 146 (MVPI) managers.

Theme 1 – Challenge of Influencing Upward

Many Chinese coachees have challenges in situations where they need to influence upward. This may include their ability to communicate and convey ideas during meetings and discussions; appropriately engage in confrontation instead of avoiding it; actively managing expectations, which requires the ability to say no sometimes; or the ability to gain more support and resources by proactively reaching out for help.

Chinese leaders are often quite cautious in presenting themselves in front of senior-level people. In meetings conducted in another language like English, language difficulties could be a potential reason for this, but it appears that language tends not to be the main reason that Chinese leaders do not speak up in meetings. Chinese leaders prefer to be well prepared before speaking, and thus may feel more comfortable doing presentations rather than engaging in open discussions in which they have little control. Also, discomfort with confrontation prevents them from speaking up and sharing their views, especially when they have a different perspective. Some Chinese leaders don't speak up because they simply don't want to be seen as overly competitive with others. Thus, if someone else has already mentioned any points, a Chinese leader would be unlikely to add on or repeat the points even if it is important to show their support. As a result, leaders from other countries may view Chinese leaders as lacking in engagement or confidence, or they may even think they are arrogant.

Nancy has also observed that another challenge for Chinese leaders in influencing upward is they are not very good at sharing and discussing challenges and difficulties. In traditional Chinese culture, such behavior would be viewed as weak or even disgraceful. As a result, Chinese leaders may try to solve all problems by themselves, rather than bringing them to the attention of senior-level leaders, even if such actions could gain more resources or support. If a leader's results are good, HQ may continue to raise expectations while the problem might still remain, thus making it even more challenging year over year. And if a leader's results are not meeting expectations, this could be perceived as a lack of communication or transparency in sharing information in advance, affecting a leader's credibility within the organization.

Coaching can often help leaders close perception gaps and help them understand that being a part of the discussion process is just as important as completing their goals. By leveraging Chinese leaders' preference for being prepared, Nancy recommends that leaders can start thinking about the subject prior to the meeting and learn to guide the discussion through questions to avoid potential confrontations. They can use the opportunity of reaching out to build trust. Instead of focusing on the challenge, focusing on what and how HQ can support them to better cope with the challenges would make it easier for them to start talking about difficulties. Over time, as they start to see the positive effects of this type of leadership style, their approach in leading their own team also gradually evolves.

Theme 2 - "Overly Confident" - The Dark Side Personality

In contrast to the challenge of being reluctant to influence upward, many Chinese managers and leaders have a strong influence and impact within their own organization where they have more control. The signature behavior for this type of leader is being overly confident, dominant, and having difficulty admitting their mistakes. Many Chinese leaders are successful because of their determination and strong drive under pressure as they evolve in their career ladder. The problem is that the higher in responsibility they go, the greater the expertise in their team below them. These leaders cannot be more expert than all their deputies. This type of leadership style can cause more harm than good, sometimes pushing organizations into taking very risky actions that bring the organization to the precipice of disaster. There have been many cases of failed Chinese leaders who make very bold decisions rather than listening to the advice of their experts; this can cause their organizations to achieve quick success but also quick bankruptcy all within just a few years.

There are many challenges associated with coaching leaders like this: 1) They often surround themselves with mostly people who will agree with them and not challenge their decisions. Their level of tolerance for different opinions is quite low; this makes quality feedback gathering rather difficult. 2) Their level of openness is quite limited; thus, it is often challenging to help them see anything beyond what they believe on their own 3) Their dominant side sometimes is hidden/not evident during the coaching session, making feedback and reflection more difficult.

Therefore, timing is crucial as coaching works best when leaders are experiencing challenges and difficulties; this helps increase their level of openness and also makes it easier for the coach to see coachees' reactions to stress. For gathering feedback, in addition to reinforcing the confidentiality when conducting interviews, Nancy has found that the opportunity to sit in the coachee's team meeting often provides very rich information. It provides the opportunity to gain feedback about the coachee's leadership style and its impact on others, and to gain an understanding about how their team members respond and about the overall team dynamics. Such live information allows space for the coachee to reflect and consider multiple perspectives while taking others' reactions into consideration.

References

Fan, J, Gao, et al. (2012) Testing the Efficacy of a New Procedure for Reducing Faking on Personality Tests. *Journal of Applied Psychology,* Jan 12, 2012.

Shalhoop, J and Sanger, M. (2012). Understanding Leadership in China: Leadership Profiles of State-owned Enterprises, Multinational Corporations, and Major Economic Trading Partners. In *Advances in Global Leadership,* Volume 7, 321–348. Emerald Group Publishing, Ltd.

Chapter 6.
The Influence of
Chinese Culture on
Leadership Coaching
in China

Axel Kuhlmann and Alan Babington-Smith

"The single biggest problem with communication is the illusion that it has taken place."

   -George Bernard Shaw

Abstract

The previous chapter addressed the importance and value of using data to support the coaching process. In this chapter, Alan, originally from the U.K., and Axel, from Germany, offer their thoughts on the effects of culture on coaching in China. They speak of cultural context, including Confucianism, "face," communication style, the role of the individual, education, and emotions. They also speak about coaching issues, including relationship in the organization, management efficiency, and the coaching "triangle." Let's join their conversation.

Cultural Context

Alan: It is generally acknowledged that China is culturally exceptional. What is less generally acknowledged is the importance that modern China still attaches to that exceptionality, both in principle and in detail.

To frame this chapter, let's start with a basic commercial point. In principle, potential clients of foreign coaches in China comprise four distinct categories:

1. State owned enterprises (SOEs)
2. Foreign multinational firms (MNCs)
3. Joint ventures (JVs) and
4. Small- and medium-sized enterprises (SMEs, typically Chinese), and some individuals

In practice, the most likely coachee will be a foreigner working in an MNC or JV. There are a few exceptional foreigners who can coach Chinese coachees (usually working in an MNC or JV)—when the coach has tolerably fluent Chinese, and the Chinese coachee is tolerably fluent in a foreign language—but these are exceptions to the general rule that in a foreign language you may be able to reach the head, but rarely the heart. (And, of course, supporting a shift in mindset or attitude is what distinguishes coaching from training.)

For a foreign coachee in an MNC, the main issue is how to be effective in that particular organization. In the case of a Chinese coachee in an MNC, the emphasis shifts to adapting from Chinese culture to the MNC culture. Understanding Chinese culture is essential in both directions.

In this chapter, we will first explain the importance of Chinese culture, then explore and try to explain it, making some distinctions and illustrating how these play out for coaches and coaching in China. We will then try to answer the fundamental question of how and where a foreign coach can add value.

To put these cultural questions in context, perhaps we can start with some history and recent anecdotal experience.

There are two lessons from Chinese history that are particularly important for coaching in China. The first is that China has developed, over 5000 years, a unique culture that is an "outlier" when measured by characteristic Western measures of culture. The second is that China has developed, over the past 40 years, economic success at a scale and speed unparalleled in history.

For coaching overall, the implication of these two factors is that China feels that it has at least equaled the West, playing the Western game without losing its cultural integrity. The immediate, detailed effect of that on coaching is that while China remains friendly to the West, it is no longer as respectful as it was over 15 years ago. The implication of this for coaches is the intense need for self-awareness, not just understanding the culture but also respecting it. The implication of this for people looking to become coaches in China, or looking for coaches for Chinese staff, is that sufficient understanding of and respect for Chinese culture need to be key criteria.

China's success over the lifetime of most of its population, and particularly over the lifetime of a typical 25-year-old, or 45-year-old, coachee has fed into a natural pride in China's culture systems and significantly reduced respect for foreigners. At the time of writing (November 2020), and probably at the time of publication (early 2021), China will be a nation largely without COVID-19, even if it lacks elections. The Chinese people have no doubt about their preference, and they are bound to wonder what lessons the West can offer in the area of corporate governance if national governance is so ineffective. Doesn't China now have as many self-made billionaires as the West? Isn't Huawei at least as well-managed and led as GE? Does the West have a communication and payments app comparable to WeChat? Jack Ma of Alibaba has, generally, been entitled to ask higher-level questions about the whole financial system when his company created one of the key electronic payment systems used throughout China.

Axel: As Alan mentioned, it is important for expatriate coaches to connect their coaching with Chinese culture. For too long, and too often, foreigners didn't (and often still don't) integrate Chinese culture into their behavior. In a proud Chinese, this "laowai" (foreigner) ignorance, even arrogance, finds a powerful opponent. Showing respect for Chinese culture produces positive "vibes" that serve as a foundation for collaboration.

Alan: The extent to which China is a cultural outlier (even compared with the rest of Asia) can be seen in daily life: the distinct food, the importance of personal relationships over contracts, dress sense (mixing Western with Eastern clothes in what may seem an incoherent way) and its unique language structure. This can also be illustrated by my own anecdotal experience. Almost every day I find myself saying, after observing some incident in an office or on the street—such as two men on bicycles carrying a pane of glass between them, a boyfriend carrying his girlfriend's handbag, and a courier sorting piles of documents on a pavement—"Only in China!"

Perhaps I should mention that I am writing this in early November 2020, having just returned to China after seven months in the United States, and finding that even though I have lived in China for more than 20 years, and have a broad cross-cultural background and experience, I am still being surprised.

There are those who argue that these cultural differences are superficial, that human nature is fundamentally the same worldwide, that any Chinese exceptionality is of minor importance.

People everywhere have similar needs, aspirations, and satisfactions, and they respond to the same motivations and incentives. This is, to some extent, borne out by the success in China of the whole-person coaching approach with which I've worked. This approach has been equally successful in over 80 countries, ranging from most countries in the Americas, to Africa, the Middle East, and Asia, including Singapore and Japan. In my view, the whole-person approach is exceptional, but even this requires acute cultural antennae.

Confucianism

Alan: The underlying cultural structure in China is hierarchical Confucianism, which is roughly as influential in daily life as Christianity is in Western Europe and the Americas. It is the basic foundation, even if unconsciously present in daily life. The relatively recent integration of Communism with Confucianism, for almost three generations now, has reinforced the obedience aspects of Confucianism.

Axel: In my view, conscious self-reflection is a key element in coaching. The coach should inspire the coachee to reflect, to dive deeper into events and actions, and to see correlations between actions and re-actions and the role of the coachee in these correlations. The coachee can then start to think about options for changing her/his own behavior and actions, within the values, motifs, emotions, and knowledge the person operates within.

But what if you never learned to self-reflect? What if you've been told what to do, and how to act or react, for most of your life? What if you realize that, as an outcome of a coaching process, you could take full responsibility for your actions, with the risk of losing face or making someone else lose face? The last points sometimes cause emotional struggles even in Western cultures, but quite often in Chinese culture.

The underlying principles of Confucianism in China are still valid. Some of them have been more enforced in the middle of the last century, like the ordering of relationships. The interpretation taught was that son has to follow father, the subordinate the superior, the younger the elder, and so on. This created a hierarchical mindset. While it may have been believed to be useful for specific purposes like face-saving, maintaining order, and respecting traditions, it also diminished critical thinking skills.

Let me provide an example. We were a group of people who wanted to support teachers in China with coaching. We thought this could also be useful for students. My colleagues started to contact schools and authorities in China. Due to the ambivalent answers we received, we hoped that the door to a possible acceptance of this proposal was still being considered. Over time, we realized that the idea didn't fit into the academic structure in China at that time. We realized that ambivalence is actually a sign of no interest.

Another experience. Many Chinese manager coachees have asked me and many of my coaching colleagues for advice. Even though most coaches have declined to do so due to the endangering effects on coaching's inquiry-focused method, many coachees repeated and repeated these requests. Once, a coachee shared, very openly, that he really struggled to use the questions I asked to help him develop other solutions. "We never really learned to think critically, in an open way. We had to learn, memorize, and repeat. To develop our own thinking was not on the learning list."

Face

Alan: The most fundamental Chinese cultural concepts are "mianzi" and its corollary "pingjia," conventionally translated as "face" and "judgment," respectively. These two factors tend to dictate many reactions or responses for Chinese. Face is probably well understood, in a general sense, but the breadth and depth of its implications may be worth elaborating. Chinese people want and need recognition from parents, school, and work. They crave the feeling of being recognized as individuals, and for their accomplishments. This means that when they receive any kind of pingjia (judgment, criticism), they can become hyper-sensitive and react, unfortunately, by closing down and concealing their reactions and emotions. This closing down can have profound negative consequences for dealing effectively with the issues for which they received feedback.

As an example, one clear result of moving up the management ladder is the need to increasingly delegate to and empower subordinates. In China, traditionally, the assumption was, and often still is, that anybody who delegates anything is really demonstrating that he or she is incompetent to do the delegated work themselves. As a result, the use of the Johari window may take more time to discuss and conceptualize with coachees. In the Johari window model of self-development, self-awareness and self-reflection on one's actions are keys to developing improved rapport and trust with others the coachee works with.

Axel: A major area for coaching in China is coaching managers, an area related to the eagerness of young Chinese managers to grow and become better leaders. As a coach in China, it is important to address a challenge to this growth, a mindset which basically translates as, "I lose face if I have a coach."

This is one of the major, if not the largest, hurdles of personal development in China and other Asian cultures. Losing face is, in Western cultures, something one puts up with. In China, it is much more important, because it is connected not only to the individual but also, likely, to the family of the individual. This creates a lot of pressure and traditionally leads to extreme cautiousness, which presents an obstacle to taking responsibility. Given this, the coach has to create a positive approach, especially for men, which addresses this "I'm being fixed" mindset.

As coaches, we should support the coachee's eagerness to grow and to increase understanding. This approach tends to be well accepted, as some role models exist. In many of the companies we have worked with continuously over the past 10-15 years, several coachees have gained multiple promotions, requiring and reflecting great personal and professional growth. These individuals have proved to be powerful and encouraging role models within their companies.

Communication Style

Alan: With regard to communication style, China's is very clearly among the most contextual and indirect. Examples of this indirectness abound in the areas of communication generally and teamwork specifically. For coaches, a lack of direct communication can appear from the very start of the engagement, because even the coachee's superior can be reluctant to tell the coach or coachee what the real issues are.

In the coaching organization in which I worked, a "triangle" session between the superior, coachee, and coach was a mandatory part of the process. The superior was often very reluctant to describe what s/he considered the real issues to be. This was true even in a one-on-one conversation with the superior. It is left to the coach to tease out from the coachee what the issues might be. This is clearly a less than optimal situation for coaching. A paradoxical consequence for communication is an exaggerated emphasis on the *human consequences* of a decision or solution, compared with the Western focus on process and structure. In China, how people—colleagues, team members, or family—might be affected can override operational efficiency. A contemporary layer of complication should also be noted: the speed of China's development has created such a shortage of skilled managers that superiors are very reluctant to criticize such colleagues for fear of losing them.

Axel: There is another aspect that any non-Chinese coach should be aware of. China is one of the strongest "high context" cultures, as Erin Meyer (*The Cultural Map*) and others describe it, and many foreigners in China experience it. High context means that communication is not as direct and clear as it is in some other countries. Germany and the Netherlands are relatively straightforward in their communication style; according to the Culture Map, these are considered "low context" cultures.

The tendency of Chinese people to describe things in a not-so-concrete, intangible way stems in part from the cautiousness mentioned earlier. If one is not very precise, it leaves space for different interpretations. This approach helps to avoid conflict and the "loss of face" of oneself or the other person.

For coaching, this means that the coach has to carefully try to help the coachee to come to a possible conclusion. This may take more time than expected and require a range of tools and techniques.

This is indeed different across China itself. In cities with MNC manufacturing zones, typically cities with populations of over 5 million, coachees are more likely to be used to the Western, relatively direct communication style. The communication style also depends on the corporate culture the coachee is embedded within. It is valuable to be aware of this underlying pattern.

Individual Context - The personal situation of coachees

Alan: People now working, aged 45-50, having joined the workforce 20 or 30 years ago, are facing management challenges that nothing in their family background or education prepared them for. The world of modern work is particularly stressful in the paradoxical areas of taking individual responsibility and teamwork.

Over the past 20 years, more and more young people have learned from their parents, who themselves have been involved in Western-style work. Nevertheless, I am always astonished and impressed that typical 25-35-year-olds, being coached to take on managerial roles in a typical MNC or SME, do not have a permanent nervous breakdown, as they are being asked to cope with challenges that lie outside their previous life experience and, in many cases, outside the life experience of anyone they know.

In addition, almost all the people being coached are single children, which poses great challenges for learning to cooperate and work in a team. As China has developed over the last 20 years, the younger people now have much higher expectations for themselves within the organizational system, expectations that are not always well-related to the realities of organizational life. They are very competitive, want faster gratification, are impatient, and keen to get on and to move up Maslow's pyramid. For many coachees, their challenges outside work, especially the "san shan," or "three mountains," of buying a house, educating a child, and providing for aging parents are just as important as the challenges inside work. Even the great pressures of China's education system do not prepare them for the heavy pressures of work and the rest of life, where making choices is critical.

This doesn't mean that Chinese cannot adapt. For example, one of my coaching engagements was with 300 aircraft maintenance staff, where the goal was to improve safety maintenance. The coachees ranged from junior technicians to foremen of teams. The engagement was a success, even though most of the coachees were already in their 40s to 50s and, in their own words, "hadn't read a book in the last 20 years." Nonetheless, by appealing to their pride (some might say to their basic human nature), these staff members applied themselves and made huge personal and operational changes.

Education

Alan: The education system reinforces Confucianism and communism: it requires rote-learning and discourages independent thinking; for every question there is only one right answer. For coaching, this grounding affects where coaching in China now sits on the spectrum between absolute coaching and training. Language is relevant. Normally the translation of "coaching" (the noun and the verb) is "zhaolian," with the coach being addressed by the coachee as "laoshi" (teacher). The implications of these words are important. Zhaolian implies supporting someone to do or practice a skill that s/he can use to achieve a result—as, for example, a sports coach teaching a tennis player how to serve into the back corner of the serving box. Laoshi is the term used, normally with great respect, for a teacher at a school or a university whose role is to add knowledge, to tell you something you didn't know, regardless of whether you want or need to know it (except to pass an exam!).

The implication for coaching in China, of course, is borne out by every coach's anecdotal experience that, either explicitly or implicitly, the coachee is asking for actionable *solutions* to their issues. I believe that there are very few coaches active in China who can say they spend 90% of their time asking questions and only 10% giving answers. This, to a great extent, overrides the common perception that a coaching environment or coaching culture has been adopted within an organization. In my experience, such an environment or culture is often only skin-deep. Its creation depends very much on whether the client is a Chinese company or an MNC.

The issues that coaching deals with have also, of course, changed over time, partly due to changes in China's economy, partly due to the different aspirations of each generation. The post-1980, post-1990, and post-2000 generations each have very different cultural backgrounds and ambitions.

Axel: I have had many conversations with my peers about this "giving solutions" situation, and it has turned out that the understanding of Western-style coaching in the Chinese market and society has increased steadily over the last 8 years, and especially in the last 3-4 years. Before that, it was necessary for many coaches to soften the "official" coaching approach in order to make a living from coaching. "The client gets what s/he wants to pay for" was a phrase I heard a lot from other coaches. At that time, a blend of coaching, mentoring, and training was the formula for success in China.

My answer to these requests for advice was to separate the disciplines, offering separate sessions for training or teaching, so that it was clear to the coachees when coaching was occurring and when it was not.

During my tenure as president of the Shanghai Coaching Circle, I promoted coaching as the ICF and many others (including DVCT, a German association) defined it. I also discussed this situation with guests like Marcia Reynolds, Philippe Rosinski, and others. They were all familiar with this difficulty that coaches worldwide can become trapped in.

Emotions

Axel: I personally experienced some surprising stories with my Chinese coachees. A remarkable outcome occurred with Mr. Chen, an engineer who was a third-line manager in a technical company. Chen was identified as a high-potential employee and promoted into his first leadership position, without any training. The general manager (GM) used mentoring, and tried to work closely with Chen to help him grow. The GM, however, didn't deeply understand the special pressure Chen was under: becoming the boss of a team of which he had previously been a member.

This situation led to a number of behavioral clashes. Chen overruled his team members often. If they expressed their frustration with his directive leadership style, he showed a disturbingly offensive, if not aggressive, reaction.

When we first met, I couldn't see this aggressive person whom HR and others had described. We began to examine Chen's Chinese leadership style and experiences. Since he had no further knowledge about leadership, but had begun to read about it, he asked me some questions. As usual, in the Chinese coaching environment, I explained that asking was my job, not his. That made him laugh, and he became more interested and engaged. By talking about his reading experience and his learnings thus far, Chen discovered the fun of reflecting in a structured way. Within a sometimes-humorous atmosphere, we developed a serious and strong connection.

In our first sessions, stimulated by a systemic coaching approach that included inquiry into both organizational and personal contexts, Chen started to speak about his personal life. His job stress also caused stress in his marriage. Chen couldn't spend as much time with his small child as he and his wife wanted. He was working dozens and dozens of overtime hours.

The coaching inquiry led Chen to realize that the lack of team trust was generated by his behavior, which increased disengagement and caused Chen to shoulder tasks alone. Worse, he felt that the team wanted him to lose face. So he fought more and worked more hours. He recognized this vicious cycle and started to think about how to break it.

Chen's solution was to create more trust by shifting to a more collaborative style, more like the style he demonstrated with colleagues before being promoted. This worked, and Chen created a positive, reinforcing cycle with his team. The feedback he received became more positive, the team more engaged.

Finally, Chen shared with me that, through adopting this different mindset and behavior, his marriage also returned to a lovely, positive emotional state, because he was clear about the time he wanted to spend with his family. When he shared this private information with me, I was not only surprised but also touched.

While this is a beautiful story, it is also a rare one, as when it comes to emotions, Chinese people learn to hold back. This is another hurdle to coaching, as behavioral coaching often touches emotions as the main drivers of behavior. To open this door to one's own emotions requires patience and solid trust between coachee and coach. As mentioned above, and in other chapters of this book, a profound knowledge of Chinese culture and history is an important foundation for coaching success.

Relationship with Employer

Alan: Engagement (i.e., emotional attachment to an employer), often thought of as a key means of promoting retention, is a key issue in Chinese companies. A recent survey in the U.S. showed that roughly 30% of employees feel that they have engagement with their employer. While that may seem a low figure, in China the figure is even lower, only 6%. Good people are scarce so as a result, many younger people respond to ambition, eagerness, and impatience to climb the career (and money) ladder quickly, and are quite open to better paid offers from other firms. This situation has eased a bit in recent years as other factors, like self-development, a healthy environment (for family and children) and broadening one's international network of contacts have become more important. Large local employers like Alibaba and Tencent, for example, are attempting to offer more than money. This also affects the market for leadership-development or organizational development services. The adage "People join a company and leave managers" is now recognized in China just as it is elsewhere.

Self-Management Efficiency

Alan: Another area in which coaching has generally proved to be more useful than teaching is the basic issue of time use and prioritization. In almost every case of coaching I've come across, the concept and application of prioritizing time use towards "high-payoff activities" has had the biggest impact on work and personal life. During individual feedback sessions at the end of the coaching process, the coachee almost always reports that he or she is not only handling their work more effectively (handling, say, three projects easily where they were struggling with one earlier), but is also now regularly taking their child swimming every Saturday.

Triangle Coaching Relationship

Axel: It is also important to keep the relationship between the coach and the coachee transparent and the discussions confidential. My colleagues and I have often experienced requests to share the content of coaching sessions with either the coachee's boss and/or HR. These colleagues felt that they had the right to such data because they were sponsoring the personal development journey of the coachee. So it is very important to thoroughly clarify the "rules of engagement," via solid contracting, with all parties at the outset of the engagement. Even when you've done this, don't be surprised if such requests still arise from time to time. A good solution can be to ask the sponsor for a meeting together with the coachee (if the coachee agrees). These requests will tend to diminish if you continue to refer to what was earlier agreed in the contract. Such "triangle meetings" can also enhance communication within the company.

Conclusion

Western coaches might wish that all Western concepts were as easily transferable and applicable as time use, but the reality is otherwise. The good news is that Western coaches and their coaching techniques and processes will continue to add value for some time to come, provided Chinese culture is fully taken into account. The not-so-good news is that, on a macro level, given recent global political and economic changes, the Western "brand" has been damaged, and Chinese people are beginning to feel that their need for Western concepts and approaches to life has been surpassed. In this book, we are continuing the conversation to keep what is relevant and useful and to be ready to adapt as the need arises. While we are constantly "on the lookout" for the effects of differences in cultures, we also find that we are more 80% alike than 20% different when it comes to priorities in life.

Daniel Denison and Bryan Adkins

Chapter 7.
Coaching in Context

*Bringing Organizational
Context into Coaching Engagements*

"Over the short term, the culture of an organization has a strong influence on the behavior of individuals within it ...But over the longer term, the people make the place (Schneider, 1987) --the culture is created by the individual members, and especially by the leaders"

- Denison

Abstract

The previous chapter addressed the critical importance of a solid knowledge of, respect for, and accommodation to Chinese culture during the coach's interactions with Chinese coachees. This chapter focuses on the value of integrating and aligning leadership development with organizational development as part of the coaching process, so that leaders are developed in a way that anticipates the future vision of the organization's culture.

Introduction

It was early November of 2017, and we were sitting in a small conference room near Shanghai, engaged in a difficult discussion with the leadership team about quality. Quality problems with the plant's medical electronics products were still a big concern in this entrepreneurial, family-founded firm, even two years after their acquisition by a global manufacturing leader. A visitor from corporate headquarters in the States was explaining the importance of robust quality solutions that would make the local approach compatible with the corporation's global manufacturing standards. The discussion was tense—as admirable as the Quality VP's standards were, they seemed impossible to the local team in Wuxi. Afterwards, at lunch, the Engineering VP, Li Xiu, explained to me, "The corporate quality standards are impressive, but they are way beyond what we can achieve in the short term. I've been here three months, and we can't even find the original drawings of the circuit boards that have just malfunctioned!"

A couple of years later, I was sitting outside a conference room near San Jose, watching the leadership team of a Chinese company's U.S. subsidiary interact with a visiting group of Chinese leaders. The U.S. subsidiary was facing some very difficult challenges in meeting their parent company's expectations, and the parent company itself was in the middle of some serious retrenching on their global strategy. After the meeting, the Chinese-American CFO, who had been recruited from Goldman Sachs to lead the IPO of the US subsidiary, was sharing his frustration. "Our CEO's vision for how to create the ecosystem that would enable our strategy wowed me at first, but I always expected that there would be much more than just a futuristic aspiration to guide us. The business environment in the U.S. for our products is tough, and the Chinese leaders don't really have much interest in understanding the complexities."

These stories point out the critical importance of understanding organizational *context* as a key part of coaching engagements. Leadership skills are usually successful only when they work in the organizational context. Nonetheless, most coaching engagements, and most assessment methods, focus primarily on the leaders themselves, often with the help of feedback from those immediately around them. This chapter focuses on the importance of understanding the broader organizational context when coaching individual leaders. In this chapter, we present a method and framework that we have developed to integrate leadership development and organizational change within a coaching engagement, and illustrate this method with reference to our work with one of our global clients.

Coaching in Context

Finding the right connection between organizational contexts and leadership competencies in coaching engagements can be difficult. Competencies are assumed to be a characteristic of the individual, and the purpose of the engagement is to improve the effective deployment of those competencies. Context is often deemphasized, especially when the focus of the coaching engagement is on the psychological or behavioral skills of the executive. Even when context is included in the discussion, the primary sources of "data" about that context are often limited to the executive's perception of the context, as that perspective emerges during the coaching session itself. Experienced coaches often complement their work with broader input from key stakeholders, but a clear sense of the broader organizational context can be hard to come by.

This chapter starts by first presenting a case study from one of our clients, illustrating our approach to coaching in context, and the insights that it provided for aligning leadership development and organizational change. We then go on to present a framework showing how the organizational context in which a leader is working can dramatically influence the key priorities in a coaching engagement.

Aligning Around Our Organizational Culture Model

Our approach is enabled by using a common model for assessing both leadership competencies and organizational contexts. For this, we build on our organizational culture model (see Figure 1 below), which serves as a basis for both our organizational culture assessment and our leadership development assessment (Denison & Neale, 1996; Denison, Hooijberg, Lane, & Leif, 2012; Denison, Nieminen, & Kotrba, 2014). Both of these assessments are based on the common model presented in Figure 1 below.

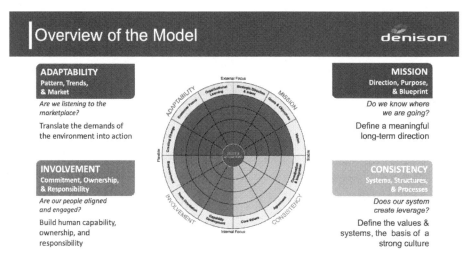

Figure 1

This model focuses on managerial behavior and values, and was developed from research on four cultural traits—involvement, consistency, adaptability, and mission—which predict aspects of business performance such as profitability, growth, and customer satisfaction (Sackmann, 2011; Denison, Nieminen, & Kotrba, 2014). At the organizational level, these four traits are measured through a set of 12 indexes that are benchmarked against a global sample of firms. At the leadership level, the four traits are measured through a set of 12 indexes that ask a parallel set of questions about leadership behaviors. The model is supported by extensive research and a long-standing focus on business performance, including a recent time-series study that helps address the direction of causality in the culture and performance studies (Boyce, Nieminen, Gillespie, Ryan, and

Denison, 2015; Denison, Hooijberg, Lane, & Leif, 2012). The four core traits are highlighted below.

Mission. Successful organizations have a clear sense of purpose and direction that allows them to define organizational goals and strategies and to create a compelling vision of the organization's future. While leaders play a critical role in defining the mission, it can only be reached if it is well understood, from top to bottom. A clear mission provides purpose and meaning by defining a compelling social role and a set of goals for the organization. We measure three aspects of mission: *strategic direction and intent, goals and objectives,* and *vision.*

Adaptability. A strong sense of purpose and direction must be complemented by a high degree of flexibility and responsiveness to the business environment. Organizations with a strong sense of purpose and direction can often be the least adaptive and the most difficult to change. Adaptable organizations, in contrast, quickly translate the demands of the organizational environment into action. We measure three dimensions of adaptability: *creating change, customer focus,* and *organizational learning.*

Involvement. Effective organizations empower and engage their people, build their organization around teams, and develop human capability at all levels. Organizational members are highly committed to their work and feel a strong sense of engagement and ownership. People at all levels feel that they have input into the decisions that affect their work and feel that their work is directly connected to the goals of the organization. We measure three characteristics of involvement: *empowerment, team orientation,* and *capability development.*

Consistency. Organizations are most effective when their values and actions are consistent and well-integrated. Behavior must be rooted in a set of core values, and people must be skilled at putting these values into action by reaching agreement that incorporates diverse points of view. These organizations have highly committed employees, a distinct method of doing business, a tendency to promote from within, and a clear set of do's and don'ts. This type of consistency is a powerful source of stability and internal integration. We measure three consistency factors: *core values, agreement,* and *coordination and integration.*

Like many contemporary models of leadership and organizational effectiveness, this model focuses on a set of dynamic contradictions or tensions that must be managed. As Schein and others have noted, effective cultures always need to solve two problems at the same time: external adaptation and internal integration. Thus, four tensions are highlighted by the model: the trade-off between stability and flexibility and the trade-off between internal and external focus. In addition, the diagonal tensions between internal consistency and external adaptability, and "top-down" versus "bottom-up" tension between mission and involvement, exemplify some of the competing demands that organizations face.

For each of these dynamic contradictions, it is relatively easy to do one or the other, but much more difficult to do both. Organizations that are market-focused and aggressive in pursuing every opportunity often have the most trouble with internal integration. Organizations that are extremely well-integrated and controlled often have the hardest time focusing on the customer. Organizations with the most powerful top-down vision often find it difficult to focus on the bottom-up dynamics needed to implement that vision. Effective organizations, however, find a way to resolve these dynamic contradictions without relying on a simple trade-off.

At the core of this model, we find underlying beliefs and assumptions. Although these deeper levels of organizational culture are difficult to measure, they provide the foundation from which behavior and action spring. Basic beliefs and assumptions about the organization and its people, the customer, the marketplace and the industry, and the basic value proposition of the firm create a tightly-knit logic that holds the organization together. But when organizations are facing change or encountering new challenges from the competition, this core set of beliefs and assumptions, and the strategies and structures that are built on this foundation, come under stress. When that happens, the organizational system and the culture that holds it together need to be reexamined.

A Compelling Case Study

This case study comes from our work with a large global client in the energy sector. Our work with this firm included both the assessment of the cultures of many different sub-units of the organization, and the 360 assessment and coaching of many different leaders throughout the organization. As our work evolved, it became clear that the agenda for the change-focused organizational culture work and the development-focused leadership coaching work converged in an interesting way. For example, at the organizational level, the firm was increasingly concerned with its lack of agility. This issue often emerged in the individual coaching sessions with the executives. But it also became clear that there were a large number of executives who did show a high level of adaptability, as judged by their direct reports, peers, and bosses.

When we began to look at these results more systematically, an interesting pattern appeared. The overall culture profile clearly showed the organization's limitations in areas of adaptability, and especially in the area of creating change. But when we looked at the leadership 360 composite for those leaders who scored above average in adaptability, it quickly became clear that this organization definitely had the leadership talent needed to become more agile. See Figure 2 below.

Leadership drives culture

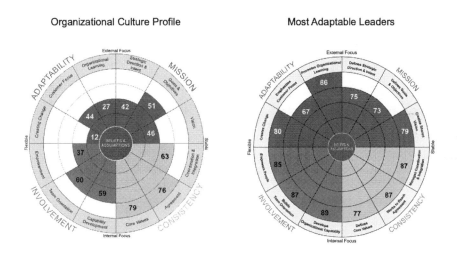

Figure 2

We recommended that the firm mobilize this group of leaders to help define the changes that would generate greater agility in the firm. These leaders were a cohort that actually felt that the organization was holding them back, and they felt they had the extensive experience and credibility to contribute to the change process. Awareness of this contrast between the leader's data and the culture data for their part of the company became a useful asset in our coaching sessions.

Coaching in Context: A Useful Framework

This insight led us to develop a framework for viewing leadership results in the organizational context to help improve the coaching process. This framework builds on our earlier research and the experience that we've gained through our practice (Nieminen, Biermeier-Hansen, & Denison, 2013). The framework contrasts the strengths and challenges of the individual leader against the strengths and challenges of the organizational culture. This allows us to define four major categories for coaching in context: "Starting from Scratch," "Getting up to Speed," "Becoming a Change Agent," and "Building on Strengths."

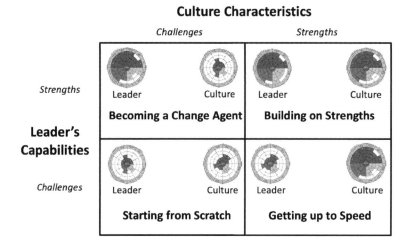

Figure 3. A Framework for Coaching Leaders in Context

Starting from Scratch. When a leader has real limitations in an area where the organization also has significant challenges, this makes for a difficult coaching challenge. There are few role models and helpful mentors in the organization, and the individual leader is starting from the beginning. This means that the coach's most important contribution may come from their ability to import outside resources or expertise to help define the next steps. Support for the leader's development within the organization may also be quite limited. "Why do we need that?" may be a common response. But with a clear picture of the limited support for development that may exist within the leader's environment, a talented coach may be able to help build the case for identifying other forms of support.

As an example, consider the coaching work we did with Katie Chan, who was in the local CHRO role of a tech company in Guangzhou. Katie's background was in compensation, and she was doing well until her firm acquired a competitor and she was chosen to lead the integration team! Then she struggled. Her 360 results showed that she was not doing very well in her role. But the culture results also showed that her organization did not have much experience or expertise in this area. So, her challenge at this point was leading a strategic change in organization that didn't have much experience in managing strategic change. Her coach helped her the most when he provided her with outside examples in her own industry and even introduced Katie to several of her peers in Hong Kong who had successfully made the transition to a strategic HR role.

Getting up to Speed. When a leader's limitations occur in an environment in which the organization has significant strengths, the dynamic is entirely different. Initially, these results may be quite a bit more intimidating, and the leader may feel like they are "on the spot," and that they need to improve dramatically to fit in and be accepted. But the upside of this situation is that the leader is in a setting where there are rich resources and examples to draw on. Opportunities for role models and mentors are rich, and there are many opportunities. In this situation, the coach does not need to import expertise into the leader's environment—it is already there. The coach just needs to build awareness of the context and how the individual can connect with internal stakeholders who can help them build an agenda for their development.

Henry Liu was a talented individual contributor in a key account role in a financial technology firm. Henry had recently been promoted as the new leader of his team, and he had been asked to take on a more strategic role. This new role required Henry to provide vision and strategic direction for the team that he had been a member of just months before! He was not well-prepared for this role. But the culture results for the firm showed that his company had a very strong sense of strategic direction, and this made both Henry and his coach aware of the abundant resources that were available to support Henry as he learned these new skills. A key part of the coaching engagement involved connecting Henry with several senior leaders who mentored him well and supported the development of these strategic skills.

Becoming a Change Agent. This situation is more closely aligned with the general pattern outlined in our earlier case study, described in Figure 1. The leader actually has extensive skills in an area where the organization is quite limited. At first blush, this may appear to be a situation in which the individual is just defined as "high potential" because they possess skills important to the organization. It is actually also a great opportunity to try to leverage the individual's skills to try to improve the organization. In this situation, a coach's knowledge of the organization's agenda for change and improvement become critically important. Opportunities to leverage a leader's strengths by connecting them to important activities designed to improve the organization may also have a positive impact beyond just gaining visibility for the leader's talents and experience in applying them.

Lisa Zhang was an experience line business leader who was promoted into the finance function in the global energy company that we featured in our example in Figure 2. Their goal as an organization was to become more agile. And the line management experience that Lisa brought into the function had helped her to lead a number of successful projects designed to make the function more responsive to the needs of the line business leaders. This showed through clearly in her excellent 360 results! But there was one problem. The feedback that Lisa received from her boss was not very good. His perception was that she was pushing too hard and not working very well with her mostly male peers and direct reports. But when the coach asked the boss to consider the culture results that described the context that Lisa was working in, he slowly began to accept Lisa's tremendous value as a change agent in an organization that needed to become much more adaptable. He also became much more committed to helping her manage the friction that some of her innovative ideas had caused with the group.

Building on Strengths. The final category focuses on situations where the individual leader has strengths that are well established in the organization. The leader's strengths are a good fit with the organization, and there are many opportunities to collaborate with others who share these same strengths, as well as a rich set of resources for continuing to learn and develop in these areas The coach may have a challenge explaining that the positive skill set the leader possesses is not very unique and thus unlikely to provide a solid base for a competitive advantage in their career. However, the coach may be able to help the leader build a strategy to define their unique contributions with the solid foundation of knowing that they share a critical set of skills with the rest of the team.

Leo Peng had done so well as a technical leader that about a year beforehand, he had been promoted to a strategic role in a large consumer products company in Qingdao. He learned fast in his new role and his 360 feedback showed the results of his progress. His success in his new role had put him in the company of a very dynamic group of peers who were also successful in an organization that was doing very well. The coach's insights about the strengths in Leo's capabilities and the strengths in the organization led to a series of discussions about focusing on "raising the bar" for the next step of Leo's development. This meant that a key part of Leo's action plans were to engage with the other leaders who were in strategic roles to plan for the next stage of evolution in the strategy function in his business division. Both Leo and his peers were operating at a very high level already, but this coaching engagement helped generate a plan for moving the group to the next level.

Discussion: What Goes Around Comes Around

As culture guru Edgar Schein once said, "Culture and leadership are two sides of the same coin" (Schein, 1985). So, we must always be aware of the need to deal with both at the same time. Over the short term, the culture of an organization has a strong influence on the behavior of individuals within it, and the individual needs to concentrate on how to fit into the context in order to be accepted and to perform well. But over the longer term, the people make the place (Schneider, 1987) —the culture is created by the individual members, and especially by the leaders (Denison, 1996). So, leadership development and organizational change must be closely linked, so that leaders are always being developed in a way that anticipates the future vision of the organization's culture. Otherwise, as the change gathers force, it is in danger of faltering, because the leaders have all been developed to fit well with the organization's past, not its future.

Many organizations complicate this situation by keeping these leadership development and organizational development activities quite separate. The talent agenda is not well-integrated with the change agenda and, in some cases, these two activities are even in competition for resources and attention. The more powerful approach is to integrate them directly, then align the two activities so that they are complementary. This helps to generate a future-oriented perspective for both activities that helps to maximize this long-term investment.

The people make the place

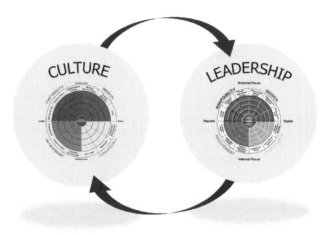

Figure 4

Experienced leadership coaches in China, and around the world, understand this dynamic intuitively and use these insights as an essential part of their practice. But a more systematic approach to coaching in context can also help to generate greater leverage by integrating these two activities in a more mutually supportive way.

References

Boyce, A., Nieminen, L., Gillespie, M., Ryan, A. & Denison, D. (2015). Which comes first, organizational culture or performance? A longitudinal study of causal priority with automobile dealerships. *Journal of Organizational Behavior, 36*(3), 339–359.

Denison, D., Hooijberg, R., Lane, N., & Leif, C. (2012). *Leading culture change in global organizations: Aligning culture and strategy.* San Francisco, CA: Jossey-Bass.

Denison, D. (1996). What is the difference between organizational culture and organizational climate? A native's point of view on a decade of paradigm wars. *Academy of Management Review, 21*(3), 619–654.

Denison, D., & Neale, W. (1996). *Denison organization culture survey:* Ann Arbor, MI: Aviat.

Denison, D., Nieminen, L., & Kotrba, L. (2014). Diagnosing organizational cultures: A conceptual and empirical review of culture effectiveness surveys. *European Journal of Work & Organizational Psychology, 23*(1), 145–161.

Nieminen, L., Biermeier-Hanson, B, & Denison, D. (2013). Aligning leadership and organizational culture: The leader-culture fit framework for coaching organizational leaders. Consulting *Psychology Journal: Practice and Research, 65*(4), 177-198.

Sackmann, S. (2011). Culture and performance. In N. Ashkanasy, C. Wilderom, & M. Peterson (Eds.), *The handbook of organizational culture and climate* (2nd ed, p. 188-224). Thousand Oaks, CA: Sage Publications.

Schein, E. (1985). *Organizational culture and leadership.* San Francisco, CA: Jossey Bass.

Schneider, B. (1987). The people make the place. *Personnel Psychology,* 40(3), 437–453.

Tianran Yin, Cindy J.W. Su
and Joey W.K. Chan

Chapter 8.
Immunity to Change

"Between stimulus and response there is a space. In that space is the power to choose our response. In our response lies our growth and our freedom."
- Viktor E. Frankl

Abstract

In the previous chapter, the authors described the importance and an approach for integrating and aligning leadership development with organizational development, as part of the coaching process with the belief that leaders are developed in a way that anticipates the future vision of the organization's culture. In this chapter the authors address the concept of VUCA (volatility, uncertainty, complexity, ambiguity). VUCA was first expressed in the late 1980's after the fall of the former Soviet Union and how this event sent ripples through out the rest of the world. It pointed out how the world is increasingly faced with events that were not anticipated. The authors introduce Kegan's and Lahey's Brain (Mental) Complexity model, as described in their book *Immunity to Change* (ITC), as a way to help individuals become aware of how they might frame their world through different lenses—lenses that provide a different, broader perspective as the individual advances. The authors also provide insights into how they have successfully applied the tools of ITC and adult development into their coaching and consulting practices in China.

Background

According to Global Human Capital Trends survey (2019), the majority of organizations rated the need for leadership development a high priority for their organizations, but only 40% think their organizations are ready or very ready to meet their leadership requirements. The demands of the rapidly evolving, technology-driven business environment require capabilities such as leading through ambiguity, managing increasing complexity, being tech-savvy, managing changing customer and talent demographics, and handling national and cultural differences. The survey shows that the top 5 worldwide new leadership requirements to be:

1. Ability to lead through more complexity and ambiguity
2. Ability to lead through influence
3. Ability to manage on a remote basis

4. Ability to manage workforce with combination of humans and machines

5. Ability to lead more quickly

Research conducted by CCL, gathering input from 763 middle- and executive-level leaders in organizations from China/Hong Kong, Egypt, India, Singapore, the United Kingdom, Spain, and the United States, showed that these six challenges are the most important that new leaders have to face around the world:

1. Honing effectiveness

2. Inspiring others

3. Developing employees

4. Leading a team

5. Guiding change

6. Managing stakeholders

We found that both of these studies mentioned the core element "change." If there is anyone who still has no clue about VUCA, the COVID-19 pandemic has provided us with a profound example. The shock caused by the COVID-19 pandemic seriously impacts every aspect of life, including leadership coaching. People who have been working on "development" (either individual or organizational) have suddenly been impacted and their clients are responding in different ways. Some have cancelled all external programs due to uncertainty and others are continuing, believing that development cannot stop and they must be ready for whatever comes next.

In China, the expectation on "development" has been there for thousands of years. There have been the traditional ways of pushing people to "grow and develop." However, in terms of coping with the changes of rapid economic growth since 1978, both individual and organizational growth and development have been facing their biggest challenge ever, long before the COVID-19 disruption.

Brain (Mental) Complexity and Adult Development Theory

Drs. Kegan and Lahey's book *Immunity to Change,* (Kegan and Lahey, 2009) introduced three levels of mental systems: the socialized mind, the self-authoring mind, and the self-transforming mind. These systems are used by adults to make sense of the world. The theory suggests that adults operating within each of these three systems use them to make sense of the world in profoundly different ways.

Based on moving from one level, e.g., socialized mind to self-authoring mind, people will have more success in crossing the gap between a world that is "too complex", as they experienced it, and the complexity of their mind at the same moment. Kegan and Lahey (2009)also indicated:

> *Skillful as such managers may be, their ability will no longer suffice in a world that calls for leaders who cannot only run but reconstitute their organizations, its norm, mission and culture-in an increasingly fast changing environment.*

It is interesting to note that ITC has a corollary and long history in Chinese culture. The concept of "mental complexity" can be tracked far back to Confucius' thoughts.

At fifteen, I set my heart upon learning.

At thirty, I had planted my feet firm upon the ground.

At forty, I no longer suffered from perplexities.

At fifty, I knew what were the biddings of Heaven.

At sixty, I heard them with docile ear.

At seventy, I could follow the dictates of my own heart; for what I desired no longer overstepped the boundaries of right.

It has been the spiritual guidance for leaders in long Chinese history. It is related to the concept of wisdom, which is generally related to age. To some extent, it is considered the true belief for many people when they manage their career and life.

Brain (mental) complexity theory, a philosophy from the West perfectly echoes the old wisdom from the East. Moreover, it brings the process and tools to make this old wisdom more practical in the context of "learning and development" in many organizations. Brain (mental) complexity is well understood and immediately related to Confucius' philosophy. Most Asians who have grown up with Confucius' theory are open to discover more details in this and are eager to learn more when "technical challenges" and "adaptive challenges" make them realize how they are stuck in their limitations causing their own immunity to change.

OD (Organization Development) and an Everyone's Culture
Almost at the same time when brain (mental) complexity and adult development theory were first brought to China in 2012, organization development (OD), also

from the Western world, became known in China. A lot of organizations realized it was critical to unleash the power of both organization and individual potential so they could succeed when facing business challenges.

Some organizations found the traditional way of development, such as hiring an external trainer, coach, mentor, or consultant, did not achieve the goal of their organization and employees being developed.

Neither the organization nor the individual can be changed if there is no self-awareness which leads to motivation, drive, or will to do so. Traditional training and development programs can provide knowledge and describe a process for making changes. However, without insight and supporting motivation, the desired change is not likely to happen. Many professionals in the development area started to search for new methodologies and tools to help their clients and coachees gain insight and develop the motivation to change.

Immunity to Change as a Powerful Tool for OD and Leadership Coaching
Leadership coaching played an important role in the recent 10+ years in leadership development in China. Leaders became aware that there could be a mismatch between the world's complexity and their own mental complexity schema or level. Leaders need to know the need for change, the gap between their reality and the reality of their organizational environment. Learning alone will not help much in individual and organizational development. Development may include learning, but it also requires personal insight into the gaps between what is needed and how one currently understands how things work. For change to occur, Kegan and Lahey (2009) posit that the learner must understand themselves and be motivated by the opportunity to change.

Leadership coaching provides an effective way for leaders to improve their self-awareness as well as the awareness to other people and the whole environment. Within leadership coaching, the use of brain (mental) complexity and adult development theory provides another roadmap for leaders to see the match/mismatch between their mind and the world. ITC provides an extremely powerful tool to connect the challenges the coachee is facing with their personal insight into what is blocking them from making desired changes.

When leaders identify these blockages and develop themselves, the development efforts are more apt to help the organization deliver business results that are sustainable.

How Brain (Mental) Complexity Theory Arrived in China

Starting in 2012 and through 2020, there have been a number of publications and events in China that sowed the seeds showing the value and use of brain (mental) complexity theory.

In July 2012, *Harvard Business Review* (Chinese version) published "Why it's hard for people to change" - an interview with Dr. Robert Kegan introduced the Chinese business community to the importance and relevance of Immunity to Change. One year later, in July 2013, another article "To change, find another self-first" written by Li Jinghua, a local ITC practioner, was published in the same journal and further spread word of the benefits of ITC as a coaching tool.

Besides publishing in Chinese, there were six forums organized in China and over 600 professionals in total had attended those forums. In 2012, with the theme of "Breakthrough Leadership - Overcoming the Immunity to Change," three conferences were held: one at the CEIBS School of International Business Administration in Shanghai, one at the ChangAn Club of Beijing, and one at the University of Macao. In 2013, with the theme of "Enterprise Development through Change," a conference was organized by Shanghai Young and Middle-Aged Intellectuals Association. In 2015 and 2019, Dr. Kegan gave keynote speeches on "Global Educational Leadership" and "Future of Organization Exploration: The Deliberately Developmental Organization" at East China Normal University.

In addition to these publications and speaking events, Dr. Kegan conducted certification workshops in China. From 2012-2015 sponsored by Keystone Group, there were four ITC mapping certificate programs held, and 97 senior consultants and coaches attended. As a result of these workshops, coaches and consultants were certified to conduct interviews and to provide feedback to individuals about their current level of mental complexity and how to overcome their own immunity to change.

Application of ITC as a Tool for Leadership and Team Coaching in China

As a result of these certification workshops, ITC has been applied in various OD and coaching initiatives in China for nearly 10 years. From the approximately 100 Chinese-speaking ITC alumnus, who frequently applied ITC in their OD and coaching projects, we selected three coaches and consultants to complete a semi-structured interview to give us a better understanding of how the theory and related tools were being used. Those interviewed were:

Faculty and student practicing coaching in class as a means of learning to apply coaching skills. (Keystone Group, Inc.)

• Joey Chan (Senior OD consultant, ITC team coaching application in Mainland China, Hong Kong and Taiwan.)
• Cindy Su (OD consultant, PCC, ITC leadership coaching application cases of MNC in mainland China)
• Dr. Callas Yang (OD consultant, ITC leadership coaching application cases of SME's in mainland China)

The purpose of these interviews was to understand: 1) if ITC can bring some unique value for leadership and team coaching; 2) how does ITC impact the effectiveness of their work; and 3) what are the opportunities and challenges of future application of ITC. Our interviews were guided by five open-ended questions. What follows in this section are the answers and reflections on these questions.

Experience and Expertise in Using ITC in China

The first two questions we started each interview with were: "How do you get to know ITC and adult development theory?" and "To what kind of projects do you apply ITC?" The following are insights we gained about how they learned ITC and how they have used it in China.

In 2008, Joey Chan went to the US to study adult development theory with

Dr. Kegan. He was the first Chinese who engaged in the adult development theory and ITC world from a consulting approach in China. Following his work with Dr. Kegan, he applied the theory in his practice for several years in Taiwan and Hong Kong, and then came to mainland China where he started to introduce adult development theory and ITC to local OD consultants and coaches.

Dr. Callas Yang was one of the OD consultants who learned adult development theory and ITC tools from Joey's workshop.

Cindy Su participated in the first ITC mapping workshop delivered by Dr. Robert Keagan in China in 2012. She is one of 97 certified ITC mapping coaches who has kept applying ITC in coaching since then.

Even though these are ITC consultants, coaches, and trainers with ten years of experience using ITC in their consulting and training work in China, adult development theory and ITC are still far from being well known and broadly applied in China, a country of over 1.4 billion people served by only about 100 ITC coaches.

Value Derived from Using ITC in OD and Leadership Coaching in China

The next question we asked these three professionals is, "What special value does the application of ITC and adult development theory bring to your OD work?" Their answers show they all had much help and inspiration from adult development theory and ITC in their consulting practice.

Joey Chan was practicing Theory-U in his consulting workshops before he mastered adult development theory and ITC mapping. He said:

> I have a new perspective to see how coachees succeed and don't succeed, however, I have to give credit to the Theory-U approach developed by Otto Scharmer. ITC is a perfect tool to support Theory-U. ITC provides a perfect practical tool for a Theory-U road map.
>
> In U theory, after an open mind, you need to have an open heart, and you don't need to go too fast. Open heart means you need to have an emotional connection to your thoughts. Everyone has some deep personal doubts and worries that are largely unconscious and block their ability to make meaningful changes. These have to be addressed or the individual will not be able to address their fears and overcome their immunity to change.

In his ITC workshops, Dr. Kegan refers to this as a "worry box." Your worry comes from deep within and is a powerful motivator or impediment to change. When dealing with multiple people in a team, everyone's point of worry is related to their work and personal experience and is potentially different than their team members. In a team, the personal worry point of each person can be put together like a jigsaw puzzle to help the team deal with individual resistance and to develop a team view of how change can happen. For ITC participants to discuss and reveal their "worry box," trust is required as most of these issues are personal. Therefore, it is critical that ITC consultants are well experienced and certified to work with the ITC process.

Joey Chan also mentioned that the challenge of each individual always relates to their work, and people have different challenges. In a team, the challenges of each person can be put together like a jigsaw puzzle, and the challenges that may affect the team performance can be reflected. This is a very smart way to integrate individual ITC coaching and team ITC coaching in OD consulting workshops.

For Dr. Callas Yang, the value of adult development theory and ITC mapping is very clear and important. She said:

[ITC] lets customers see what the real mechanism is that is impeding them from succeeding. Of course, sometimes, seeing clearly does not necessarily predict change success immediately, but it is almost impossible to change if you can't see what is blocking you clearly.

As a practitioner certified in ITC mapping in Dr. Kegan's workshop and who keeps and practicing the use of the tool, Cindy Su declared:

To some extent, my OD job is highly related to the concept of a deliberately developmental organization. It has been my true belief that an organization can only be continuously developing if it helps in individual development, a so called "everyone culture." ITC and adult development theory (mental complexity) provides a clear roadmap and powerful tools for me to serve my clients, and it is compatible with Confucianism theory so there is a cultural connection for participants in China.

Finally, we asked the three professionals to share some representative cases.

As one of the most highly regarded OD consultants in China, Joey Chan brought the ITC mapping tool to different kinds of organizations in Taiwan, Hong Kong, and mainland China.

At an individual level, Joey shared one case about an executive from a Taiwan public department who was known for procrastination.

> *With ITC mapping help, he found that it was always him that wanted to move quickly, and it demonstrated that he is not like the other people who need to plan well in advance. He had to learn that not everyone had to approach work the same way. He had to accommodate others pace of change and action for their comfort in making change. His big assumption was that speed was most important in achieving change, but he had neglected the safety needs of others. He learned this from ITC mapping.*

Another case Joey shared was also working at the individual level in Hong Kong. This individual was the successor of a family business.

> *When the founder of the enterprise went through the ITC mapping, he realized that he just bundled who he is with the company he created. This was his big assumption, which prevented him from getting the whole organization to follow changes he felt were important, such as let his son takeover the company.*

In the two cases Joey mentioned above, ITC mapping helped executives to enhance their self-awareness, which is definitely a milestone in their self-development journey. In fact, both the Taiwan public officer and the Hong Kong entrepreneur had achieved important self-breakthroughs that enabled them to make meaningful changes.

In mainland China, the very dynamic economic environment created a significant OD challenge. Challenges also come from business success. Joey also applied ITC mapping in large local firms in mainland China. He shares two cases at team level, one from a famous fintech company, the other from a media company. In the fintech company, he supported the whole security team of the company to go through ITC mapping.

> *The purpose was to try to improve the cross functional cooperation, be proactive and do valuable and creative things. But when they went through ITC mapping, they found they had a collective assumption which is they are the fixers for the company, because they are focusing on solving problems after they occurred.*

To solve problems effectively, they had to better understand what the company was trying to do, recognize potential threats and come up with ways to stop them from happening. This change of mindset (their big assumption) was from cleaning up messes already made to eliminating the risk of having a mess to have to clean up.

Based on this awareness and using ITC, I helped them to study the future technology trends, which opened their eyes and gave them a new perspective of seeing the future and predicting technology security risks. This new perspective taking, can reform their job description and purpose, to be more proactive and creative.

Another team coaching case shows that a rapidly growing local firm in mainland China had the risk of lack of efficiency.

When there is not enough communication and mutual understanding, it reduces understanding and reduces engagement. Because of lack of communication and mutual understanding of the goals, the organization was put into a reaction mode. People would refuse to do time consuming things, be afraid of being challenged and see disagreements as leading to conflicts. They rushed to achieve their data driven KPI, which they believed was the key to satisfying their investors. They felt their investor needs must be satisfied by achieving their KPIs so the team focused on understanding and resolving the immediate problem, otherwise they would hurt their team, may lose their jobs and lose the company.

This was their big assumption for their whole company. This assumption resulted in their not spending sufficient time in building a clear road map to improve the working efficiency of the marketing team. Other teams in this company face similar challenges.

Cindy Su shared an ITC coaching case from an MNC in China in the following example.

It was a leadership coaching case in a global firm. My client was a senior director and going to be promoted to VP within two years. She was very smart and energetic. The first time I met her, I had an impression that she could achieve anything she pursued.

However, after first two sessions with her, I was informed that she had become seriously ill and had to postpone the rest of her sessions until after her return to work. When we restarted after about 3 months, she appeared worried and was wondering if she should take greater responsibilities. On one hand, she was still striving for excellence, but on the other hand, she was too exhausted by an extremely busy schedule and her health status was still a concern. Our sessions were going deeper and deeper when she wanted more and more to examine the meaning of her life.

The tool of ITC helped in these sessions tremendously: my client saw her desires and dreads so clearly that she realized how this fear stopped her from achieving what she wanted and how she was limiting herself. She felt that she had so much potential but was gripped by fears about her ability and physical stamina. Together, we designed some actions for her and tested these in the last few sessions. By the end of our coaching process, she was promoted as planned. More important, she was able to manage priorities more effectively than ever and had more confidence in her health and well-being.

Dr. Callas Yang shared a local SME case:

My typical case is dealing with a senior executive. ITC helps them to see the conflicting and somewhat confusing action of stepping on the accelerator and stepping on the brake in the process of leading the team. The executive wants to support the growth of subordinates, but at the same time, feels it is more time consuming to answer questions, or risk them making mistakes, so he can't help but be furious or do it himself. On the one hand, the executive understood that this behavior was confrontational and he wanted to change, but on the other hand, was always regarded as a bad-tempered leader who looked down on subordinates.

ITC helped another executive to see his inner worry: part of the sense of security was that it was necessary to be much better than subordinates. The executive realized that trusting others created some misgivings and discomfort at first. However, there was a realization that there was a new way to build a sense of security, a strong subordinate and a new sense of teamwork and trust in others.

In brief, the ITC mapping application cases covered both leadership coaching and team coaching. When there is readiness on the coachee side, the ITC mapping can really help them to get much better awareness, especially facing change challenges. Most people fail to make changes because there is some fear or some worry that will not allow them to make changes and once they see this, it becomes easier for them to adapt.

These cases help us understand that if Chinese OD consultants and leadership coaches have a clear understanding of the value of brain (mental) complexity and adult development theory and ITC, they will have more confidence to use these tools in their coaching practice. According to Cindy Su, she is delighted to see adult development theory (brain complexity) accepted and applied by more OD consultants and coaches. She said:

> *Even in my WeChat Moments, I see the words of "socialized mind," "self-authoring mind," "self-transforming mind" quite frequently. But ITC applications are still relatively new. I guess it is partially caused because only a few professionals are certified. Some OD consultants asked me about when would be the next time that Drs. Kegan or Lahey will come to conduct another ITC workshop. I hope that I can do something for these people who are so eager to learn.*

Dr. Callas Yang shared her opinion in just a few sentences:

> *I think the ITC tools alone will be relatively thin, and the consultation and coaching skills behind the tools are the key. Professional HR, OD, or organizational leaders need to study and practice ITC to create real value.*

Joey Chan concluded:

> *ITC mapping and its use in coaching put forward high demands on coach's and consultant's knowledge, coaching and facilitation skills. ITC mapping is a beautiful tool, but to really make it powerful, coaches need to develop their own practical skills and learn how to listen to the coachee carefully, and be able to relate to their individual fears that are impeding their ability to make meaningful change. It is clear that the ITC practitioner must have a high degree of empathy and trust with their clients.*

He confirmed that there is still a big shortage of the real qualified ITC mapping coaches in the market.

Future of ITC in China

To end our interview, we asked the last question: "We believe that with the application of adult development theory, ITC can better help organization development and executive leadership development. What else can we do to increase the use of theories and tools?"

All three interviewees suggested that we initiate more OD and leadership development forums, conferences with workshops in which we collect more learning needs, demo what we have done so far, and invite more people to practice together. These activities will help to present the value of adult development and ITC by showing that we have successful ITC applications in China. There was agreement that more HR/OD work needs to be accepted as a practice in enterprises in China and there is a need to train more people in ITC mapping. Further, more ITC mapping practical experiences need to be shared between coaches to acquire a better understanding and to develop relevant skills for it. This could be added as a separate section in future coaching conferences in China.

There is a great deal of strength that can be derived for individuals and organizations by applying ITC in OD leadership coaching. Brain (mental) complexity and adult development theory is inspiring both for being cutting edge and for echoing of old wisdom. As mentioned earlier, the ideas presented in ITC emanated from the West, yet, they are seamlessly connected to traditional Confucian philosophy elements rooted in China.

In terms of coping with changes in a VUCA world, ITC consulting brings light for people to explore different directions for them to overcome their own immunity to change. The light does not come from any master or expert, but through ITC coaching techniques that allow organizations and individuals to find it from their own heart – from understanding the emotional blockage that stops them from making changes they want to make, illuminating a new path forward.

ITC, together with brain (mental) complexity and adult development theory, is a robust tool. It supports sustainability for people who are willing to learn and develop continuously. It integrates with Evidence-Based Coaching as it requires a philosophy of appreciative inquiry and use of effective listening. Based on these interviews and work with other practitioners, the following summarizes some things that could be done to increase the use of ITC in China in the future.

Challenges to Promoting ITC in China

One of the key challenges to promoting the use of ITC in China is that there are few practitioners who understand the tools and are certified to use them. Even within the professionals who are certified, only a few of them keep practicing and accumulating related experience. In addition, there is little support for them to promote their practices and experiences.

Opportunities to Promote ITC in Leadership Coaching

Leadership coaching and organization development are a growing trend for organizations that are looking for effective solutions to address organizational issues and change. Many are willing to move beyond traditional means, such as training and educational programs for their leaders. ITC can play an important role in terms of development, for it reveals the core assumptions that can be a barrier to "development." It helps uncover what we really need to develop, what can we really change, and what can we do to influence others.

Traps that may mislead understanding of ITC?

Generally speaking, ITC is quite safe, and if a qualified and experienced practitioner clearly follows the process and applies the tools, it will not do harm. That is the beauty of the tool and approach.

The short conclusion: ITC is not a clinical tool and most coaches are not certified to explore psychological dysfunctional domains with clients. The purpose of the ITC process is to allow the individual to see more clearly the assumptions they hold that block them from achieving their desired outcomes. There is a place for coaching and a place for clinical psychology. If an ITC practitioner wants to be cautious about the process, they only need to observe the ICF ethics guidelines and avoid getting into the domain of clinical psychology

The ITC roadmap is there to help individuals understand what assumptions the individual has built that causes them to think and act the way they do. Why do they have trouble trusting subordinates? Why do they not communicate more completely? What is stopping them from achieving the goals they set?

In their book, Kegan and Lahey point out that only about 10% of annual New Year's resolutions to lose weight, stop smoking, save more money, etc. actually happen. Using ITC, people can increase the effectiveness of their change efforts and help them achieve their goals without frustration. Using the ITC process map enables people to see what big assumptions they have that are blocking them from achieving their desired goals. The results of using ITC as a leadership coaching tool adds one more important and useful tool to the professional coach's tool kit.

References

Kegan, R., & Lahey, L. (2009). *Immunity to Change: How to Overcome It and Unlock the Potential in Yourself and Your Organization* (Leadership for the Common Good), Harvard Business School Publishing. Boston, MA.

Chapter 9.
Challenges to Building a Leadership Coaching Business in China

Leadership Coaching in China:
Context, Challenges and Ways Forward

Gary Wang and James C. Warner

"By three methods we may learn wisdom: First by reflection, which is noblest; second by imitation, which is easiest; and third by experience, which is the bitterest."

- Confucius

Abstract

In chapter 8, we saw how coaching that incorporates adult development theories and tools from *Immunity to Change* can lead to successful change for individuals and organizations in China. In chapter 9, we will examine the context in which leadership coaching in China takes place, including shifts in the business and social environment over the last 40 years. We dig deeper into how cultural norms and a focus on short-term business results lead to a focus on leadership development that may have a negative impact on long-term leadership success. We look at how these factors create challenges for the use of leadership coaching in China and offer suggestions for how organizations preparing leadership coaches and business leaders can address these challenges, including expanding the recognition of the value and benefits of leadership coaching in China.

Business Changes in China

To understand leadership coaching in China, it is useful to understand the environment in which coaching takes place and the changes therein. There are two primary underlying factors affecting leadership coaching in China: the shift from a centrally-planned to a market-driven economy, and adherence to Confucian principles, as a number of authors have noted.

Perhaps at no other time in history have economic and social changes occurred for such a large proportion of the global population, and at such scale and speed, as have happened in China since the late 1970s. Since the "Great Opening," sparked by Deng Xiaoping in 1978, China has moved toward a more open society while still maintaining its adherence to "socialism with Chinese characteristics." Implications of this shift included a transition from cooperative farms and central planning of production to a semi-free market economy, including the growth of entrepreneurship (Rudoph, J. 2018).

Other changes included the individual ownership of property and businesses, retention of profit by individuals for their contributions, and greater decentralization of decision-making. As a result, many people took risks to start businesses meeting unfulfilled needs. Others, finding that foreign investment had created job opportunities at new factories in cities such as Guangzhou and Shenzhen in Southern China, left their families behind and migrated to take jobs in the now-burgeoning manufacturing sector.

It is estimated that 400 to 600 million people were lifted out of poverty due to this shift as GDP increased at nearly 10% per year for thirty years. This increase in GDP enabled a 25-fold increase in per capita income during this period (Rudoph, J. 2018)—a significantly higher income growth per capita than in any of the developed markets in the same period. (Nunn, R & Shambaugh, J. 2018).

As China opened up, Foreign Direct Investment (FDI) increased substantially year over year. Along with this investment, Western multi-national companies (MNCs) sent their experienced leaders to oversee the transportation, installation and operation of businesses operations in China. To ensure their continued development, these leaders were given access to global leadership development processes, including leadership coaching. Many MNCs during this time supported providing access to leadership coaching to their expatriate staff and high-potential local leaders. These organizations routinely stated that they found the investment in coaching to be beneficial to executive performance as well as retention. This was a primary reason for the growth of leadership coaching in China and an opportunity for coaches to grow their businesses in China.

Even before the Chinese economy started to slow in 2016, a number of MNCs started "localizing" the leadership of their companies by reducing the number of expat leaders based in China. Some of these companies also reduced budgets for leadership development including for leadership coaching.

In this same period, because of government policy changes, there was a shift in ownership of Chinese companies. Large, state-owned enterprises (SOEs) were gradually broken into smaller units and often spun off as privately-owned enterprises (POEs). In addition, due to changes in China's financial policy and the growth of newly educated business leaders from institutions like CEIBS, CKGBS, and Fudan and Tsinghua Universities, new entrepreneurs started businesses using leverage and other sources of finance, which resulted in a rapid expansion of the number of small-to-medium enterprises (SMEs). Many of these POEs and SMEs, such as Midea, Haier, Alibaba, and JD.com, reached IPO status and became large, publicly-traded companies. As China entered the WTO in

2001, many of these companies set their sights on operating beyond China's borders with leadership including both Chinese and foreigners. This became a second source of clients for coaches in China to grow their coaching practices.

Between 2005 and 2015, the demand for leadership coaching grew at a slower rate, for a number of reasons. One reason was that SOEs had their own leadership development practices, which included the rotation of Chinese Communist Party (CCP) officials in senior leadership positions, many of whom had other avenues for leadership development provided by the party. In addition, a number of POEs and SMEs were led by Chinese leaders who had not experienced the benefits of, or were simply unfamiliar with, leadership coaching. This lack of experience and familiarity with leadership coaching is one of the greatest barriers to the expansion of this effective leadership development approach in China today.

Challenges Business Leaders in China Face Today
To understand how Chinese companies, especially the POEs, operate and grow their market standing, one must start with the backdrop of China business, which leads to engagement challenges of the workforce.

In the last 20 years, thanks largely to its entry into the WTO and increased market attractiveness to MNCs, China has made great progress in many sectors, including infrastructure, electronics, high-speed trains, mobile phones, electric cars, and eCommerce. Yet, the country still lags behind leading Western countries in technology, innovation, and productivity.

Most Chinese companies follow a low-cost, large-scale strategy, and are unable to command higher profit margins that their global competitors often enjoy. Rather than low cost and large scale, foreign competitors leverage the two ends of the famous "smile curve": technology and innovation at one end (as Apple, Microsoft and Disney do) and brand leadership at the other (as P&G, Nike and Starbucks do). When you can't compete on the technology (innovation) or branding (marketing) fronts, you can only live on scale and low margins. Consequently, competition is rampant in most industries in China, and it is hard for most companies to make significant profits.

Take the smartphone industry, for example. Out of the global top 10 players, 5 are from China: Huawei, Oppo, Vivo, Xiaomi, and Lenovo. There are no major players from Europe or Japan, with Apple the only American player and Samsung the leading Korean brand. The smartphone market offers revealing insights on how hard it is for any brand, local or foreign, to succeed in China. Few companies can afford financial losses for years, like the legendary Coca-Coca, which lost money for 30 years before making a profit in China. To survive, companies need to resort to either innovation or marketing. Staying at the bottom of the smile curve runs the risk of becoming irrelevant. Generally, in consumer products, if a company is not in the top 3 brands, retail outlets don't want to provide shelf space. However, in an increasingly on-line business distribution channel, even numbers 4, 5 and 6 brands can compete without substantial disadvantage.

Since most Chinese companies must compete from the low-value point of the smile curve, their immediate need is to stay alive. Unlike global leaders in technology, products, and brands, who invest heavily in R&D, marketing, and distribution, these Chinese companies rely on economic scale and rapid response to stay ahead. Driven by their need to stay afloat, many Chinese companies, including such local icons as Alibaba, Huawei, and Meituan, have developed a savagely inhuman overtime culture. While this culture has indeed helped make some companies powerful competitors in the domestic market—for example, Alibaba fares much better than Amazon in China, Huawei leaps Ericsson and Nokia in 5G and Apple in smartphones, and Tencent is a formidable rival of Facebook—their success comes, sadly, at the expense of their employees, who habitually function under extreme stress and lack of work/life balance—a concept often ignored or ridiculed by top management.

The struggle to survive, involving ever-greater speed, cost-leadership and efficiency, have given rise to a typical Chinese phenomenon: the "996" culture—work that stretches from 9 am to 9 pm, 6 days a week. This 996 phenomenon is especially common in tech companies, where time is money, and speed is critical to survival. Widely criticized, companies with the 996 culture manifest a fear of lagging behind and choose to make speed a strategic edge.

Need for Increased Digital Presence
Digital transformation is a buzz phrase these days, not just in the business community, but also in the public sector. As one of the global leaders in the digital economy, China has strategically invested in its digital infrastructure and become a forerunner in a number of areas, including eCommerce, smart payments, electric cars, robotics, 5G, AI, IoT, smart city, and smart public service. Reflected in its ambitious "Made in China 2025" strategic plan, issued in

2015, the central government sees the digital economy as an opportunity to catch up with, or even leapfrog, the Western countries in key manufacturing sectors, with digitalization as a strategic enabler. While the government has backed off on promoting this policy because it inflamed the Trump administration, there are still concerted efforts to improve the quality of manufactured products and manufacturing processes in China.

Another example is the automobile industry in China. China had zero relevance in the automotive industry, and it was initially unable to compete with established Western and Asian leaders, such as Germany, Japan, and the U.S. in conventional car manufacturing. Thus, the chosen national development strategy was to invest in technologies of, and supply chain for, electric cars. Today, China produces 70% of the world's electric cars and boasts the best battery technologies in the world.

In addition to improving agility and efficiency, companies can also use digitalization for innovation in their business model, and in China, this embrace of digital innovation is taking place across the board. Thanks to the pioneering Rural Taobao movement initiated by Alibaba (China's digital leader, think Amazon, eBay, and PayPal combined), farmers in remote provinces, leveraging the power of the internet, can sell their products anywhere in the country. In addition to hearing of the success of large Chinese companies "going digital," you may be surprised to learn that revenues from online sales of products on Taobao's platform, from 740 townships and villages in coastal Chinese provinces, recently exceeded US $14 million.

In today's business context, digital transformation is not just a winning strategy but a survival strategy. Companies that can't compete effectively via digital transformation will soon lose the game and become irrelevant. The good news is that the number of companies embracing digital transformation is growing rapidly, a trend validated by the boom in digitalization consulting businesses. Large consulting firms in China, such as Deloitte and PwC, have seen strong revenue growth from their digitalization consulting, and some of the smaller consulting firms are either receiving institutional investments or aggressively hiring in spite of the COVID-19-induced slowdown.

Disruptions of Supply Chains Caused by the Trade War, the Pandemic, and Political Changes

Since its WTO entry in 2001, China rapidly emerged as the world's factory floor, making exports accounting for as much as 35% of its GDP in 2005-2006 (World Bank). As the best demonstration of the country's dependence on exports, China used to command as much as 40% of global exports of textiles and clothing and 20% of furniture exports. China's exports in electronics, machinery and equipment are equally remarkable, accounting for 38-42% of the global total.

With the ongoing trade war between the US and China, COVID-19, and political confrontation, governments and companies have started rethinking their supply chain strategies. Both the US and Japanese governments, for example, have offered subsidies to companies willing to consider moving manufacturing jobs back to their home countries.

These actions have generated limited results, given China's advantages in cost and turnaround time. For many products, the cost to manufacture in the US and Japan is still higher than it is in China. Additionally, Chinese companies have integrated the complete value-chain from design to delivery and become highly-efficient, able to deliver products much faster than their counterparts in the US, Europe, and Japan. This is due to an innovative and flexible design and manufacturing approach, a well-established supply base, lower labor costs, a flexible labor system, and a system fueled by millions of internal migrant workers willing to work long hours for the additional pay they are eager to send home.

Though China will remain a competitive option for manufacturing for the short term, more and more companies are moving their operations to such ASEAN countries as Thailand, Vietnam, and Cambodia to minimize the supply chain disruption. In the long run, this should prove a safe bet.

Competition in the Talent Market as the Supply of Talent Diminishes

Due to an unprecedented GDP growth averaging about 8% annually for 40 years, talent had become the hottest currency in the China market. Most businesses could have grown faster were they not hampered by a common shortfall of talent. In the first 25 years since the open-door policy, most local talent chose to work for MNCs, as these promised an open company culture, provided better learning and development, and generally paid more.

Here is an example from a Chinese family. The head of the household worked for Sony, DuPont, and Dell. The wife worked for Global Sources, RR Donnelly, and Domino's. The sister in-law worked for BASF and Nike, and her husband worked for Gillette, Ford, and Nu Skin. As one can see, many of these companies are Fortune 500 firms. In fact, in coastal cities such as Beijing, Shanghai, and Guangzhou, MNCs trained a whole generation of Chinese professionals like this family, many of whom have assumed senior positions in local companies such as Alibaba, JD.com, and Ping'an, China's largest private financial group.

However, a shift has taken place in the last 15 years as a result of the rise of such Chinese internet giants as Alibaba and Tencent, and the success of other Chinese companies, such as Huawei, Oppo, Vanke, and Anta (a local sports brand that has acquired global brands including FILA, Solomon, Arc'teryx, and Wilson). Top talent now often prefers to work for local companies, especially the listed internet and IT companies, not only because they pay more than most MNCs, but also because working for Chinese companies evokes national pride. This intensifying talent war between the MNCs and local companies has increased the cost of talent acquisition so much that senior managers in Shanghai now make more than their counterparts in Hong Kong, something unimaginable 10 years ago. The higher acquisition cost of talent plus the risk of making a selection error have increased the interest in leadership coaching to ensure smooth onboarding of newly promoted or new hires.

Boosting productivity has become a top priority for companies as they strive to grow. Organizations now realize that good leadership and a high-engagement culture are dependable sources of productivity. "People join the company and leave the manager" now rings as true in the Middle Kingdom as it does elsewhere.

Changing Values of the Millennial Generation Related to Income and Work Contract Expectations

In the last 40 years, three powerful forces have fundamentally changed and redefined our world: the rise of the internet, the rise of the millennial generation, and the rise of China. Because these are all profound global events, their impact is felt by everyone in every aspect of life.

The millennial generation literally means the same thing for a Chinese, an American, and a European. However, how the generation affects society, business, and organizations varies greatly in these different geographies.

Unlike their counterparts in most Western countries, millennials in China face a number of uniquely Chinese pressures. Firstly, millennials in China tend to have supervisors who have grown up in a predominantly top-down, authoritarian culture that is largely responsible for the country's famous low employee engagement, the lowest among the world's major economies (7% compared to 30% in the US, Gallup Engagement Survey 2019).

Secondly, Chinese millennials face notoriously high home prices in coastal cities, prices that are substantially beyond the means of average millennial salaried workers. This situation contributes to another modern-China phenomenon: frequent job-hopping for higher pay. Changing jobs every 2-3 years, even every 1-2 years, is common among young office and blue-collar workers, making workplace loyalty a concept foreign to many.

Why this phenomenon? Because in a country where home ownership is a national value, and job opportunities are plentiful because of the long-standing economic boom, increasing income through job hopping is an easy option to cope with high home prices.

Thirdly, Chinese workers are the product of a highly dysfunctional educational system in which rote learning, standard answers, and ruthless competition for good grades and schools have long consumed a significant portion of family resources. In a society motivated by money-worship, young professionals in China are widely known to lack commitment, maturity, independent thinking, creativity, and a life and career guidance. Education has strayed from what it was supposed to be; all work and no play has made Jack a dull boy with limited soft skills. What is the extent of the liability? Only 10% of university graduates are regarded as competent enough for their first corporate job according to a MindSpan survey of 140 HRDs in MNCs, 2017-18. Often, the selection process in organizations does not do a good enough job of convincing candidates why they should join the organization. Engagement is built from the bottom up.

This has set the scene for a harsh reality for the millennial generation in China and posed a huge challenge for companies. When 93% of your employees are either not engaged or are actively disengaged, what valuable level of productivity is even possible? What other agonizing organizational inequalities keep owners and CEOs awake at night?

And when one adds a mere 10% university graduate job competence to the discussion, it is apparent that we are in a workplace catastrophe. In my personal opinion, workforce inadequacy (low engagement and low job competence levels) is the biggest waste for China. This supports the need for greater investment in the organizations selection process and providing onboarding feedback to new hires, letting them know why the organization hired them in addition to incorporating strong and more effective leadership coaching programs.

Barriers to the Use of Leadership Coaching in China

A 2020 ICF survey compares barriers to the use of coaching in general in China with other countries. Similar to other countries, these barriers include untrained individuals calling themselves coaches and marketplace confusion about the benefits of coaching (ICF, 2020).

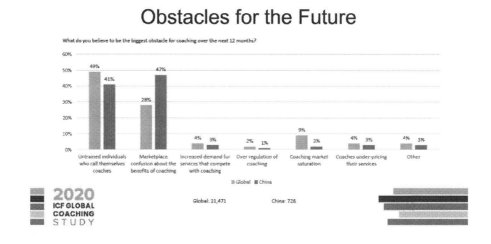

When we consider leadership coaching specifically, there are other barriers to its use in China. One major barrier is the pressure caused by the rapid pace of business growth and the need for quick decisions. Because Chinese businesses have grown rapidly and significantly in the last 20 years, seeking first-mover advantage often outweighs the use of long-term strategy and introspection about markets, processes, and data. The result of this pressure to focus on results has left little time for and interest in developing leadership skills. In addition, leaders have been known to make comments such as investing in the development of their organization's talent simply provides them with an opportunity to move easily to other, better paying employers, leaving the "investor" with little to show for their investment. There is little awareness of non-monetary motivators for workers.

As noted earlier, the first-mover advantage is starting to decline as many Chinese businesses are now in industries facing their second generation of growth and greater competition in their business life cycle. While earlier in the China industrial era, a business leader with a good idea, above-average skills, and access to financial backing could start a business that would easily disrupt the slow and outdated approach of many of the SOEs. These businesses succeeded by being somewhat better than the status quo and disrupted through modest innovation and lower-cost approaches and because there was limited competition. Today, as competition grows within more mature industries in China, businesses need stronger and faster innovation, better management and leadership talent, and rapid development of processes and market insights if they are to continue to grow.

Also, as wage structures have increased the cost of talent, there is less and less opportunity to "poach" talent from other companies with a promise of additional pay. This is especially true for young workers who are looking for opportunities for their own development, work-life balance, and leaders who treat them with respect for their individual contribution.

History of Results-Oriented Leadership Tenets

A second barrier is a shift in the type of leadership skills needed to compete in a rapidly developing economy. A study of business leaders conducted by Korn Ferry (Dai, et. al. 2015) found that "those who best met the leadership requirement (in China) in the past were highly directive, action-oriented, and task-driven." They scored much higher in the skills of driving results and ensuring execution than Western leaders.

The Korn Ferry study also found that as the business environment in China changes, "leaders most likely to succeed will excel in influencing across generations and cultural groups, situational adaptability, dealing with paradox, building networks, cultivating innovation, managing change, and thinking strategically with a global perspective." Compared with Western business leaders, Chinese business leaders scored much lower in these skills. These are skills that are coachable but often not seen to be of value by current business leaders in China.

In this case, coaching is a much better investment than training as it allows the individual manager to reflect and discover how they can change their behavior when it is required rather than trying to change themselves. This is where personality assessments are quite valuable to the coach and coachee. They can start to relate how their pre-dispositions in personality can affect their effectiveness in certain areas of the leader's job. These assessments can focus the coachee on certain competencies they need to further develop.

Hierarchical and Confucian Culture

A third and less visible barrier to the adoption of leadership coaching in China is Confucianism, whose cultural tenets inform much of the behavior of leaders here. Wasserstrom & Cunningham (2018) summarize these tenets as "education, rituals and relationships," which serve as the basis for social order. They expand on this to say that "followers are expected to obey supervisors" to create a "harmonious society." Leaders are expected to be individuals who have been educated, know the rituals or processes of business operations, and are not challenged. As a result, few subordinates will raise concerns about their supervisor's directions or desires, even if they have concerns. This reduces the opportunity for leaders to practice what is viewed in the West as a "participative or coaching style of leadership," where followers are asked for input or suggestions. Because leaders are expected to be experts, asking such questions may cause them to be seen as incompetent. During opportunities to engage in coaching, the Johari window framework can be useful to help the Chinese leaders understand that others may have a different perspective and enable the leader to understand the importance and value of feedback from subordinates and others. It can also create an environment for sharing information about themselves with their subordinates to develop mutual trust.

Further, because leadership coaches are viewed as "laoshi," or teachers, they are often expected to impart business or content knowledge during coaching sessions. Peterson (2010) describes 4 roles of leadership coaches, including imparting content knowledge. Peterson goes on to say that the successful leadership coach, in addition to providing content knowledge, helps the coachee to learn new skills and to develop approaches for their own ongoing development, which will sustain the coachee for the longer term. While this last is consistent with the International Coaching Federation's (ICF) competencies and tenets of coaching, it is often not considered the most pressing need of the coachee in the results-driven China business milieu. Unless leadership coaches have the ability to provide business or content knowledge, they are not likely to be given opportunities to coach executives in Chinese companies, or may be considered as failing to provide sufficient value.

A related barrier to culture is the need for "saving face." In this tenet of Confucian philosophy, it can be understood that in return for the leader being obeyed by the follower, the leader has the responsibility to take care of his or her followers. Some may interpret this "care" to include not giving development feedback, lest the person feel "harmed." In general, giving feedback is used less frequently by Chinese leaders than it is by Western leaders in the same company (Van Katwyke, 2012). As a result, the use of a coaching style of leadership may be vague when it comes to delivering messages to the leader's followers, not being specific enough to help them to identify situations or skills that would help them perform more effectively in their current role or advance in their career. Rather than helping individuals recognize that what they did is not effective, there is a concern that such feedback may be seen as a negative reflection on the person's value.

A leadership coach who engages in "direct communication" with a senior leader may find that the leader feels s/he is losing face, even if the conversation is important for them to understand what might be limiting their success. Direct communication, while an essential skill for leadership coaches, is something that can be difficult to deliver effectively in China. However, if the coach is senior enough age-wise, this may mitigate the discomfort. It is especially important in China for the coach to be trusted by the coachee for this relationship to develop.

Lack of Promotion of Coaching as a Scientific Approach for Leader Development

Additional barriers that limit the ability of leadership coaches to grow their business in China include the desire for secrecy, a lack of trust and openness, the lack of strong leadership development practices in many Chinese companies, and the lack of effort by professional coaching organizations in China to spread the message about the benefits of effective coaching.

In China, individuals with an idea for a business or product are often reluctant to share that idea with others. One potential reason for this is that, until recently, there has been little IP protection in China. If someone copied your product or process, it was difficult to say that it was your idea and that you deserved the fruits of developing it. Also, as China became more Westernized, or modernized, people had greater opportunities for more individual achievement (e.g., social status and wealth). Yang (in Bond, 2008) hypothesizes that this resulted in less social concern for others' success and a greater focus on individual achievement, resulting in less desire to share confidential information. As a result, Chinese business leaders are often reluctant to share intimate personal stories or business information with individuals in a leadership coaching relationship. The ICF (2020,b) indicates that building a strong, trusting relationship between the coachee and coach is core to a successful coaching engagement; the failure to build that trusting relationship can be a barrier to the success of coaching. Coincidently, this is also important for leadership effectiveness—unless a trusting relationship is built, it is difficult for leaders to win anything but tacit support from their teams.

Lack of a Strategic HR Function

In Western companies, successful HR functions are those that are involved in developing and implementing the business strategy. Bersin (2010) lists practices implemented by advanced HR leadership. These include the identification and targeted development of individuals thought to have "high potential." Leadership coaching has been reported to be one of the most effective approaches for accelerating the development of these individuals.

Many senior executives in China describe the role of the HR function in their organization as "administrative." While they feel the value provided is important for hiring, delivering development programs, and administering performance management processes, they do not look to HR to ensure that processes are implemented to ensure the organization has talent ready to execute business strategies. Boudreau & Ramstad (2007) suggest that there is an evolution of HR, from administrative to strategic, which takes place over time. Because strategic thinking itself is less well-developed in Chinese businesses, and because HR is a relatively new function, few HR departments in Chinese businesses are prepared to take advantage of and implement systematic leadership coaching to accelerate the readiness of talent to meet strategic challenges. In an effective organization, the HR leader will be of equal importance as other key direct reports to the CEO, such as the CFO, chief marketing officer, and chief production officer. They will be a key business partner to the CEO as well as their peers who report to the CEO. They will often have conversations outside of business hours, and "at the table" where they may be asked for insights into the potential impact of key talent availability and quality on business strategies.

Lack of Business Support for New Coaches

Another barrier to accelerating the use of leadership coaching in China is the focus of coach development organizations on the preparation of coaches, rather than promoting the benefits of leadership coaching, or helping their alumni find sufficient coaching engagements to sustain their practice. While a number of university programs in the US and Europe prepare leadership coaches and help MBA and EMBA students learn to apply coaching skills in their leadership roles, there are few such programs in China. Many of the coach development programs in China are operated by private organizations teaching a broad spectrum of coaching skills useful to a variety of specializations, including life coaching and career coaching. However, few focus on teaching the skills needed for a person to become a leadership coach specifically. While a deeper discussion about is what is needed to prepare leadership coaches will be covered elsewhere, suffice it to say that there are many coaches who are not well prepared for this specialized area of coaching.

In addition, professional organizations, such as the ICF and the Asia Pacific Alliance of Coaches (APAC), focus on helping individuals to become coaches and to advance their professional skills. Few organizations help coaches manage their coaching *business*, or promote the profession to potential clients. As a result, unless they have worked for some of the larger human capital development companies that operate in China, many individuals who learn to be professional coaches find it difficult to find clients and to sustain their business at an adequate level, resulting in lower income for coaches in China than in other countries (ICF, 2020b).

A related concern is that many individuals who seek to become professional leadership coaches in China have not worked in sufficiently large businesses, leading to a lack of understanding of the business environments and complexities executives face in their work. In the US, many coach training organizations provide internships or practicums for their students. Most human development consulting companies in the US and Europe that provide leadership coaches to their clients ensure that these coaches have sufficient experience working with executives inside large organizations. Because businesses of this size and scope are relatively new and rare in China, companies that provide leadership coaching services must either find coaches who have had such experience, or provide an apprentice development path for them to gain relevant experience working with executives. Many coachees may have difficulty relating to a coach who has never been in an executive position in an organization and/or is quite a bit younger than they are.

Talent and Leadership Challenges

As described earlier, low employee engagement poses a cardinal challenge to Chinese companies, and the resulting low productivity is a monstrous impediment to the Chinese economy. According to the IMF, Chinese productivity is about 12% of that of the US. We have explored some of the key drivers for this, including ample jobs and pay increase opportunities due to rapid economic growth and high home prices. But the more essential reason is a widespread lack of experienced leaders. Who an organization puts into a key position is often not subject to enough rigor. Selection is a business process that can be learned and managed like any other business process, and leaders need to take selection seriously. Once in the position, in China, leaders are often left to their own means with little support from their bosses when they face difficulties.

"Training and Development can help great people be even better—but if I had a dollar to spend, I'd spend 70 cents getting the right person in the door."
— Paul Russell, Director, Leadership and Development, Google

Local leaders are products of a highly-authoritarian and hierarchical social structure, and they usually operate with a command-and-control style without being fully aware of the impact of this style on employees predominantly born after 1983. The younger generation grew up with the internet, and they demand more autotomy, equality, and respect. For this young generation, leading through using personal influence is far more effective than leading by using position power. This is a critical leadership lesson for leaders of the young generation.

Rise of Millennials Who Desire Greater Leadership

In many ways, Chinese millennials are not that different from their counterparts in Western countries. They are equally curious, open-minded, creative, and seek autonomy, recognition and meaning in what they do. However, Chinese millennials do stand out, uniquely, in a number of ways. One is that most of them are the only child to their parents, given the one-child policy first imposed by Mao Zedong, modern China's first leader. This policy had a tremendous impact on this generation. Given the focus of attention of 2 parents and 4 grandparents, this generation is generally more self-centered, psychologically vulnerable, and spoiled, making them more challenging employees than their predecessors. Engaging, developing, and retaining them constitutes one of the biggest workplace challenges. They don't share a loyalty mentality, they are less mature and empathetic, they are more self-centered and direct in their materialistic pursuits when under financial pressure, and they tend to not be very patient.

Understandably, leading and engaging Chinese millennials in this daunting backdrop is challenging, and companies and leaders must figure out how to be effective in doing so. While many MNCs have found their way, often through the use of coaching leadership, most Chinese companies are still struggling. They are slow to realize the value of coaching because their closed and directive culture has blocked the opportunity.

We have listed a number of barriers to the use of coaching at the beginning of this chapter, but we would like to point out a few more here. These include late adoption of coaching as a development tool, limited experience in working with leadership coaches, market confusion, and a low awareness of the value of coaching.

Leadership Coaching in China Is Still New

Confusion in the market about what coaching is, and the difference between training and coaching, as well as the differences between personal/life coaching and leadership coaching, has limited the use of coaching as a tool for executive development.

Since leadership coaching is largely still a novel concept in China, much education is required. Most local companies have never had exposure to coaching, and they can't distinguish it from training, mentoring, consulting, or facilitation—the latter services also being new practices to local firms. This situation is not only true with leadership coaching; it is also true with personal/ life coaching or parent coaching, too. One may be curious: is psychological counselling popular in China? The answer is relative. Counselling is recognized and available, but if we compare it with Western countries, especially the US, penetration of this service is still quite low.

In spite of its exponential growth in the West in the last 10 years, leadership coaching is much less well understood and supported as an effective leadership development approach in China. Less than 1% of companies in China actually pay for coaching services, compared with over 80% of companies in Australia and New Zealand, for example. Out of this 1%, about 75% are global companies such as Microsoft, J&J, Ford, Mars, IBM, Nike, Roche, AstraZeneca, BMW, and Deloitte.

As a young industry that began gaining recognition in China around 2008, leadership coaching promises huge potential in the long run. The tipping point will take place when Chinese companies become as serious about coaching as MNCs. If one takes the essential cultural factors into account, a best guess is that it may take 5-7 years before Chinese companies demonstrate similar appreciation of the value of coaching as MNCs do.

One heartening sign is the extraordinary popularity of ICF-accredited coach certification programs in the country. Some of the world's best-known certification programs are all doing well, generating a steady supply of good, certified coaches to help meet the increasing demand and to promote the industry. These programs include Ericsson, CTI, IECL, Keystone Group IBC, ICA, Progress U, Coaching Australia, MMS, and MindSpan. Thanks to these programs, the number of ICF ACC, and PCC-level certified coaches in China is growing rapidly.

Why have Chinese companies been slow in embracing coaching? I think three barriers have been identified:

• First, China has an almost 3000-year history of hierarchy. Even though the Berlin Wall was torn down 31 years ago, autocracy is still a Chinese political reality. When command-and-control is a dominant leadership norm, especially in typical Chinese companies, it is hard to sell coaching to them. The good news is that, with more open company cultures in new-economy setups and executive movement from MNCs to local companies, coaching has begun to be introduced to Chinese firms. Success stories include Huawei, Alibaba, Tencent, JD.com,

Midea, Huazhu, and DiDi, the Chinese counterpart of Uber.

• Second, a great number of Chinese companies are still operating from a day-to-day need for survival, which puts business at the top of the agenda. They care much more about business results than about people and organization development. As a result, having been in that mode so long, the business focus still dominates the organization, even though the company has become bigger. People are less cared for, a signature feature of Chinese companies.

• Third, given a significant lack of maturity, most Chinese company leaders can't tell learning from development. Many of them grow all employees through buying training programs, as training is the only thing they know: MBAs or EMBAs for senior leaders, workshops for managers, and classroom training for frontline staff. Company culture tends to be top-down, repressive, impatient, and much less open or progressive. 360-degree feedback and psychometric instruments are much less used or trusted than in MNCs. Even if they do employ these tools, the validity of data is very low because people don't tell the truth and give open feedback. In such an environment, everything is based on short-term considerations, business numbers top the company agenda, and people and leadership are not valued, let alone part of the culture. However, the fact that high-quality psychometric assessments are used in selection in some Chinese companies assures that they are available for use in coaching as well.

One emerging positive shift is that action learning programs (AL) are gaining popularity in more open-minded Chinese companies who are using them to try to promote problem-solving and cross-functional collaboration. Focusing on business issues, not people, leadership, or organizational challenges seems to promise safety, and is therefore easier to introduce.

In trying to make sense of all this, one can bear in mind that China was one of the poorest countries in the world before its 1978 "Great Opening." At that time, GDP per capita stood at $178, vs. $10,560 for the U.S. The China index was 1/59 that of the U.S. Today, after 40 years of runaway growth, the same index is 1/6, with the China GDP per capita exceeding $10,000 in 2019. When economic development level is so low, modern-society infrastructure, processes and software are inevitably scarce, even nonexistent.

In addition, the reputation of coaching was tainted, early on, by the fall from grace of TopHuman, once a towering coaching success story in China, which disrupted the development of the industry. Founded by a Hong Kong coach trainer, entrepreneur and the first Chinese MCC, TopHuman once had 700 employees and \$60 MM in revenue, and in 2007, the company was cracked down on by the Chinese government. It had operated as a pyramid-selling organization without a license. To make things worse, their powerful marketing machine and the hype it created fostered the belief by some people that they were a cult. After a few years in jail, the founder's name was no longer mentioned in the coaching community, but the damage was inflicted and took a toll on the coaching industry in the country.

As highlighted earlier, MNCs in China have been fueling the demand for leadership coaching services, and Western-trained HR and business leaders have been mainstream participants in coach certification programs, promoting the awareness and practice of leadership coaching. In order to develop local talent demanded by rapidly-growing business, leading global companies bank on leadership coaching with most of them reporting positive results. In the experience of Keystone Group and MindSpan, two market leaders in China, over 90% of client projects are rated as successful, very much in line with conclusions from global surveys. The open and developmental company culture has been the primary contributor.

While there have been coaching successes with Chinese companies, such as the "Leader as Coach" project in Neusoft, an outsourcing giant, and in Huazhu, a leading Chinese hotel chain, the majority of coaching experiments in Chinese companies have evinced less encouraging results. Many coaching programs are launched as one-off interventions, rather than as part of a systematic approach, managing it as part of the fabric in a talent development masterplan. While you can testify that there is a people and coaching culture in companies like Microsoft, Google, J&J, Mars, and Deloitte, you can't declare that you see the same culture in any big-name Chinese companies. Some of these may have used coaching now and then, but there isn't a systematic attention to people and leadership development with a coaching component.

Creating Opportunities for Increasing Coaching Usage

That coaching is powerful is no secret. There are a number of ways that we, as coaches and coaching company leaders, can increase the use of coaching by Chinese business leaders. Some suggestions include the following.

• **Promote the effectiveness of business leaders who use a coaching leadership style.** Though coaching is still relatively new in China, the country has already been home to numerous stunning coaching culture successes such as Deloitte, Ford, Roche, AIA, Aramark, Neusoft and Huazhu. These successes need to be better promoted by coaching industry leaders.

MJN China is also a world-class coaching culture success. Led by an Australian who, upon becoming China President in 2010, devised a culture change movement called GGCL (Growing Great Coaching Leaders), the movement aimed to shift the culture from leading from position power to leading through personal influence. Over the course of 6 years, the top 140 leaders were trained through a 6-day, internally designed coaching program and were measured by their team satisfaction. The company transformed itself completely, boasting the following "Mission Impossible" feats:

1) The China operation overtook that of the US, to become the company's biggest market;

2) China contributed the lion's share of global profits;

3) Cities of presence increased from 28 to 200;

4) Employees jumped from 800 to more than 5000;

5) Market share increased from #5 to #1;

6) Turnover rate dropped below 10%, half of the industry average, and

7) There was zero turnover among the top 20 leaders.

The GGCL program was so successful that the China President was offered the global COO role. Takeaways from this exceptional MJN China success are inspiring:

1) Culture defines business results;

2) It's a CEO thing;

3) It takes time to change a company culture; and

4) The secret to organizational performance is always people. Another learning—coaching is probably the best tool for culture change.

Promoting such success stories plays well into the pragmatic Chinese psyche, and helps spread a belief in human potential. Once the legendary MJN CEO shared his success with a luxury company, and with the China retail CEO becoming a follower of coaching leadership, business results improved significantly, and the CEO was promoted to be the Greater China Head. We can draw a number of conclusions from this experience.

• **Influence Business Leaders through New Channels.** It is important to shift the channel of influence to business schools and pitch the practicality of coaching to CEOs as well as to Human Resources Directors (HRDs). Innovation and entrepreneurship are required in order to spot new ways to extend influence. While converting HRDs remains a safe bet, it's always more direct to work through CEOs. Marketing platforms, such as Keystone Group and MindSpan, should learn from McKinsey, whose partners insist on speaking with CEOs, not HR VPs. Another great example is Lingjiao Gongfang, the Chinese counterpart of Vistage. The company only speaks with owners and CEOs for business development.

• **Provide Free Leadership Coaching to MBA Students.** Apple has been successful by selling their Mac product line to business schools at a very low price point. This is the equivalent of planting seeds that grow into relationships with future business leaders to invest in their future. Keystone Group, MindSpan, and other coaching training companies are providing free or low-cost coaching to MBA students to help them make career choices and develop additional insights into their long-term development.

• **Form Alliances with Leadership Development Platforms.** It is equally important to form alliances with leadership development platforms that focus on local companies such as Lingjiao Gongfang and Hundun University, and to open a door for coaching. My prediction is that the tipping point in this market may arrive in 5-7 years, in that Chinese companies will become major customers of coaching services. While MNCs in China are low-hanging fruit, Chinese companies will be the future of the industry. Whomever has mastered connections with Chinese companies will own the market of tomorrow. Building alliances with leading gateways to Chinese companies, such as Lingjiao Gongfang and Hundun University, is a smart strategy.

• **Offer Free Coach Training Programs.** It is also important to strategically offer free programs, such as *Leader as Coach* workshops, to leading Chinese companies, plus furnish exposure and experience. Partly because HR is not perceived as a strategic partner, Chinese companies tend to be conservative and risk-averse. By offering low-cost trials, such as Leader as Coach workshops, we open new doors. MindSpan has used this strategy effectively to open doors to Alibaba and JD.com.

• **Create and Promote Compelling Business Cases.** We must seek to create compelling business cases in using coaching to empower millennials. The global need for leading and empowering millennials has given rise to a huge business opportunity: the coaching culture. To lead millennials effectively, it is important to understand what really motivates them. Besides good pay, they value meaning, significance, autonomy, recognition, and a collaborative relationship with their manager. There are so many success stories in this line; Huazhu is one of them.

• **Invite Global Coaching Experts.** Keep planting seeds by inviting global gurus such as Marshall Goldsmith, Robert Kegan, Alan Mulally, and Dr. Cherie Carter-Scott to interact with Chinese business and coaching communities to enhance awareness of coaching. Keystone Group's partnership with Fielding Graduate University (FGU) and their highly-qualified faculty to present webinars about advances in leadership coaching is another example. Incorporating FGU Press's new book, *Innovations in Leadership Coaching* into study and reading groups distributes recent PhD research in coaching to China.

In the last 10 years, we've been taking these steps and finding them useful in promoting the leadership coaching industry. We will continue making investments by creating exciting learning opportunities. In 2021, for example, we will bring the Courageous Leadership program, based on Brené Brown's "Dare to Win" program, to clients.

• **Organize Regular China Leadership Coaching Conferences.** Since 2011, MindSpan has organized 4 such conferences, and the 5th conference will be held in Shanghai in November 2020. In addition to leadership coaching conferences, Mindspan will also host the 6th APAC Coaching Conference in Shanghai in 2022, where it is expected to draw 700 participants from around the world.

• **Sponsor Research to Support Coaching and Coaching ROI.** Mindspan has been sponsoring APAC Coaching Surveys and will continue to support this most serious coaching survey in China and Asia. In addition, PhD alumni of FGU are actively engaged in creating new coaching and coach development theories and practices that reflect the unique culture of China. Some of this research will focus on the ROI of coaching as well as approaches that work well in China.

• **Promote Famous Coaching Titles.** There are many great books that many Western leaders are familiar with that espouse the value of using a coaching leadership style. Examples include *What Got You Here Won't Get You There* by Marshall Goldsmith, *Trillion Dollar Coach* by Eric Schmidt and Jonathan Rosenberg, and *Immunity to Change* by Robert Kagan and Lisa Lahey. It is critical that we continue to bring such ideas to CEOs of local companies to help them gain insight into why coaching works for top companies such as Google and Apple. Many coaching vendors have given away hundreds of copies of such books, and they have used them in their training programs for corporate executives and HRDs, and have discovered that this simple act is one of the most powerful ways to promote leadership coaching.

Conclusion

There have been rapid changes in the business environment in China over the last 10 years. These changes created an opportunity for the start and growth of leadership coaching in China, but they have also led to the decline, in recent years, of opportunities for new coaches. We believe that, as the China economy transitions to seeing more local leaders in key leadership roles, things will change. Chinese companies face greater global competition as they expand their reach and operations beyond China. As leadership philosophies and approaches change from autocratic and directive to more participative and coach-like, the need for leadership coaching will continue to flourish.

It is up to coaching providers and business leaders to ensure that this happens by promoting the value of coaching and providing an ecosystem to help newly-certified, capable coaches to succeed and offer value to their clients.

References

Bersin, J. (2010). *The new talent management framework*. Bersin & Associates. Retrieved October 6, 2020: https://joshbersin.com/2010/05/a-new-talent-management-framework/.

Boudreau, J. & Ramstad, P. (2007). *Beyond HR: The new science of human capital.* Harvard Business School Publishing. Boston, MA.

Dai, G., Et. Al. (2015). *China's new business leaders.* Korn Ferry Institute, Los Angeles.

International Coaching Federation (ICF). 2020. ICF Core Competencies Update: November 2019. Retrieved October 6, 2020: https://coachfederation.org/core-competencies.

International Coaching Federation (ICF). 2020b. *2020 Global Coaching Study.* Retrieved November 2020: https://coachfederation.org/research/global-coaching-study

Nunn, R. & Shambaugh, J. (2018). *If wages aren't rising, how is household income going up?* Brookings Institution. Retrieved October 5, 2020: https://www.brookings.edu/blog/up-front/2018/10/04/if-real-wages-arent-rising-how-is-household-income-going-up/

Rudoph, J. (2018). *The China questions: Critical insights into a rising power.* Harvard University Press. Boston.

Van Katwyke, P. (2012). "Differences in skill use by Chinese and Western Leaders." *Personnel Decisions International.* Presentation to AmCham, Shanghai.

Wasserstom, J. & Cunningham, M. (2018). *China in the 21st Century.* Oxford University Press. London.

Worldbank (2005).

Yang, K. in Bond, M. H. Editor (2008). *The psychology of the Chinese people.* Chinese University Press. Hong Kong.

SECTION II.

THE FUTURE OF COACHING IN AN EVOLVING MARKET

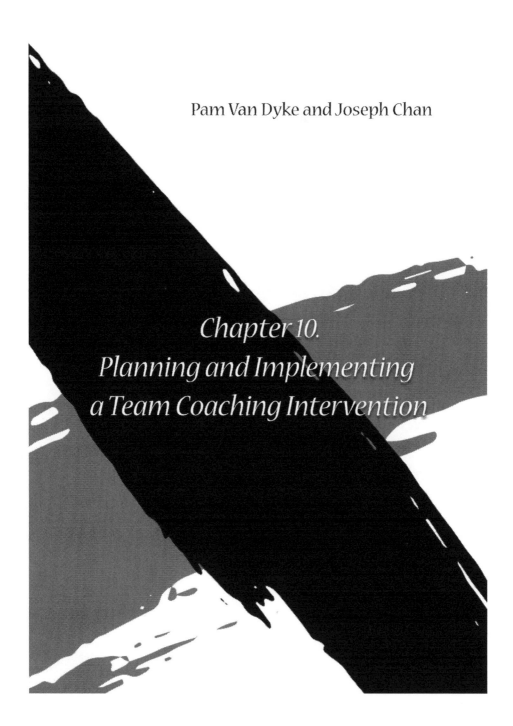

Pam Van Dyke and Joseph Chan

Chapter 10.
Planning and Implementing
a Team Coaching Intervention

Coming together is a beginning. Keeping together is progress. Working together is success.

    – Henry Ford

Abstract

In the previous chapter, we examined in some detail the context in which leadership coaching in China takes place, examined challenges that must be overcome to increase the use of leadership coaching, and offered some suggestions on how to overcome these challenges. In this chapter, we provide some background on practices that leadership coaches can use, based on research, to make team coaching effective in improving leadership teams. These include how to diagnose when team coaching might be an appropriate intervention, alternatives to team coaching, and how to implement a team coaching intervention. While there are cultural barriers to incorporating team coaching and leadership coaching in China, we provide a short case of how the principles described in this chapter were used in a real situation in China.

Introduction

Since more and more organizations are leveraging the power of coaching in their workforce, it has created more opportunities for coaches who wish to expand their coaching offerings beyond just individual leadership coaching.

International Coaching Federation (ICF) celebrated its 25th anniversary in 2020 while also exceeding 23,000 members in 161 countries. The focus of ICF and other coaching organizations has been on standardizing individual coaching. It was not until 2019 that ICF began discussions about team coaching competencies. Dr. Van Dyke was honored to be invited to serve with a panel of team coaching thought leaders and experts to help contribute to the discussion on team coaching standards. At the time of this writing, Dr. Van Dyke and this panel have met together four times with coaches from all over the globe, and we are working hard to establish standards; it is a work in progress. As the coaching field continues to mature, we will become more and more knowledgeable about things that fall outside of individual coaching, such as team coaching.

While much of the content of this chapter is based on her research and extensive experience in team and group coaching in the US, many of the foundational principles are likely to apply as the use of team coaching grows in China as well.

Growing Interest in Team Coaching

As organizations have become more and more knowledgeable about coaching, they have become more involved in the *what, who*, and *how* of coaching. This change has been positive because it has forced the field of coaching to mature in its dialogue about coaching approaches, methodologies, philosophies, and standardization of competencies, i.e., PCC markers. All things that have helped to strengthen our field.

As this evolution has taken place, more and more coaches have sought to expand their coaching offerings to include team and/or group coaching. This expansion has in turn encouraged more accredited coaching schools to begin to offer courses in team and group coaching. This is goodness! Having felt like a voice crying in the wilderness for over 10 years regarding "more-than-one-coaching," which incorporates models for team, group and peer coaching, we are elated we are finally having the dialogue and looking for ways to train coaches beyond the basics.

When we think of why team coaching and why now, we have come up with the 4 top reasons that we see within organizations:

1. Innovative Leadership Development Option

For years, organizations have offered off-the-shelf leadership development programs, and for some, they have been very effective. But for others, these programs are too generic and do not address the real issues leaders are facing. Providing coaching for teams provides an innovative approach to leadership development to those who might not otherwise experience coaching.

2. VUCA - Volatility, Uncertainty, Complexity and Ambiguity

Although this acronym has become a trendy managerial term, it speaks to the ever-changing nature of our work environment. Most corporations today are experiencing VUCA in a variety of ways, which in turn, has forced organizations to stay on their toes regarding providing the right kind of assistance to keep their workforce productive.

3. Cost Effective

In recent years, coaching within organizations primarily started at the C-suite level or the executive level (or however the organization defined "executive," i.e., director, vice president or senior vice president). As these individuals experience the benefit of coaching, there has been an interest in cascading the experience further down into the organization. This is especially true for organizations who are seeking to create a coaching culture. Fast forward to 2020, and now more and more organizations are offering coaching to other levels within the organization as a way to develop and retain their talent and to do so in a cost-effective manner. Team coaching allows other levels of the organization to experience the benefits of coaching. It has become a win-win. Employees on teams get exposed to coaching and the organization benefits from the productivity that follows. This is especially true in China where leaders are more focused on results than in the development of talent.

4. Multi-Generational Work Environment

In the US, or Europe, it is not uncommon for organizations to have four different generations within the workforce (Baby Boomers, Gen X, Gen Y, and Gen Z). In fact, in rare circumstances, there could be five generations, i.e., including the Silent Generation. While these generations in China have different names (e.g., 40+-year-olds, single child, etc.), the principles of generational differences and working together as a team apply in China as well. This convergence of different generations on the same team can produce some difficult situations. Team coaches are often called in to assist in helping teams leverage the different generational perspectives.

In China, a big factor in generational differences is due to the single-child policy and the influx of children from this generation into the workplace. These differences require a different leadership style when they are present in a team. Children born in the single-child policy generation are the object of the attention of 2 parents and 4 grandparents, and they had no cousins and few peers with whom to socialize. They were often given special tutoring and enrolled in special classes to ensure their advancement in China's rigorous school admissions and promotion programs. As a result, many of these children, like millennials in the West, expect leaders to treat them with greater respect. When told to do something, they often ask why it should be done and are not motivated if they don't understand the reason or purpose. They also expect regular feedback given in a supportive and respectful way. This has forced organizations to offer training to their leaders to equip them to possess more of a *coaching style* of leadership. In that vein, team coaching has become a natural way to improve; in fact, in some situations, it has become an expectation.

Planning a Team Coaching Intervention

There are many different approaches a coach can use to impact a team's performance. Much depends on the skill set and diagnostic abilities of the coach and/or consultant as well as the desired outcomes of the team involved.

When planning a team coaching intervention, it is important to work with the sponsor and gather some information about the current situation, why they want an intervention at this time, and to reach an agreement on the purpose s/he sees for the intervention. It is important to gather additional information before committing to a specific approach. At this point, the coach can suggest a general approach about what might be the best approach.

If after the conversation with the team leader or sponsor, or after observation of how the team functions, it may be appropriate to recommend an approach that does not start with team coaching. This is particularly true if there appears to be a low level of trust between team members. If people seem closed and distrustful about sharing information, it may be better to start the intervention at another point on the Team Coaching Continuum, shown in Figure 1.

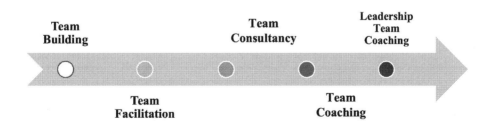

Adapted from P. Hawkins, 2014

Figure 1 reflects the continuum that should be considered when working with a team. Not all teams are ready or need team coaching. It is important that the coach understands each of these interventions in depth and has diagnostic skills and abilities to determine which stage of development the team is in, and what level of intervention would best help the team meet their desired objectives. Figure 2 provides a deeper description of the focus of each of these approaches.

Figure 2

INTERVENTION	FOCUS
Team Building	Most appropriate when helping a team bond during the initial stages of team development
Team Facilitation	Managing the process so that the team can focus on the tasks at hand
Team Consultancy	Provides reflections and suggestions on "how" the team is performing their tasks – Practitioner is consulting on a "known issue" and provides advice and solutions
Team Coaching	Combines both the performance and the process through reflection and dialogue. The role of the coach is to lead from behind
Leadership Team Coaching	Combines coaching with systems thinking. Helps leaders understand their impact both individually and as leaders with special emphasis on those that report to them and how collectively they impact the organization

If the sponsor agrees with the general approach, it is helpful to meet with other key stakeholders to get further insights into the level of team functioning. Some information we have found to be valuable includes the level of understanding of clarity of team purpose, processes, and level of commitment to the success of the team. This includes asking questions about the capabilities and commitment to the team members. Other areas to gather information include team processes around team coordination and communication approaches – do they coordinate their activities with each other? Do they communicate effectively and on a regular basis?

Another area to consider is that of the atmosphere, or attitude, of team members toward the entire team and toward individual team members. Questions such as, how much respect do team members show for each other? What is the level of conflict? What is the nature of the conflict? What prevents team members from collaborating on critical tasks or activities? What is the level of tension within the team? What do you think is creating this tension? What types of emotions are exhibited in team meetings?

Some of the critical criteria in creating a detailed team coaching plan include the degree to which it is necessary for the team to operate as a team—that is, do they have a common purpose and is there a team leader? Another critical criteria is if there will be the need for coaching individual team members, or if all the coaching can take place in a group setting. A final consideration is who will conduct the coaching—will it be the "coach," or will there be opportunities for peers in the team to coach each other? These are all important elements in planning the intervention, and at times, they will not be fully known until the intervention has begun.

Some team coaching engagements can proceed well without the leader or executive sponsor being heavily involved either with individual coaching or as part of the team when group sessions are held. If you believe the team leader or sponsor does not have the necessary leadership abilities, it is important for the plan to include individual coaching for the team leader or sponsor to ensure the intervention is successful.

Launching a Team Coaching Intervention

If an intervention includes the team leader or sponsor being present during team coaching sessions, the role and actions expected of the team leader or sponsor should be discussed and agreed in advance. To ensure a high level of trust during the team coaching sessions, transparency should be established so team members know what to expect when dealing with team issues.

When holding the first team coaching session, it is necessary to observe team dynamics as well as fulfilling the coach role you feel is appropriate for the intervention. Sometimes, it is valuable to sit in on a team meeting in advance of the first team coaching session. Some of the things to observe include body language, level of participation, quality and quantity of communication, and the content of conversations. If you are not already familiar with them, there are many good references on team dynamics and team processes that can help you be more effective in your team coaching. Some evidence you may see during a team meeting that would suggest areas to focus on during the team coaching are listed below. These were all present in the case study presented later in this chapter.

• Lack of eye contact when talking to each other
• Palpable tension
• Quick to disagree with each other
• Defensive posture
• Withholding information
• Lack of camaraderie—no small talk before or during the meeting

Team Development Stages

The behaviors observed during team meetings and team coaching sessions provide insight into the developmental stage at which the team is currently performing. There are five stages of team development, according to the psychologist Bruce Tuckman, who developed a model of team development in 1965. He posited that teams go through five stages as they grow and mature in their development as a team (Tuckman, 1965). The following brief description of what occurs in each stage is helpful in determining where to start the intervention.

Forming

When a team first forms, they are in the evaluation stage of getting to know each other and understanding their boundaries in the context of the team. Members are trying to figure out what is expected of them. This is the stage when the group sets ground rules and team tasks are discussed.

What is manifested during this stage is open-ended questioning in an effort to familiarize themselves with the goals and responsibilities. You may also see questions related to getting to know each other and the part each person brings to the table. You may also see testing of the leader and the system in which they operate. Sometimes team members are associated negatively with the part of the organization they represent, not for who they are personally. It is helpful to understand conflict or animosity between different functions or departments represented by team members.

Figure 3

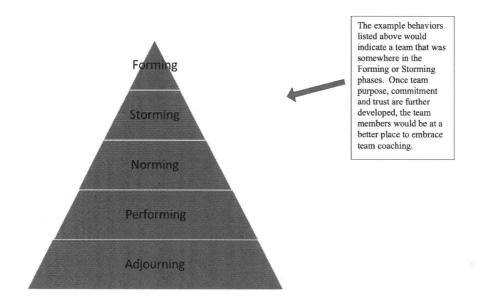

The example behaviors listed above would indicate a team that was somewhere in the Forming or Storming phases. Once team purpose, commitment and trust are further developed, the team members would be at a better place to embrace team coaching.

Bruce Tuckman's Model (1965)

Storming

As a team or group begins to evolve and make decisions, the personalities of the members begin to emerge. This emergence is sometimes met with resistance and power struggles. It is also common during this time for members to create cliques and form factions. Personality characteristics and idiosyncrasies emerge, and members begin to feel frustrated and annoyed. The need for compromising must happen or the team's progress is hindered.

Norming

It is during this stage that the team begins to gain agreement and consensus on roles, responsibilities, and direction. The commitment and unity among the team members is strong.

Until a team works through their differences, norming cannot happen because the respect and agreement of the team and its leader is not evident. The role of the leader during this stage is required.

Performing

During this stage, the team has worked through its differences and established clarity around roles, responsibilities, and direction. This allows the team to have strategic awareness and execute on tasks.

It is not until the team has worked through its differences and established expectations that they can begin to work towards goal achievement. It is also during this stage that the team needs little to no direction from the leader.

Adjourning

The stage is more applicable to teams that are formed on a time-sensitive project because it entails the break-up of the team once their task is completed successfully and its purpose fulfilled (Tuckman, 1965).

If you observe a team is at the forming or storming stage, it may be more helpful for the team to engage in team building exercises before attempting team coaching.

It is natural for coaches who work with individuals to assume that when a team needs assistance, team coaching is the most appropriate application. However, there are times when team coaching is contra-indicated or may not produce the expected benefits because the team is operating at a lower level of functioning. Some indications that a team is not ready for team coaching include the following:

• A team in the early stages of team development (Forming or Storming)
• There is a lack of trust among the members
• Confusion exists around roles and responsibilities
• Team members are unclear on direction and purpose of the team

Helping the team gain clarity around basics in team functioning is generally best done with team building and team facilitation activities. These approaches can, and in some situations should, be used as a pre-curser to team coaching. Team coaching is best initiated once the team is clear on a few critical components. The following are indications a team may be ready for team coaching.

• Clarity of team membership and how each team member links to each other
• Team members share the same goals and objectives

• Reporting structure is clear
• A shared purpose exists, is clear and is agreed on
• Team members understand and accept their individual performance is tied to the whole team
• There is clarity around who the leader of the team is and other key stake holders
• There is an openness to learn, grow and develop both its processes and performances

It may be hard to ascertain what stage a team is in or how they are functioning until the coach has had an opportunity to be with the team and assess their level of functioning. It is often prudent to wait to commit to a final team coaching plan until the coach has had an opportunity to observe the team interacting with one another, and to ask some diagnostic questions. The following are examples of questions that are helpful in determining the level at which a team is functioning.

• How aligned are the values of each team member with each other and with the organization?
• Is each team member clear on the roles and responsibilities of this team?
• How open and honest is each team member with each other?
• How would this team describe their ability to work together?
• How would you describe the functioning level of this team?

When working with teams, using a team assessment that includes some of the questions listed above will help the coach know the level of intervention that is appropriate for the team.

Evidence-Based Team Competencies
We firmly believe it is important to equip oneself in the areas of specialization in which one plans to coach. Continued education should be coupled with one's interest in the services offered, not *winging it*. Adding to and sharpening one's tool kit will only help to ensure effectiveness.

To add to that, one of the most common misperceptions encountered when working with coaching students who are interested in doing team and/or group coaching is their belief that because they know how to do individual, 1:1 coaching, they can easily parlay those skills into doing team coaching. Although training and experience as a 1:1 coach clearly prepares one to do team coaching, it should not take the place of acquiring and building specific team coaching competencies.

What follows is a list of the 3 main competencies that emerged from the research Dr. Van Dyke conducted on team and group coaching.

Competency: Coach Self-Awareness

One of the insights often overlooked is that you bring to each coaching engagement your life experiences. And some of these experiences include those from your family of origin—your "first team." Your early experiences regarding your first team matter significantly in who you are and how you react to those around you. Whether your family experiences were positive or negative or a combination of both, they can impact how you *show up* as a team coach. Taking time to reflect on what you learned from your family and how they can either help or hinder you as a team coach is time well spent.

There are a number of areas in which it is helpful to increase your self-awareness in regard to your first team. Use the questions below to help reflect on each of these areas.

Communication – What were the communication patterns in your family? Did family members communicate open and freely with one another, or were the communication patterns subversive and covert?
• How did you learn how to communicate?
• As a coach, what do you need to learn or unlearn about communicating and communication patterns in order to be effective?

Conflict - When there is more than one person present, there is the potential for conflict. We are not all the same, and from time to time, we are going to disagree. Conflict is natural, necessary, neutral and in some cases needed in order to grow and develop.
• How was conflict handled in your family? Was it embraced, avoided, or distorted?
• As a coach, how comfortable are you when things get heated and people disagree?

Cohesive - The dictionary defines *cohesive* as how things unite and fit together. In families, this is sometimes measured by how close a family is with one another. Some families seem to naturally mesh and fit together while others have to work at it.

• Do you know what is feels like to be in a tight-knit family? Was a level of closeness important to your family?

• As a coach, are you aware when a team lacks cohesion and the feeling of closeness among members? If so, do you have the necessary skills to help a team experience cohesion?

Committed – There is a saying, "When the going gets tough, the tough get going." High-performing teams get things done. History is filled with examples of committed teams doing miraculous things.

• What happened in your family when things got difficult? Did people leave, or did they roll up their sleeves and get going?

• As a coach, how will you help a team get and stay committed when the chips are down?

In this age of digital bombardment, a 9, 9, 6 work requirement, and multi-tasking it is imperative that coaches develop the habit of "staying up to date with themselves." It is easy to quickly lose touch with ourselves and how we are feeling. We're focused on our coachees after all. Taking a break to spend time with ourselves to simply think and reflect on how we are feeling, what we are doing, why we are doing it and how we are doing is all central to being self-aware practitioners.

Here are a few habitual activities that I do, and I encourage those I coach and supervise to do them as well:

• Sit by yourself at least once a day, even if it is for 5 minutes, to just "check in" with yourself; be cognizant of how you are feeling.

• Put some efforts in, either through meditation, prayer or positive readings.

• Take personality assessments when given the opportunity; don't allow yourself to get rusty just because you've "already taken the MBTI." Seek out other assessments that can provide insight into yourself and others.

• Practice a program of rigorous honesty with yourself. Although it may be easier to push things under the carpet or delay a crucial conversation, don't. Life's too short.

• Value "deep work" practice, i.e., be a disciple of depth in a shallow world. Take time to "turn off" the world of distraction around you and crave going beyond the surface.

The discipline of staying up-to-date with yourself will sharpen your ability to be in tune to others around you. As a team coach, a critical skill is being able to pick up on what is being said and what is *not* being said. Those who practice self-reflection and awareness are more sensitive to the surroundings of what is happening with others.

Competency: Coach Social Awareness

This competency is about being able to create psychological safety for your coachees. We have found that it is beneficial to ask students learning team coaching to describe the atmosphere the last time they hosted a party or social gathering. What things did they do or not do to make the guests feel comfortable? What things did they do to create the kind of atmosphere you wanted? Another approach is to ask them to reflect about a party or social gathering they attended that was uncomfortable. Both approaches are equally helpful.

These actions and behaviors are some of the same types of behaviors and actions you can do when coaching teams and/or groups.

Here are a few tips for creating safety in teams:

• Be yourself. When you are at ease, it models the role for others to be as well.
• Be predictable. Say what is going to happen and then act accordingly.
• Eliminate distractions.
• Take time to survey the surroundings for possible barriers to safety, i.e., space, seating, logistics, soundproofing, etc.
• Create an open emotional space. Demonstrate behaviors that connote being non-judgmental.
• Communicate in a transparent and honest manner to create trust.
• Answer questions and concerns in a timely manner.
• Model the role around being open and transparent.

Competency: Understanding Group Dynamics

The most basic description of group dynamics is the interactions that occur between and among people in a group. Those interactions can involve but are not be limited to, communication patterns, verbal and nonverbal behaviors, and decision making. Kurt Lewin, a social psychologist that began his work in the 1940s, contributed a lot to our understanding of group dynamics. He noted that people tend to behave differently when in a group than when they are working alone. The study of groups is fascinating and often covers group process as well.

When working with more than one in a coaching engagement, the coach owes it to the people they are working with to have a good understanding of group dynamics. One's ability to understand group nuances will strengthen their ability to facilitate growth.

There are other competencies that emerged from my research that are important to success as a coach in a group setting. Some of these include the coach's ability to be organized, psychologically accessible, able to facilitate discussion, and have technological knowledge based upon the medium the team was using, i.e., virtual coaching.

Case Study – Reshaping Company Culture - European Medical Equipment Company in China

This case is shared by Joseph Chan, a seasoned leadership coach who has lived and worked in China for over 20 years.

Overview

I was approached by Mr. Wu (not his real name), the Asia Pacific CEO of the captioned manufacturing company, initially to help improve the learning culture. Mr. Wu had tried various ways to improve the culture of the company, including one-on-one leadership coaching for his direct report to promote the employees' learning interests and self-initiative as he believed those were the keys for sustainable business growth. He was lost and could not understand why no one seemed to appreciate his intention and efforts.

With his introduction on the company background, key team-member situations, and expectations for the coaching engagement outcome, we agreed that cultural reform would take at least one year, and we would start with the development of the management team members through leadership coaching. Later on, we would use a facilitative team approach to better align vision and goals. Subsequently, team coaching could be deployed for further team development. The choice of leadership and team coaching approaches were due to its innovativeness and effectiveness in tackling individual learning needs.

The Process

Phase I – Leadership Coaching for Management Team Members

The CEO and the management team members were assigned a coach to address their individual development needs for 6-9 months. The CEO did not require a report of the details of coaching provided to his team in order to ensure confidentiality and provision of a safe space. This is not easy in China as it is culturally accepted that the sponsor of a development project has the right to know about the details, which typically results in the coachee's reservation in revealing true thoughts.

Phase II – Setting Goals for Culture Change

Several strategic planning workshops were facilitated over a period of time beginning about four months later to assist the management team in developing the next 5-year vision and key initiatives for the business. One key deliverable of this phase was enabling the management team to reach consensus on reshaping the management team's culture. This included establishment of learning organization culture and realization of a high-performing leadership team capability. In planning this phase, I used many of the principles described earlier in this chapter by Dr. Van Dyke.

Diagnosing the Organization's Existing Culture

China is a large country with 56 official ethnic groups that differ widely in the culture and even in the language spoken. In a large organization like the subject organizations, employees typically come from different parts of the country carrying different ethnic characteristics and beliefs.

One common challenge of a leader to gain alignment of thoughts and values across and within all team members. Responsible leaders take the time to present, check and clarify the vision and direction of the company with subordinates. Even so, the current fast-paced working environment and high market demand hinders such efforts in most cases.

For a culture reshaping initiative to be successful, a team coach or coach-like leader must focus on cultural competence development, as well as essential social emotional awareness and relationship management practices. These are essential skills in quickly reducing the barriers to mutual understanding the direction of the company and obtaining aligned and effective execution.

In working with the team, I paid particular attention to the beliefs and values of myself and others, and how they interplay to ensure quick integration. I noticed the relatively big difference in understanding and reception of the company vision and value among the management team members. Some members even had opposing views of the current company policies and practices. This was all valuable information to plan for the intervention approach.

Phase III – Launching Team Coaching

After arriving at the aligned intention of the management team to create a high-performing culture, we formed a core project team consisting of the management team with some selected next-level employees and deployed team coaching.

The initial project meetings were initially partially facilitated by me as the team coach to ensure modeling of behaviors of a learning culture. The approach used was not just to run through the project routines, but more importantly, to explicitly set the stage for learning, mutual respect, and collaboration to co-create future successes and sustainability.

As the project progressed, I took the observer role and provided intervention when required. In most Chinese business settings, people prefer not to display their talents and capabilities in the beginning, particularly in a public way. Modeling by the coach helps introduce a gradual and comfortable example to start the culture shift and to ensure thorough understanding of the process.

Team coaching is still new in China, and people have yet to grasp its value. Besides, business leaders have the pressure to deliver quick results, and this makes the developmental part of team coaching less of a priority. To ensure we get the most out of team coaching, the ability to understand and address sponsors' and team members' goals and needs is essential. Based on the observations and findings, we also require proper balancing and prioritizing to form the coaching intervening plan. To this end, understanding team dynamics including power interplay is vital. In China, people are less direct in expressing themselves, but the force of the undercurrent from what they are not saying or committing to can be very impactful. Neglecting this will trap the team into limiting their understanding of underlying barriers and stall progress.

Key Deliverables

The combination of leadership coaching, meeting facilitation, and team coaching in this case resulted in individual development of leadership capabilities of the management team. It also resulted in better alignment of organization and team vision, mutual understanding, and jointly defined behavioral practices.

The cultural reshaping initiative was successfully launched company-wide and sustained by supporting structures and reinforcement activities; these actions were conducted by internal employees as the new approaches, cultural expectations, and behaviors were cascaded down through the organization. This was attributed to the involvement of key next-level employees who willingly served as change agents and advocates after joining and learning from the core project team. This demonstrated that team coaching intervention played a sizable role throughout this process.

In addition, the attitude of the operations director changed significantly. He shared that he benefited from the program by gaining new awareness of what a coach-like leader could do to improve leadership and results. He used to doubt the company and regularly argued with his boss, as he was not clear on the company's direction and his role. He expressed that he became more efficient and collaborative in the management meeting as he became better aligned with his boss and could see things from the company's point of view. He took a less directive approach in interacting with his production team by giving them more space to experiment with new ideas and find out root causes of problems. I commented that this change would be difficult to achieve with mere one-on-one coaching as the broader company perspective may not be discerned and experienced so personally. The participative and co-creative experience through team coaching greatly helped to pave the path.

It is rewarding to see the positive impact of coaching in supporting the challenging cultural change of a company. I believe when coaches and leaders integrate and apply some of the team coaching essentials described in this chapter and are mindfully present, we can co-create more success stories in China.

Chapter 11.
Coaching That Addresses
Educational and Vocational
Guidance in China

Joyce Yuan Gong

"The future belongs to those who can give the next generation reasons to hope"
- Pierre Teilhard de Chardin

Abstract

In the previous chapter, we saw how team coaching could be used as a practice to enhance the performance of leadership teams in China. This chapter by Joyce Gong serves as encouragement for us to look at how coaching practices can be employed to provide educational and career guidance to students in China. Students in China are moved along based on their capabilities in subjects, often not taking into account their interests, which drive their motivation. Parents and teachers are well meaning and tend to push students into areas they are good at but may not be motivated to do in life. By combining capabilities, interests, and personality, we may be better able to guide the student to focus on the most likely career choice and then look at the educational program that will provide the best preparation for the student. Research has shown that people who pursue an educational path based on career motivation, and moderated by their capabilities and personality, are more likely to graduate on time, have higher grade points in their major, and have less risk of dropping out. For instance, a student who says they want to be a rock musician, but has only moderate singing or musical instrument capability, may find that they could still be in the music business but use their capabilities in management to be a talent agent or a musical producer. This is an area that the coaching community could become productively involved in to make a difference in students' future.

Introduction

Career development is a lifelong journey, starting from childhood, becoming much clearer during adolescence, and turning pragmatic and realistic in adulthood (Porfeli, Lee, Hynes, & Hirsch, 2012). Career guidance is defined as the activities to assist individuals to make educational and career choices (OECD & EC, 2004). Globalization, advances in technology, the rapid changes in genetics, artificial intelligence, digital technology, robotics, nanotechnology, three-dimensional printing, biotechnology, smart systems and electrical grids represent the arrival of a Fourth Industrial Revolution, which has been transforming society and the work (World Economic Forum, 2016). With the rise of information overload and social anxiety, to thrive in a world where change is constant and learning never stops, calls for a new consideration of career development and career guidance by shifting focus from job matching and searching to skills development to be both agile and creative (Gillmore, 2018).

Career choice is influenced by multiple factors including personality, interests, self-concept, cultural identity, globalization, socialization, role model, social and family support, and available resources such as information and finances (Kerka, 2000). Bandura, Barbaranelli, Caprara, and Pastorelli (2001) pointed out that an individual's career trajectory is influenced by several factors including the context in which they live, their personal aptitudes, social contacts, and educational attainment and most importantly, their perceived efficacy is the key determinant of their preferred choice of work and life. However, among all factors influencing career choices of young adults, the influence of parents, the most pivotal one, is often neglected.

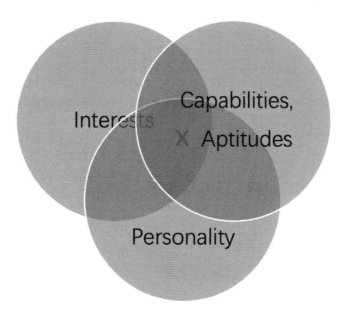

Figure 1. Model of Career Preference Intersection of Interests, Capabilities and Personality

In 2010, a program to provide career guidance in high school was initiated by the Ministry of Education of China followed by the announcement of the *Outline of the National Mid- and Long-Term Plan for Educational Reform and Development 2010–2020* (Huang & Wang, 2014). Extensive efforts have since been made by some pioneer high schools on a variety of projects mainly from teachers and students' perspectives, such as training courses to change teachers' mindset, coaching services to develop their capabilities, and occupation exposure curriculum to students. However, the role of parents and the connections between students and parents, and parents and teachers, have been generally ignored by these new policies, even though parents exert important influences on Chinese students' career choices (Zhou, Li, & Gao, 2016).

Education in China is viewed as a major path to advancement and the critical way of changing life. Many families raise children with such values (Shek, 2007). Unlike the Western belief that the level of ability leads to success, Chinese parents have high expectation on their children's academic success due to China's outcome-based education system. Chinese parents have typically paid attention to the issue of career development when their children reach university or before graduation from the university. Under deeply rooted tradition of filial piety based on Confucian philosophy, students tend to be more obedient and follow parents' directions, including education and career choices (Leung, Hou, Gati, & Li, 2011). Having identified the absence or low quality of career-related parent support in high schools in China, a great deal of coaching efforts is planned to apply in the education sector in China.

Career Guidance and Career Development Theories

Career development theory and practice have shifted from quantitively oriented, trait-and-factor approaches, and job-matching model to the qualitatively oriented, constructivist and social constructive approach, and developing model (Arulmani, Bakshi, Leong, & Watts, 2014). Career guidance and counselling started in the early 20th century as a result of the growth of industrialization (Keller & Viteles, 1937; Watts, 1996) and evolved in the 21st century with theoretical models and empirical tested approaches. Career theories have evolved along with the changing work contexts, shifting from individual to systems, from content to process, and to the mix of content and process (Arulmani et al., 2014; Patton & McMahon, 2014). Prior theories and practices served career development needs in the 20th century and were mostly Western-based. However, in the dynamic world of work in the 21st century, they are not sufficient in addressing the challenges of globalization and technology disruptions.

Over the 100 years of history, there are five major theories of career development that guided career guidance and counselling practice along with research in the United States as well as internationally (Leung, 2008). They are (a) theory of work-adjustment, (b) Holland's theory of vocational personalities in work environment, (c) the self-concept theory of career development formulated by Super and more recently by Savickas, (d) Gottfredson's theory of circumscription and compromise, and (e) social cognitive career theory.

The theory of work-adjustment and Holland's theory of vocational personalities in work environment is job-related with a focus on matching and environment fit. The theory by Super (1980, 1990), a life-span, life-space approach to career development, among the many theories, receiving much attention in the world, suggests a developing model. The self-concept theory has received wider attention and has been tested in different cultural settings in the world. Gottfredson's theory is a more recent contribution, representing theory of both content and process (Leung, 2008; Patton & McMahon, 2014). Among the big five theories, the three based on developing model and constructive approach are widely used in career guidance.

Self-Concept Theory of Career Development

Donald Super's life-span, life-space approach has been tested, refined and advanced over the years since 1950. According to Super (1990), self-concept is a product of complex interactions among a number of factors, such as physical and mental growth, personal experiences, environmental characteristics, and stimulations. The career model, also known as Life-Career Rainbow, is based on the belief that self-concept changes over time and develops as a result of experience. Super et al. (1992) developed the theories based on the extension of Eli Ginzberg's work on life and career development stages from three to five. The stages include growth, exploration, establishment, maintenance, and decline.

However, Super neglected the fact that people may not develop each of their career stages one after one. Savickas (2002) developed a new way of approaching and understanding career, with concentration on processes of development first, and then on the content. He initially worked under Donald Super, and there is a very clear legacy from Super in Savickas' work. The concept of career maturity was widely used to describe the degree of a person's development. Savickas used the term *life designing* to describe the process of individuals constructing their careers (Savickas, 2005). Savickas takes a developmental approach to career and particularly focuses on the self-concept, how we see ourselves, as a fundamental aspect of career.

In terms of life design, researchers such as Savickas and his collaborators (Nota & Rossier, 2015; Savickas, 2012; Savickas et al., 2009) conceptually clarify these constructs from a historical perspective. They identify three keystones of career theory and intervention: individual differences or traits, career development or tasks, and life-career design or themes. The central goal of career counseling shifts from choosing an occupation or charting a career path to championing a meaningful work life that matters to the person and to society (Fan & Leong, 2016).

Super, Osborne, Walsh, Brown, and Niles, (1992) identified fives areas to be considered when assessing career development. They are career planning, career exploration, decision-making, world of work information, and knowledge of preferred occupational group. It increases with the age and grade-level increase during the adolescent years. Savickas (1997) proposed career adaptability as a replacement of the career maturity concept since adaptation servers as a bridge constructs to integrate the four segments of Super's life-span, life-space theory: individual differences, development, self, and context. Adaptability could be conceptualized using developmental dimensions. Recent research has advanced career adaptability along three primary dimensions of planning, exploring, and deciding (Creed, Fallon, & Hood, 2009; Hirschi, 2009; Johnston, 2018; Koen, Klehe, & Van Vianen, 2012). Maree (2017) mentioned that recognizing the constraints and the limitations by use of a biologically-based term, career maturity was replaced by the concept of career adaptability due to the mixed results obtained in empirical research. The practical implications of career adaptability as it relates to career guidance. The gap can be found by use of assessments such as the Career-Adapt-Abilities Scale, the Career Adaptability Inventory, the Students' Career Construction Inventory and the Career Future Inventory, and then a targeted career intervention can be applied (Johnston, 2018).

Gottfredson's Theory of Circumscription and Compromise

In the development of career theories, cognitive growth and development are popularly discussed. Gottfredson's (1981, 1996) theory, assumed that career choice is a process requiring a high level of cognitive proficiency. In recent revisions of the theory, Gottfredson's (2002, 2005) elaborated on the dynamic interplay between genetic makeup and the environment. Genetic characteristics play a crucial role in shaping the basic characteristics of a person, such as interests, skills, and values. Yet their expression is moderated by the environment that one is exposed to.

Even though genetic makeup and environment play a crucial role in shaping the person, Gottfredson (2002, 2005) maintained that the person is still an active agent who could influence their own environment. Hence, career development is viewed as a self-creation process in which individuals looked for avenues or niches to express their genetic proclivities within the boundaries of their own cultural environment (Leung, 2008). Gottfredson (2005) developed four stages of circumscription, with the fourth stage called *orientation to the internal, unique self,* which is at ages 14 and above. By age 13 and 14, adolescents have developed two cognitive competencies related to career development: self-concept and perceptions about occupations (Gottfredson, 2005). It is the adolescent time of individual, in which the self-concept such as personality, interests, skills and values, become prominent. Compromise is the response to external realities and to accommodating personal preferences to achievable choices in the real world. Although Gottfredson's theory remains untestable in many aspects, it serves well as a conceptual guide to career guidance program development, especially in a school setting (Leung, 2008).

Social Cognitive Career Theory

The Social Cognitive Career Theory framework has been widely used to guide career development practice. Bandura et al. (2001) outlined that the course of life is shaped by many choices made during the formative period of development in an individual. This theory is based on Bandura's self-efficacy theory. Self-efficacy relates to a person's perception of their ability to reach a goal (Bandura, 1986). It plays the central role in the cognitive regulation of motivation. Perceived self-efficacy is proved as a pivotal career choice and development (Bandura et al., 2001). The theory offers three interrelated segmental process models, centering around three core variables: self-efficacy, outcome expectations, and personal goals (Leung, 2008). The three segmental processes are the development of academic and vocation interest, how individuals make educational and career choices, and educational career performance and stability. Social Cognitive Theory stresses the importance of self-efficacy in one's choice and behavior. Career self-efficacy is influenced by individual variants and contextual factors such as family background and learning experiences (Lent, Brown, & Hackett, 2000).

Young adults can develop interest in activities when they feel efficacious with predictable positive outcomes associated with the activities. With the reinforcement between self-efficacy and outcome expectation, the interest would lead to a personal goal. The intertwining relationship helps form a stable pattern. Bandura et al. (2001) claimed that familial socio-economic status influences parental perceived efficacy and academic aspirations, which, in turn, affect their children's perceived efficacy, academic aspirations and career achievement. The children's perceived efficacy and academic orientations shape their perceived efficacy for different types of career pursuits, which, in turn, plays a determinative role in the careers they choose and those they actively shun.

Strategic career intervention will positively impact young people in the context of social cognitive career theory. It provides a well-rounded framework for young people to understand the development of career interest, career choice, and performance (Leung, 2008). This has been studied and verified in many cultural settings internationally. For example, by using this framework, Nota, Ferrari, Solberg, and Soresi (2007) did a research studying the career development of Italian youths when they attended a university preparation program. The study generated many findings consistent with the social cognitive career theory career choice models; most importantly, the authors indicated the lynchpin of family support to career decision and efficacy.

The above-mentioned theories offer a conceptual foundation for career guidance and career development. The matching theories fail to provide insights on how to guide individuals' development. The developing models of self-concept over life-span and social cognitive model are more appropriate in support of effective career guidance in the 21st century workplace. The changing global social contexts call for an important skill set development: lifelong learning (Herr, 2008). The emerging social re-arrangement of work has been reflected in career theories by the conceptual move from career development to career management. The construct of stages as developmental periods has been replaced by learning cycles, which pushed people to actively plan and lifelong learn to construct their best possible future (Savickas, 2008).

Career Guidance in Educational Settings

Career development theories and career guidance practices have been applied in education settings and been validated in many countries and under different culture settings for a long time. Gysbers (2008) stated that there were increasing similarities in career guidance provisions, although differences in conceptualizations across countries remained. During the last decade of the 20th century and in the first decade of the 21st century, the efforts on developing a robust career guidance program in educational settings were strengthened. Providing career guidance in education settings shared a common purpose of life career development, which is defined as self-development over the life span through the integration of the roles, settings and events in a person's life (Gysbers, 2008).

In the global era, the increasingly intensive international economic competition and accelerating flow of information across national boundaries have brought about significant changes in education, the labor market and the professional lives of individuals (Van Esbroek, 2008). The career paths of individuals are becoming more and more complex and fragmented, and people are switching to new jobs, some that they create by themselves. The job growth in the next decade is expected to outstrip growth during the previous decade, creating 11.5 million jobs by 2026, according to the U.S. Bureau of Labor Statistics (2016). Even further, it's estimated that at least 65% of children at primary school today will ultimately hold jobs that do not yet exist (Economic Graph Group, 2017). Therefore, the job matching theories will not work in the 21st century global workplace. Developing theories have laid a solid foundation for career guidance practices in education settings.

Guest (2000) argued that all the issues about careers have been viewed as an integral element of the educational process for a long time. Reimers (2006) saw a growing consensus among educators to try to use education to make sure students became architects of their own lives. He further concurred that the children could be productive citizens and fulfill the great promise of the enlightenment given the right skills to be part of a fast-changing, interconnected, digital economy. Gysbers (2008) thinks career guidance should use logical and systematic ways of instruction to help students. The knowledge students need to acquire, the skills they need to develop, along with the attitudes they need to form, are the results of the career guidance program in educational settings, thus reflecting a general presupposition of many countries that career guidance is served to achieve learning outcomes.

The Importance of Providing Career Guidance in High School
Super (1990) described that in the stage of exploration (ages around 15 to 24), an adolescent has to cope with the vocational developmental tasks of crystallization, specification, and implementation. Crystallization refers to a cognitive process involving an understanding of one's interests, skills, and values, and to pursue career goals consistent with that understanding. Specification is making tentative and specific career choices, and implementation is taking steps to actualize career choices through engaging in training and job positions. During this stage, people have the characteristics of trying out through classes, work experience, and hobbies to develop choice and skills (Super, 1992). Students are on their own in college. There is a clear gap when students shift from teacher-directed learning in high school to student-directed learning in college.

Under this globalization and digitalization circumstance, career guidance in high school becomes more crucial and urgent. The self-concept and future skills development is the key content in career guidance in high school. Many scholars have studied topics on how to prepare students for college life. However, there is little research from the family perspective to help students be their own CEO, to develop capabilities such as setting goals, to devise right learning strategies, to make sound decisions and to monitor their performance by themselves.

Self-Concept and Skills Development in High School
Career guidance is not just choosing an occupation; it is a process of self-exploration and self-evaluation (Nota & Rossier, 2015; Savickas, 2011; Savickas et al., 2009). A relatively stable self-concept should emerge in late adolescence to serve as a guide to career choice and adjustment. The self-concept will continue to develop and change when the individual gains more exposure and reflection through the developmental stages (Savickas, 2008).

In the high school years, self-concept development is important while there is more emphasis to developing decision-making skills, goal-setting, and planning skills (Gysbers, 2008). In high school, the topics of college and career readiness have been discussed for years in the United States. In 2010, the Association for Career and Technical Education (ACTE), the National Association of State Directors of Career Technical Education Consortium (NASDCTEC), and the Partnership for 21st Century Skills (P21) came together to emphasize that integrating career and technical education (CTE) and 21st century skills into the entire education system will put more students on the path to success (Hyslop, 2011).

As career development is a life-long process, adolescents start working on their careers long before they engage in actual work behaviors. Negru-Subtirica and Pop (2016) did a study on the relationship of career adaptability and academic achievement of 1151 adolescents. Results showed a reciprocal relationship, that adolescents with a strong future orientation, who were already invested in career planning activities, tended to perform better in school and vice-versa; high academic achievement further strengthened adolescents' positive outlooks on their vocational future.

Gysbers (2008) emphasized that especially in the high school years, the career guidance purpose is to develop and use decision-making, goal-setting, and planning skills to prepare for the future. It is possible to improve adolescents' decision-making skills (Gati & Saka, 2001). Therefore, both school and family should adaptively prepare youth for their future work lives. Interventions have been successfully implemented to teach career decision-making skills to high school students (Jepsen, Dustin, & Miars, 1982; Savickas, 1997). The career awareness and the acquisition of career decision-making skills are crucial, especially when students transition from high school to further education or occupation (Lankard, 1991). Providing career guidance activities and employing high school guidance counselors can provide integrated programs using career development theories as the basis for their comprehensive program (Krass & Hughey, 1999).

The Role of Parents
Substantial research has been done on the family's influence on children's development. Although schools, peers, and the living environment have some

levels of impact on the student's self-identity and career choice, the expectations and perceptions of parents on vocational fit for their children have been found to be the key players in shaping career choices of their children. The career development path, the decision-making style, and the behaviors adolescents carry out are a part of the complicated family influence (Young, Ball, Wong, & Young, 2001). Both life design approach and social cognitive approach emphasize the parents' role in children's development in several factors, such as the family forms, parents' attitudes and behaviors, culture and beliefs, and lifestyles. Parental involvement in children's education is a critical factor associated with children's socio-emotional and educational outcomes (Wang, Deng, & Yang, 2016). The level of parental education, family size, employment, and socioeconomic variables, like parental income, are major influencing factors to students' occupational goals. Young et al. (2001) emphasized that parents and children co-construct the young adult's career to address the socioeconomic uncertainty.

The first responsibility of educating a child rests with the parents; thereafter, it becomes a shared responsibility with the school and the community at large. Children learn more from parents, though schools usually ignore parental input in the education of their children and consequently their career choices. Parents who live with their children and know their interests, abilities and personalities of their children tend to have influence on decisions children make (Hoghughi et al., 2004). However, understanding the influential factors that parents have on career choice of children is not clear despite the unique and critical impact parents hold in this matter.

Life and the career development path involve millions of decisions. The school and the teacher could provide general guidance; however, the career guidance to each student should be individualized and tailor-made. Therefore, if parents have the right skills in providing career guidance, they can have personalized conversation with students to co-construct the career plan with short-term and long-term goal setting. Parents' support will help students choose, prepare, and develop skills, test interest, identify strength, and build confidence. With right career guidance, the students' motivation will be strengthened and their performance in the education will become better (Gysbers, 2008).

Bandura et al. (2001) illustrated many factors influencing career choices such as social economic status, education attainment, financial status, and family support. They can either be intrinsic or extrinsic or both. However, most people are influenced by careers that their parents favor, others follow the careers that their educational choices have opened for them, some choose to follow their passion regardless of how much or little it will make them, while others choose the careers that give high income. Morsel (2009) stated when parents made it clear that they had no specific expectations for their children's career choices, children often felt free to explore a greater variety of professions based on their own preferences instead of those of their parents.

Perry, Liu, and Pabian, (2010) mentioned that parental guidance on career choices has been recognized as an important factor in enhancing students' career confidence and planning. Adolescents who felt that they could meet parental expectations in the career and academic areas demonstrated a great capacity to deal with career-related problems (Leung et al., 2011). In collectivist culture, adolescents also anticipate that they are perceived to be in line with parental wishes, they are supported by parents, and they are able to make parents satisfied (Sawitri, Creed, & Zimmer-Gembeck, 2014).

Career-Related Parent Support Scale (CRPSS)

Sawitri et al. (2014) highlighted the key roles that students perceived parental career support in positive relationship to the expectation outcome. Career-Related Parent Support Scale (CRPSS) assesses participants' perceptions of the way their parents provided educational and career-oriented efficacy information (Turner, Alliman-Brissett, Lapan, Udipi, & Ergun, 2003). The CRPSS (Turner et al., 2003) was translated and modified to form the 24-item Chinese version of the scale. The results of the exploratory factor analysis and confirmatory factor analysis suggested that the Chinese version of the CRPSS provided adequate indicators of Chinese adolescents' perceptions of parent support for their career aspirations (Cheng & Yuen, 2012). CRPSS could be used as an evaluation tool after the implementation of the career-related parent support program. CRPSS include four subscales, which are instructional assistance (IA), emotional support (ES), career-related modeling (CM) and verbal encouragement (VE), with a total of 20 questions.

Little is known by parents themselves on how huge their impact is on career choices made by their children. Parents are seen to be most commonly consulted for young adults as influential sources of career advice. They are critical, especially in the transition from school to the world of employment, as they have influence on the career path of children. Children's perceptions of parental support have a strong impact on their abilities, their career interests and choices. Parents should have awareness of the importance of their role, and they should be taught how to increase their children's self-efficacy beliefs (Ginevra, Nota, & Ferrari, 2015). Pursuing a career is an essential factor in gaining independence, achieving social inclusion, and ensuring equal participation in all aspects of life. The ability to make quality decisions should be developed during adolescence. Guerra, Modecki, & Cunningham (2014) defined effective decision making as the capacity to anticipate real-world scenarios, to pay attention to relevant cues, to consider perspectives, and to make effective choices across varied situations and contexts, including stressful or challenging circumstances. Through self-exploration, planning and taking actions, and reflections under proper guidance from parents, young adults can sharpen their decision-making skills, identify their interest, and formulate a career goal.

Career Guidance in China

Many countries have pursued education reforms over the last decades. China has been trying to learn from the Western world about best practices and advanced theories in child development, including providing career guidance in education settings.

The development of career guidance is in line with the transformation of society and economy. China's current market-oriented economy, having shifted from the planning nature defined by the ideal Marxist system, brought a dramatic revolution to the Chinese employment system. In this context, China's career intervention was transitioned from a fully regulated government arrangement to the choice of individuals. The job-placement system was operated by the Labor Bureau in the communist planned economy to assign jobs to everyone. All the people recruited by the state sector were guaranteed lifelong jobs, and their children could take on their parents' jobs after their parents had retired. This was known as "Iron Rice Bowl" (Zhang, Hu, & Pope, 2002). Zhang, Hu and Pope (2002) introduced the history of career guidance in China starting from 1917 as the beginning of vocational guidance, moving to reorientation of vocational education and guidance in 1950 after the founding of the People's Republic of China. Career guidance was abandoned in 1966 during the Cultural Revolution. After the Cultural Revolution ended in 1976, the country transitioned to an experimental period in 1996 and an expansion period in 1990 to the current international collaboration stage starting from 1997. Although the history is long, the real development of career guidance spans just about two decades. It becomes increasingly important with burgeoning opportunities and the freedom of choice. The development history of career guidance in China has many similarities as that of Western countries.

Why Career Guidance Is Needed in China

The globalization and changing labor markets call for individualized career guidance. However, China's collectivistic and interpersonal related family-oriented culture, along with traditional Confucianism, have serious impacts on the development of career guidance in its delivery. Chinese individuals mostly turn to friends or family when they encounter career problems. They do not believe in career development professionals, and there is indeed a big gap of the well-trained career consultants in China.

Several studies state that in China, 10-30% of adolescents demonstrated emotional or behavioral problems (Liu, Tein & Zhao, 2004; Liu et al., 2000). Liu et al. (2000) emphasized that career guidance is important to the mental health of adolescents. Without career-related support, students may potentially go towards the wrong direction or make detours with less or no preparation for the 21st global workplace, which will obstruct their pursuit of a meaningful life and their continuous learning to make a positive impact on their society and community.

There are two prevalent social phenomena in China. One is the NEET (not in education, employment, or training) problem, which refers to the group of children who are living with parents and not doing anything productive in society. According to the statistic released by the China Research Center on Aging (2010), an older generation raising a younger generation is a normal existence in more than 65% of Chinese families in cities; about 30% of adults need money from their parents for part or even all of their living expense (Wang, 2011). NEET youth can be either unemployed or inactive and not involved in education or training. They generally lack the skills to improve their economic situation and rely on their parents most of the time. The other more common social phenomenon is students who become unemployed after graduation, because they cannot find a job due to a variety of reasons ("High School Students," 2017). The common attributes of the two groups are a lack of confidence, weak decision-making capabilities, and no self-evaluation or self-planning abilities. In terms of traits, they have low scores in situational self-awareness, agility, and adaptability ("High School Students," 2017).

Why Chinese Parents' Role Is Important

One recent national survey on career planning status for students in high school and university in China reported that 53% of the students stated that parents are the most important influential factor, and next were teachers with 39% ("High School Students," 2017). This survey also indicated that while enrolled in a university, 63.8% of the students did not think carefully about their career choices before university enrollment, 65.5% of the university students wanted to change their major, and only 13.9% of the students expressed interests in their current major.

The Confucian tradition has a major influence on the value and behavior of parents and children. Nelson, Badger, and Wu (2004) listed Chinese beliefs such as respect for elders, deference, obedience to authority, endurance, learning to bear one's problems, hardworking, maintaining social face, and avoiding embarrassment. Chinese value caution rather than adventure. Obedience, conformity, and cooperation are the guiding principle of many Chinese families. Parents with a collective culture imprint teach children how to control one's emotions, become less self-oriented, develop greater consideration for others, and demonstrate a commitment to others (Nelson et al. 2004). In this regard, students' choice of school, behaviors, and values are heavily influenced by parents in China.

Chinese parents are more outcome-based with little emphasis on the holistic development of students. The education of a child is the top priority for a Chinese family, and children receive more attention and care from their parents and grandparents than previous generations. Zhao, Selman, and Haste (2015) identified that parents and students are at toxic levels of exam-related stress, and China's education system produces graduates with high scores, low ability, and poor health, which has become a grave social problem in Chinese society. In China under the pressure of gaokao, the strict one-time national college entrance exam, parents are willing to invest more effort and money into strengthening knowledge acquisition to achieve high academic performance. The education courses and curriculum are test-oriented with a high emphasis on rote learning.

Chinese tradition emphasizes academic achievement and extensive parental and grand-parental involvement to promote children's school success. Parents believe that earning a high score is a guarantee to get admission to a top university, which leads to a high probability that they can find a good job (Zhao et al., 2015). Parents tend to invest more on the items that they value the most. Parents from the East invest more than those from the West on education. Data indicated that 93% of Chinese parents are willing to pay tutoring expenses, while only 23% of British parents would do so (Wang, 2017).

Parents who are against an education system that encourages memorization and deference to authority and who do not believe in test-based score-oriented selection process, choose international or private schools with plans to send their children abroad to avoid gaokao. However, most parents rely on school consultant and agencies to introduce best quality universities for their children. Under this situation, the challenge would be the question of adaption into a Western university environment without proper preparation (Zhu, 2016).

Current Policy Changes

Some key policy initiatives were enacted in recent decades, such as the Rejuvenation Action Plan for Education 2003–2007 by the Ministry of Education in 2004, and the Outline of the National Mid- and Long-term Plan for Educational Reform and Development 2010–2020 by the State Council in 2010. Since the 2000s, policy themes in education development have been centered and more focused on four national discourses in China: equality in terms of a democratic mission of education for every citizen, quality in terms of individual and social productivity, efficiency as a national priority based on practicality, and rejuvenation of the nation for nation building and global status (Li, 2017). The four major themes of policy initiatives are not exclusive of each other but are all inter-related and interdependent in many aspects. Meanwhile, these themes have been highlighted dynamically and pragmatically over time.

Facing mounting criticism of the education system, at the turn of the twenty-first century, the Chinese central government began to issue new policies on a regular basis for the purposes of narrowing gaps among schools and reducing academic competition among students based solely on test scores. In 2000, the Chinese Ministry of Education issued the "Urgent Regulations for Alleviating the Academic Burden of Primary School Students." The document set strict limits to the number of required textbooks, the amount of homework, and the time students spent in school. Later, similar regulations were also released on secondary education. The Ministry of Education called for parents to help supervise the enforcement of these regulations; however, as long as the gaokao is used as the single criterion for college admission, the Chinese education system will continue to define academic success by external indicators that impose high pressure on schools, parents, and students to focus on increasing test scores and on producing students with low levels of self-confidence and creativity (Zhao et al., 2015).

Gaokao, the national college entrance exam, is a single-time outcome-based test, and it has been playing a life-threatening role to determine students' future life chances. The exam has been criticized for overemphasis on grades and a forced division between science and liberal arts, with students obliged to choose one path or the other at an early stage (Li, 2017). Recent rounds of education reforms started in 2014, and an initial pilot project about the new gaokao system was launched in Shanghai and eastern China's Zhejiang province. Other provinces will reflect on the implementations and make modifications. It is a long process, and each city or province may have different models. The new system offers more chances and wider choices, bringing more pressure on the students to make decisions by themselves. The education reform in China and the globalization in education and workplace have provided increasing opportunities and wider choices to students in their education and career (Fan & Leong, 2016). In this context, researchers studying the Chinese context increasingly argue that career guidance in high school is urgent and critical (Huang & Wang, 2014).

In the past, university choices, including which major to take, after gaokao were usually made or heavily influenced by parents. However, with the continuous efforts on the reform of gaokao, as part of the Thirteenth Five-year National Plan (2016–2020) for Education by the Ministry of Education (2010), and the increasing popular overseas education, students and parents now have more choices and opportunities. Huang & Wang (2014) argued that the role of parents in Chinese families has started to change from just providing financial support to nurturing the overall belief and capability of their children.

Career Guidance in High School in Shanghai

Shanghai is taking the lead in the development of career guidance in China and has exerted substantial influence on other provinces. In research sponsored by the Shanghai Pujiang Program, Zhou et al. (2016) presented four stages in the development of career guidance and counseling in education settings in Shanghai, People's Republic of China, from 1977 (after the Cultural Revolution) to 2015, with an economic-political perspective.

In the first stage (1977–1992), job allocation was implemented by the government as a mandatory regulation to meet the pressing demands for trained professionals in various industries. In the second stage (1993–1999), job allocation was replaced by vocational guidance as a service. In the third stage (2000–2011), there was a growth in career education, mainly in colleges. The fourth stage (2012–2015) witnessed the boom of career counseling with the focus transferring to secondary schools (P.203).

The first National Conference of Career Guidance and Counseling was held in Shanghai in 1996 (Zhang et al., 2002). In October 1993, the Shanghai Graduates Vocational Guidance Center (SGVGC) was established. By 1999, vocational guidance was only offered to senior college students. To promote national development of career intervention, the Ministry of Education issued a document titled "Requirements on Career Curriculum for College Students" in December 2007. In 2010, SGVGC changed its name to the Shanghai Center for Student Affairs (SGSA) to provide services to both college and secondary vocational schools.

Career adaptability in high school may portend young adults' career success over time (Deng et al., 2018). High school students are facing extra pressure brought by the recent reform of the college system and college entrance examination (Liu, 2015; Qu & Zhao, 2014), which requires high school students to devote more time and energy to deciding which kind of college to attend. As such, they are expected to improve their self-exploration and self-management so as to prepare for college life ahead of time; however, they receive little support from their school and their parents. In 2010, career guidance in high school was initiated by the Ministry of Education, followed by the announcement of the Outline of Long-term Education Reform and Development (Huang & Wang, 2014). Extensive efforts have since been made on a variety of projects to enhance teachers' capabilities and students' program design, whereas the role of parents, the connections between students and parents, and between teachers and parents, were generally ignored, even though parents exert greater influences on Chinese students' career choices (Zhou et al., 2016).

Shanghai, as one of the pioneer cities practicing education reforms in China, has generated some best practices and outstanding performance, such as the superb scores of Shanghai students across all domains in the 2009 and 2012 PISA results (Organization for Economic Cooperation and Development 2016). A two-decade effort in Shanghai has been underway to research and implement career guidance programs in high school. One of the leaders of this effort, Dr. Huo, has observed that "there is no systematic career guidance support in public high schools," and the initial efforts in private high schools have been of "low quality" (Y.P. HUO, personal communication, November 17, 2017). Dr. Huo mentioned some best practices in developing teacher's career guidance capabilities and enriching the students' curriculum experience. However, parents' career-related support is neglected.

Conclusion

Facing one of the toughest eras of disruptive change, with the rise of information overload and social anxiety, thriving in a world where change is constant and learning never stops calls for new considerations of career development by shifting the focus from job matching and searching to agile and creative skills development. Staying competitive in the digital era requires the young generation to be well equipped with career and life skills for the 21st century global workplace. During adolescence, the young generation needs to have a good understanding of their interests, skills, and values and to pursue their career and life goals consistent with their understandings (Super 1992). Career guidance in high school is crucial and urgent. Gysbers (2008) emphasizes the importance of self-concept development during the high school years. Both family and school play critical roles to support and guide the students' development of necessary skills, to shape future-oriented mindsets, and to explore life meanings (Partnership for 21st Century Skills, n.d.a.). The younger generation needs individualized parental support in the age of self-exploration, and with the right parental guidance, they can master goal setting and planning, sharpen their decision-making skills, identify their interests and crystallize their value.

One of my studies in a high school in Shanghai concludes that there are strong and urgent needs for parents to provide career-related parent guidance for their children. To address these identified needs, an integrated program with three solutions is suggested for the school from providing training workshops and one-on-one coaching programs to parents about career guidance to establishing online and offline career-related parent support platforms and enhancing the family-school partnership. The three solutions are integrated, with the first one as the training program, the second as the learning platform to encourage practicing of coaching and continuous improvement, and the last one as the culture of support to ensure positive reinforcement at all stages of implementation. A CRPSS survey to students is conducted before and after the program launch. Whether students will benefit from career-related parent guidance is able to be shown by the score improvement of the CRPSS result. It is an ongoing effort, and some high schools in Shenzhen have started to pay attention to career-related parental coaching.

References

Arulmani, G., Bakshi, A., Leong, F., & Watts, A. (2014). *Handbook of career development: International perspectives* [electronic resource]. New York, NY: Springer New York

Bandura, A. (1986). *Social foundations of thought and action.* Englewood Cliffs, NJ: Prentice Hall

Bandura, A. (2000). Exercise of human agency through collective efficacy. *Current Directions in Psychological Science*, 9(3), 75–78.

Bandura, A. (2005). The evolution of social cognitive theory. In K. G. Smith & M. A. Hitt (Eds.), *Great minds in management* (pp. 9–35). Oxford: Oxford University Press.

Bandura, A., Barbaranelli, C., Caprara, G., & Pastorelli, C. (2001). Self-efficacy beliefs as shapers of children's aspirations and career trajectories. *Child Development,* 72(1), 196-206.

Cheng, S., & Yuen, M. (2012). Validation of the career-related parent support scale among Chinese high school students. *Career Development Quarterly*, 60(4), 367-374.

Creed, P. A., Fallon, T., & Hood, M. (2009). The relationship between career adaptability, person and situation variables, and career concerns in young adults. *Journal of Vocational Behavior,* 74, 219–229.

Deng, L., Zhou, N., Nie, R., Jin, P., Yang, M., & Fang, X. (2018). Parent-Teacher Partnership and High School Students' Development in Mainland China: The Mediating Role of Teacher-Student Relationship. *Asia Pacific Journal of Education,* 38(1), 15–31.

Economic Graph Group. (2017). *LinkedIn's 2017 U.S. emerging jobs report.* Retrieved from https://economicgraph.linkedin.com/research/LinkedIns-2017-US-Emerging-Jobs-Report

Fan, W., & Leong, F. (2016). Introduction to the special issue: Career Development and intervention in Chinese contexts. *Career Development Quarterly, 64*(3), 192-202.

Gillmore, M. (2018). Preparing Students for future careers. *Teach* Jan/Feb, 13-15.

Ginevra, M., Nota, L., & Ferrari, L. (2015). Parental Support in Adolescents' Career Development: Parents' and Children's Perceptions. *Career Development Quarterly, 63*(1), 2-15.

Guest, C. L., Jr. (2000). Introduction to the special issue: Career issues in education. *Education, 120*(4), 602.

Guerra, N., Modecki, K., & Cunningham, W. (2014). Developing Social-Emotional Skills for the Labor Market: The PRACTICE Model, 7123, Policy Research Working Paper (7123).

Hirschi, A. (2009). Career adaptability development in adolescence: Multiple predictors and effect on sense of power and life satisfaction. *Journal of Vocational Behavior, 74,* 145–155.

Huang, X. Y., & Wang B. X. (2014). *Regular high school student development guidance.*

Shanghai, China: East China Normal University Publisher.

Johnston, C. (2018). A Systematic Review of the Career Adaptability Literature and Future Outlook. *Journal of Career Assessment, 26*(1), 3-30.

Gati, I., & Saka, N. (2001). High school students' career-related decision-making difficulties. *Journal of Counseling and Development, 79,* 331-345.

Gottfredson, L. S. (1981). Circumscription and compromise: A developmental theory of occupational aspirations [Monograph]. *Journal of Counseling Psychology, 28,* 545–579.

Gottfredson, L. S. (1996). Gottfredson's theory of circumscription and compromise. In D. Brown & L. Brooks (Eds.), *Career choice and development: Applying contemporary approaches to practice* (3rd ed., pp. 179–232). San Francisco, CA: Jossey-Bass.

Gottfredson, L. S. (2002). Gottfredson's theory of circumscription, compromise, and self-creation. In D. Brown & Associate (Eds.), *Career choice and development* (4th ed., pp. 85–148). San Francisco, CA: Jossey-Bass.

Gottfredson, L. S. (2005). Applying Gottfredson's theory of circumscription and compromise in career guidance and counseling. In S. D. Brown & R. T. Lent (Eds.), *Career development and counseling: Putting theory and research to work* (pp. 71–100). Hoboken, NJ: Wiley.

Gysbers, N. C. (2008). Chapter 12: Career guidance and counselling in primary and secondary educational settings. In Athanasou, J., & Esbroeck, R. *International Handbook of Career Guidance* [electronic resource]. (pp. 249-262). Dordrecht: Springer Netherlands.

Herr, E. L. (2008). Chapter 3: Social contexts for career guidance throughout the world. In Athanasou, J., & Esbroeck, R. *International Handbook of Career Guidance* [electronic resource]. (pp. 45-67). Dordrecht: Springer Netherlands.

"High school student career planning status and career counseling objectives."_ Sohu Education_Sohu, 29 Sept. 2017, Retrieved from http://www.sohu.

com/a/195571555_99936945

Hoghughi, M., & Long, N. (2004). *Handbook of parenting: Theory and research for practice* / edited by Masud Hoghughi, Nicholas Long. London, UK; Thousand Oaks, California, US : SAGE.

Hyslop, A. (2011). CTE and 21st century skills in college and career readiness. *Techniques,* 86(3), 10-11.

Jepsen, D., Dustin, R., & Miars, R. (1982). The effects of problem-solving training on adolescents' career exploration and career decision-making. *Personnel and Guidance Journal,* 61, 149-153.

Johnston, C. (2018). A Systematic Review of the Career Adaptability Literature and Future Outlook. *Journal of Career Assessment,* 26(1), 3-30.

Keller, F., & Viteles, M. (1937). *Vocational guidance throughout the world; a comparative survey,* by Franklin J. Keller... and Morris S. Viteles... New York, NY: W.W. Norton &.

Kerka, S., & *ERIC Clearinghouse on Adult, Career, Vocational Education.* (2000). Career development specialties for the 21st century [microform] / Sandra Kerka. (Trends and issues alert ; no. 13). Columbus, OH: ERIC Clearinghouse on Adult, Career, and Vocational Education, Center on Education and Training for Employment, College of Education, the Ohio State University.

Koen, J., Klehe, U. C., & Van Vianen, A. E. (2012). Training career adaptability to facilitate a successful school-to-work transition. *Journal of Vocational Behavior,* 81, 395–408. doi: 10.1016/j.jvb.2012.10.003.

Krass, L., & Hughey, K. (1999). The impact of an intervention on career decision-making self-efficacy and career indecision. *Professional School Counseling,* 2, 384-393.

Lankard, B. A. (1991). *Strategies for implementing the national career development guidelines.* Washington, DC: Office of Educational Research and Improvement.

Lent, R., Brown, S., & Hackett, G. (2000). Contextual supports and barriers to career choice: A social cognitive analysis. *Journal of Counseling Psychology,* 47(1), 36-49.

Leung S. A. (2008). Chapter 6: The big five career theories. In Athanasou, J., & Esbroeck, R. *International Handbook of Career Guidance* [electronic resource]. (pp. 115-132). Dordrecht: Springer Netherlands.

Leung, S. A., Hou, Z., Gati, I., & Li, X. (2011). Effects of Parental expectations and cultural-values orientation on career decision-making difficulties of Chinese university students. *Journal of Vocational Behavior,* 78(1), 11-20.

Li, J. (2017). Educational policy development in China for the 21st century: rationality and challenges in a globalizing age. *Chinese Education & Society,* 50(3), 133-141.

Liu, J. (2015). Reconsidering life planning education in high school from the perspective of college entrance examination reform. *Educational Development Research,* 35, 32–38, doi:10.14121/j.cnki.1008-3855.2015.10.007

Liu, X., Tein, J., & Zhao, Z. (2004). Coping strategies and behavioral/emotional problems among Chinese adolescents. *Psychiatry Research,* 126(3), 275-285.

Liu, X., Kurita, H., Uchiyama, M., Okawa, M., Liu, L., & Ma, D. (2000). Life events, locus of control, and behavioral problems among Chinese adolescents. *Journal of*

Clinical Psychology, 56(12), 1565-1577.

Maree, K. (2017). *Psychology of career adaptability, employability and resilience.* Springer Verlag

Ministry of Education of the People's Republic of China. (2010). *National education reform and development program for medium and long term* (2010-2020). Retrieved from http://www.moe.edu.cn/publicfiles/business/htmlfiles/moe/moe_838/201008/93704.html

Negru-Subtirica, O., & Pop, E. (2016). Longitudinal links between career adaptability and academic achievement in adolescence. *Journal of Vocational Behavior,* 93, 163-170.

Nelson, L., Badger, S., & Wu, B. (2004). The influence of culture in emerging adulthood: Perspectives of Chinese college students. *International Journal of Behavioral Development,* 28(1), 26–36. doi: 10.1080/01650250344000244.

Nota, L., Ferrari, L., Solberg, V., & Soresi, S. (2007). Career search self-efficacy, family support, and career indecision with Italian youth. *Journal of Career Assessment,* 15(2), 181-193.

Organisation for Economic Co-operation Development, & European Commission. (2004). *Career guidance : A handbook for policy makers.* (Education and culture (European Commission)). Paris : [Brussels?]: OECD; European Commission.

Organization for Economic Co-operation and Development (2016). PISA 2015 Results (Volume II): Policies and Practices for Successful Schools, PISA, OECD Publishing, Paris. http://dx.doi.org/10.1796/9789264267510-en

Partnership for 21st Century Skills. (n.d.a). *A Parents' Guide.* Retrieved from http://www.p21.org/out-work/citizenship/a-parents-guide

Partnership for 21st Century Skills.(n.d.b). P21. Retrieved from http://p21.org/about-us/p21-faq

Partnership for 21st Century Skills. (n.d.c). P21 Life and Career Skills. Retrieved from http://www.p21.org/about-us/p21-framework/266-life-and-carer-skills

Patton, W., & McMahon, M. (2014). *Career Development and Systems Theory: Connecting Theory and Practice* [electronic resource]. (3rd ed.). Rotterdam, Netherlands: Sense Publishers

Perry, J., Liu, X., & Pabian, Y. (2010). School engagement as a mediator of academic performance among urban youth: The role of career preparation, parental career support, and teacher support. *The Counseling Psychologist,* 38(2), 269-295.

Porfeli, E., Lee, B., Hynes, K., & Hirsch, B. J. (2012). Career development during childhood and adolescence. *New Directions for Youth Development,* 2012(134), 11-22.

Qu, D., & Zhao, Y. (2014). Problems and countermeasures of the transformation and development of local undergraduate colleges and universities. *China Higher Education,* 12, 25–28.

Reimers, F. (2006). Citizenship, identity and education: examining the public purposes of schools in an age of globalization. *Prospects,* 36(3), 275-294.

Savickas, M. (1997). Career adaptability: an integrative construct for life-span, life-space theory. *The Career Development Quarterly,* 45(3), 247-259.

Savickas, M. (2002). Reinvigorating the Study of Careers. *Journal of Vocational Behavior,* 61(3), 381-385

Savickas, M. L. (2005). The theory and practice of career construction. *Career development and counseling: Putting theory and research to work,* 1, 42-70.

Savickas M. L. (2008). Chapter 5: Helping people choose jobs: a history of the guidance profession. In Athanasou, J., & Esbroeck, R. *International Handbook of Career Guidance* [electronic resource]. (pp. 97-113). Dordrecht: Springer Netherlands.

Savickas, M., Nota, L., Rossier, J., Dauwalder, J., Duarte, M., Guichard, J., ... van Vianen, A. (2009). Life designing: A paradigm for career construction in the 21st century. *Journal of Vocational Behavior,* 75(3), 239-250.

Savickas, M. L. (2012). Life design: A paradigm for career intervention in the 21st century. *Journal of Counseling & Development,* 90(1), 13-19.

Sawitri, D. R., Creed, P. A., & Zimmer-Gembeck, M. J. (2014). Parental influences and adolescent career behaviours in a collectivist cultural setting. *International Journal for Educational and Vocational Guidanc*e, 14(2), 161-180.

Shek, D. (2007). A longitudinal study of perceived differences in parental control and parent-child relational qualities in Chinese adolescents in Hong Kong. *Journal of Adolescent Research*, 22(2), 156-188.

Super, D. (1980). A life-span, life-space approach to career development. *Journal of Vocational Behavior,* 16(3), 282-298.

Super, D. E. (1990). A life-span, life-space approach to career development. In D. Brown & L. Brooks (Eds.), *Career choice and development: Applying contemporary approaches to practice* (2nd ed., pp. 197–261). San Francisco, CA: Jossey-Bass.

Super, D. E., Osborne, W. L., Walsh, D. J., Brown, S. D., & Niles, S. G. (1992). Development career assessment and counseling: The C-DAC model. *Journal of Counseling and Development*, 71(1), 74.

Turner, S. L., Alliman-Brissett, A., Lapan, R. T., Udipi, S., & Ergun, D. (2003). The career-related parent support scale. *Measurement and Evaluation in Counseling and Development*, 36(2), 83-94.

Wang, H. (2011, Jan. 30). Audit NEET children exists in over 60% of Chinese families: Study. *People's Daily Online.* Retrieved from http://en.people.cn/90001/90782/90962/7277071.html

Watts, A. G. (1996). International perspectives. In A. G. Watts, B. Law, J. Killeen, J. M. Kidd, & R. Hawthorn (Eds.), *Rethinking careers education and guidance.* (pp. 366-379). London, England: Routledge.

World Economic Forum. (2016). *The future of jobs.* Retrieved from http://reports.weforum.org/future-of-jobs-2016/

U.S. Bureau of Labor Statistics, 2016, retrieved from https://www.bls.gov/opub/mlr/2016/

Van Esbroek R. (2008). Chapter 2: Career guidance in a global world. In Athanasou, J., & Esbroeck, R. *International Handbook of Career Guidance* [electronic resource]. (pp. 23-44). Dordrecht: Springer Netherlands.

Wang, X. (2017, November 1). Parents' investment on education, East v.s. West. *China Times.* Retrieved from http://www.chinatimes.com/cn/

newspapers/20171101000804-260309

Wang, Y., Deng, C., & Yang, X. (2016). Family economic status and parental involvement: Influences of parental expectation and perceived barriers. *School Psychology International,* 37(5), 536-553.

Young, V., Ball, P., Wong, D., & Young, R. (2001). Career development in adolescence as a family project. *Journal of Counseling Psychology,* 48(2), 190-202.

Zhang, W., Hu, X., & Pope, M. (2002). The evolution of career guidance and counseling in the People's Republic of China. *Career Development Quarterly,* 50(3), 226-36.

Zhao, X., Selman, R. L., & Haste, H. (2015). Academic stress in Chinese Schools and a proposed preventive intervention program. *Cogent Education,* 2(1), retrieved from http://dx.doi.org/10.1080/2331186X.2014.1000477

Zhou, X., Li, X., & Gao, Y. (2016). Career guidance and counseling in Shanghai, China: 1977 to 2015. *Career Development Quarterly,* 64(3), 203-215.

Zhu, J. (2016). *Chinese Overseas Students and Intercultural Learning Environments* [electronic resource]: Academic Adjustment, Adaptation and Experience / by Jiani Zhu. (Palgrave Studies on Chinese Education in a Global Perspective) London: Palgrave Macmillan UK: Imprint: Palgrave Macmillan, 2016.

Jack Denfeld Wood and Katherine Xin

Chapter 12.
Coaching for
Leadership Development

A Conversation

Abstract

The previous chapter addressed the probable growth, and increasing importance, of parents in China being able to provide career coaching to their adolescent children. This chapter, a conversation between two leading professors of leadership development in China, speaks to coaching in the Chinese cultural and systemic context, and argues for a coaching focus that supports the leader's personal as well as professional development. The chapter also advocates, as the next step in the development of leadership coaching in China, that coaches endeavor to deeply understand, and to work adeptly with, psychological factors, including group dynamics.

The Evolution of Coaching

Katherine: We've known each other for almost two decades. We've worked at two business schools together—one in Switzerland, IMD, and now here in China at CEIBS. When you came to China, we began collaborating on the CEO leadership program that I directed. Given that our topic for this chapter is about coaching for leadership development in China, it might be helpful to begin by getting clarity on the difference between coaching and leadership development, on your experiences of the similarities and differences of the work here and in the West, and on how we've actually combined coaching and leadership development in our work.

Jack: When I began putting together leadership development programs at the International Institute for Management Development (IMD) in Europe thirty years ago, coaching was just beginning to be used in a management context. I was curious about what the terms "coach" and "coaching" really meant because in my experience, a coach was the guy who yelled at you during soccer and ice hockey practice drills and games in school and university. That kind of coach carried considerable ambivalence for me. The new kind of coach appeared to promise something different [1].

Katherine: Maybe we can cover how coaching has evolved, then perhaps talk in more detail about how coaching fits within leadership development—specifically group leadership development—and how we've designed it into the programs on which we've collaborated, like the CEO Leadership Program I directed and the kick-off one-week leadership module of the CEIBS Global EMBA module that you developed.

I'm particularly curious about your understanding of what you do. I have my own perspective—which I'll share—having done leadership work before and after we began to collaborate. But I am interested in your thoughts and experience about the evolving profession of coaching and in how leadership development works differently from how leadership is normally taught in business schools.

Jack: Ok. Let's unpack the meaning of the words we use: coach and coaching; leadership and leadership development; thinking mechanically and thinking psychologically; conscious and unconscious phenomena [2]; and the bias in looking at individuals rather than at groups and larger social systems.

I've always found ancient and renaissance philosophers enlightening. The 17th and 18th century European philosophers Voltaire and Locke, for example, cautioned that before you begin discussing a topic meaningfully, you have to define your terms, or you're wasting time fruitlessly [3]. Moreover, it's illuminating to understand the original meaning of root words.

Historically, the word coach derives from the 16th century [4]. The word comes from a Hungarian town, Kocs, where a new kind of enclosed horse-drawn carriage was first built. The origin of the word coach describes a protective means of transportation—a carriage—like Cinderella's coach. It carried her along to her destination: the ball. In the mid-1800s, the meaning of coach broadened to include the compartments in which steam engines carried passengers along a railway. Even today, this "compartment as a means of protective transportation" definition of coach is still present. You can choose to fly internationally in coach with the airlines, which basically means you're in a second-class enclosed compartment, as opposed to Business and First-class compartments.

About the same time, in the U.K. and in the U.S., the definitions of coach broadened still more. In the U.K., the word coach was Oxford slang for a tutor who prepared or carried a student through exams. And in the U.S., the word coach broadened still further to mean a manager and trainer of an athletic team—the guy who yells at you during practice. That was the meaning I attached to the word until I started focusing on leadership development and had to train people to work competently in a psychological way with groups of executives.

These origins of the word coach imply two things: carrying and protecting. A coach carries their client in a protective way from a starting place, say Point A, though some intermediate stage, to a specific destination, Point B. In the Oxford tutorial and American athletic cases, the destination is based on performance— carrying and protecting someone towards the accomplishment of some competitive academic or athletic achievement. This achievement orientation carries a subtle implication about the meaning of coaching, one that isn't helpful for leadership development.

Katherine: How is that? Businesses are about getting results. Making the plan. Reaching the targets.

Jack: For a decade at IMD, I was responsible for the MBA leadership stream throughout the entire year. Leadership can't be absorbed through only a few classroom sessions any more than one can learn a language from a weekend course. Leadership is not a question of knowledge. It's a question of behavior. Leadership is a skill, like flying a jet or playing golf or tennis or football. Most military organizations first train cadets in leadership. Then when they become officers, they are trained in technical skills. Corporations work the other way around: they select employees for their technical skills. Then the employees are left to figure out how to lead on their own. That's why we end up with 30- and 40-year-olds in class who have great technical skills but don't know how to exercise leadership very well.

An IMD colleague of mine, Chris Parker, used to say, "Knowledge is not behavior." Competent leadership is an integration of conscious, rational thinking and unconscious, irrational, emotions. Irrational doesn't mean crazy; it means not easily accessible to conscious and logical reasoning [5]. One has to experience this integration process over and over to get it to stick.

The idea was that if the students developed an integrated grasp of leadership and group dynamics, then that would bring those skills and insights to all their other group work: accounting, finance, operations, marketing, and so on. Leadership is fundamental. All groups need leadership. Not all groups need finance or marketing or supply chain management. Leadership crosses the boundaries of the other subjects. That is a major difference with other management topics.

Katherine: I understand why leadership is important, and even central, to organizational success, but how can an achievement orientation be unhelpful for success?

Jack: It depends on what you mean by success. An IMD colleague was responsible for the OB (organizational behavior) classes in the first module where I began the leadership stream. Student grades were based largely on group work and an important end-of-module group presentation. Students told me that my OB colleague told them in class, "Jack likes you to fail, but I like you to succeed." By that she meant that she wanted them to make good presentations and get good grades on their end-of-module presentation. She was measuring their performance against other groups. I also wanted them to succeed. But my definition of success was how much they learned about leadership and group dynamics, not whether a slick presentation from a totally dysfunctional team got a good grade, which often happened. Her grades were based on their presentations. My grades were based on their learning about and understanding of leadership. That's a very different orientation.

Katherine: For coaching, isn't an achievement orientation helpful? Your sports coaches want the team to win; the academic tutor coaches a student to ace the exam. That's good, isn't it?

Jack: The achievement orientation presents the coaching profession with something of a dilemma. The unspoken aim of this view of coaching is that success is an adaption to a socially- prescribed, competitive corporate goal. Comparative social achievement—the measuring of professional performance— is not the same as preparing someone to live a meaningful life.

Before MBA or EMBA students come to my programs, they write a 5-10-page autobiography—a personal and professional identity narrative (PPIN). The idea is that they have to know who they really are aside from their professional persona. MBA students and corporate managers are much more than their professional roles. They are fathers and mothers, husbands and wives, sons and daughters.

For me, the aim of both coaching and leadership development is not adaptation to a specific corporate demand, but the creation of frameworks that offer personal and professional development through psychological integration. Their future might be with their present employer, or their future development may require that they leave that employer and walk along a different path.

It's also important to be clear on who your client is. Is it the individual in the classroom with whom you are working, or is it the organization that sponsored them? For me, the primary client is the individual human being in the class. The sponsoring corporation is secondary. Of course, the more developed the individual employee becomes, the greater the benefit to the individual and the company—if the company is looking for talented and creative leaders and not obedient drones.

Coaching and Culture

Jack: Katherine, you've studied in the U.S., have a PhD from UC Irvine (University of California, Irvine), have taught at USC (University of Southern California), and have a daughter studying at USC and a brother who lives in the L.A. area. You also have a brother who is a teacher in China and his family still lives there. Your mother lives in China too. You're fluent in both languages. So you are the walking personification of two cultures that appear to be vastly different yet appear to have much more in common than at first appears. What are your thoughts on this?

Katherine: My personal take on culture is that we are much more similar than different. Yes, of course, there are differences across cultures. However, we are all human, and we are much more similar than different. All of us, regardless of our cultural backgrounds, would like to be treated with respect. We all value deep friendship, and we all love our families. I can go on and on. We have similar processes in grieving. Basically, psychological processes and group dynamism are the same whether we are American or Chinese. So in my mind, I always feel we are more similar than different. This is how I view culture from different countries or regions. That said, we have some differences, of course. Each culture has its distinctive characteristics. Some values are more salient in one culture than in others.

What has your impression been after having worked in China for almost a decade, Jack?

Jack: I would never presume to present myself as a China expert. I do not speak the language much, and I am sure I miss a lot of nuance. Nevertheless, when you live in another culture your internal radar kind of tunes into subtle non-verbal signals. Experts estimate that communication is about 93% non-verbal (55% body language, 38% tonality), and only 7% words. [6]

I agree with you. The conventional assertion that "cultures are different" is true, but not nearly as true as it appears to be on the surface. When you assume "people are different," you inadvertently overlook their similarities. Katherine, you and I have both worked with people from all over the world—Asia, India, Africa, North and South American, and virtually all European countries. And what do we find? People express the same patterns. Humans might dress in slightly different clothes and eat slightly different food, and sleep on slightly different beds, but we all dress, eat, and sleep. Moreover, our minds all work in the same way. This should not be surprising to anyone. Our hearts, livers, kidneys, lungs and brains all work in the same way, too. Why should the patterns of our psychological structures be any different? With analysts and leadership coaching clients and students from around the world, I've found the patterns of their relationships with their parents are similar; the images in their dreams are similar; the relationships between the sexes is similar—people fall in love and are afraid of the same things. The universality of human life becomes clear.

We have different languages, but the languages all function similarly and are all learned in a similar way—they're our mother-tongues. To enhance survival, some languages differentiate concepts more precisely than others. The familiar example is of the Inuits of northern Canada who have several distinct words related to "snow," or some African languages which differentiate several words for the word "green" that other cultures don't need to differentiate. For people of the Equator, snow is snow. For people from a desert, green is green. In English, the differentiation is between red and pink, but really, pink is just another shade of red.

Westerners generally have this stereotype of the inscrutable Asian. I have not found Asians in general, or Chinese in particular, to be particularly inscrutable—and no more difficult to read than people from other cultures. I have, however, found Chinese culture to be layered, like other social systems, but with its own slightly different accents. I can feel these layers operating within individuals, groups, classrooms and organizations. It's my impression that each layer of a culture offers a slightly different accent to a universal human pattern. That's the delight of working internationally and cross-culturally—the reassuring reality of a common human foundation with the colorful accents of different cultures. In China, I think I see maybe four or five principal layers— Confucian, Taoist, Buddhist, and Marxist thought, plus the cumulative effects of the different dynasties. These are historical realities, but they are also very much social psychological realities, even today.

Shakespeare wrote in *The Tempest* that the past is the prologue. But the past isn't even past. It's very much alive today. Furthermore, cultures carry the trauma of the past, and while the specific protagonists and events might be different, the underlying patterns are archetypal and are exactly the same. I am confronted with national cultural trauma in virtually every leadership development program I do. It becomes particularly clear in coaching sessions. National cultural traumas leave an imprint that is passed down for generations. The Americans are still trying to manage the legacy of slavery, the subjugation of native lands, and the Civil War; the Germans are still coming to grips with the Nazi regime and the holocaust and their responsibility in it; the Chinese are still working through the distresses of European exploitation during the Opium Wars, the Civil War, the Great Leap Forward and the Cultural Revolution. The Russians are still working through the pain of the Bolshevik Revolution, Stalinism, the collapse of the Soviet Union and their resentment of the West. The Israelis are still working through the Roman occupation and their own diaspora. It's an old story, and it's fundamentally the story of human life.

Chinese and Western Leadership

Jack: Sometimes I ask a class to list great leaders in the long sweep of history. Around the world, the list is the same; it includes names from all countries and all cultures, from millennia ago to today. The conclusion that stares us in the face is that there really is no such thing as a specific Chinese leadership or American leadership or Russian leadership. Leadership is leadership. Leadership is timeless and universal. That fact makes it interesting to work in different cultures.

I did a little study with a few hundred Chinese EMBA executives several years ago. I was curious about comparing their impressions of Chinese and Western leadership in business and in government. Specifically, I asked about long-term and short-term focus, what might be called a strategic orientation versus a tactical orientation. The results were remarkable. The majority of the executives characterized Western business as long-term and Chinese business as short-term. Conversely, they characterized Western government as short-term and Chinese government as long-term. I think they are right.

You just have to compare the cautious, patient, and responsible way in which the current Chinese government approaches the pandemic, worldwide economic disruption, environmental improvement, and a globally destabilized political order, with the American government of the Trump administration: the reckless, thoughtless, and dysfunctional way in which it approaches the pandemic, economic disruption, the environment, and how it contributes to the destabilization of the political order. Half the American citizenry misunderstands what makes for good and bad leadership and the fundamental instinctual nature of authority. [7]

Westerners have a curious stereotype of democracy and other political systems. The predominant Western view is binary. To perhaps oversimplify, Westerners think that democratic political systems are good and one-party political systems are bad. What Westerners fail to realize is that all political systems and all leadership is fundamentally authoritarian—that is, based on an archaic and instinctual pattern of authority and obedience, dominance and submission. This is as true of Western nations as it is of Asian nations.

The structure of all human social systems—of governments, churches, schools, hospitals, corporations, families—is basically authoritarian. The Germany of Adolf Hitler was a republic. The republic was authoritarian before Hitler rose to power, and it permitted his ascent to power. Hitler was elected to the Reichstag, and he was elected chancellor. Similarly, the United States is considered a liberal democracy. Its citizens elected Donald Trump and they elected a Republican majority in the Senate. And once a President in the United States is elected, he can behave in a completely autocratic manner and retain the support of half the citizenry. The active participation of a citizen in a democracy consists of five minutes of filling out a ballot every four years. The rest of the time, whoever is President can exercise leadership for good or ill the way they want. They drag you into wars, trade disputes, terrible environmental decisions, and safety and health fiascos. So many in the West misunderstand how human systems really work.

The U.S. and Chinese governments are both authoritarian systems—so is

Singapore—like any human system. The critical issue for human systems is not whether they are authoritarian or not, since they all are. The critical issue is whether a system—and a leader—is moral or not. Singapore's first Prime Minister, Lee Kuan Yew, was by all accounts an autocrat. But he was also a wise and moral individual. While criticized by the West for curtailing civil liberties, he retained his authority by providing stability, economic development, and security for all minorities—a non-ethnic, non-populist rule of law, rooting out corruption, encouraging religious harmony among Buddhist, Christian, Muslim, Taoist, Hindu, and other religions and non-religious segments of the population. He also established English as the common language to facilitate Singaporean commerce, yet required bilingualism in education to preserve ethnic identity of the subgroups of which Singapore is composed. "There is no other way you can govern a Chinese society," Lee Kuan Yew was quoted as saying. [8]

Social Systems Psychodynamics

Katherine: You've mentioned to me a buzzword, a "social systems psychodynamic" approach to understanding behavior. What does that really mean? What does it mean to work in a systems psychodynamic way?

Jack: It means to work with unconscious and irrational forces. It is a buzzword, and that's not helpful. It makes working psychologically in a social context seem esoteric. It's really quite simple, but also quite subtle.

Katherine: How did you come up with your particular psychological approach to coaching and leadership development?

Jack: Systems psychodynamics came out of the Tavistock Institute and Clinic following WWI [9]. Several psychoanalysts and social scientists tried to figure out why human beings kept destroying themselves in wars and destructive organizational behavior. They started to look at unconscious processes within groups, between groups, and between leaders and followers. The importance of working with unconscious processes cannot be overestimated. This had been my training at Yale, then in Switzerland I went deeper through training as an analyst at the C.G. Jung Institute in Zürich while teaching at IMD. It was a process of integrating the different developmental pieces of my life.

When I came to IMD in 1988 after receiving my doctoral degree, I was immediately put on a two-week leadership program called Mobilizing People, MP. It became crystal clear to me that virtually all leadership occurs in a small group—that the small group is the basic unit of organizational decision-making; that presidents and prime ministers make their decisions in executive committees and cabinets that are simply a small group. Leadership, I saw clearly, was not an individual phenomenon—it was a group phenomenon. And it was driven by unconscious forces. From this beginning, I put in place a program design and started elaborating on a program architecture that made a significant difference in people's lives—people from around the world—to help them make sense of the unconscious personality influences on group member behavior.

Katherine: Well, my approach to leadership development took a similar path, in a way. At USC I worked with senior executive teams from different companies. Rocky Kimble, who is a clinical psychologist by training and a pioneer in using experiential group approaches for leadership development, was a great friend and mentor. We took executive teams whitewater rafting, mountain climbing, and on survival exercises, then held peer feedback and one-on-one coaching sessions afterwards. In Hong Kong, I worked with a group of senior leadership coaches to develop a broad variety of experiential exercises to facilitate executives and EMBA students to reflect on their irrational, unconscious behaviors in a group setting to help them understand themselves and the group dynamics. I guess one of the reasons why you and I have worked well together is that we both believed in the behavioral and psychological processes of leadership development. Reflecting on cultural differences, I did not, honestly speaking, take different approaches with American/European executives or HK/Chinese executives. They find the same processes helpful in their leadership development. I know you used the same approaches to leadership development with Russian executive participants from Skolkovo, the Moscow School of Management.

Jack: When I first came to CEIBS, you asked me to collaborate in your CEO Leadership Program. We just started brainstorming what a design might look like. And we kept refining it over several years. But I'm curious. We had known each other before in Switzerland but had never worked together. I never asked you: "Why did you approach me about collaborating in China?"

Katherine: When you came to CEIBS, that opportunity presented itself. I was re-designing the CEO Leadership Program's first module. I had heard about your approach to leadership and felt that we shared a similar philosophy about leadership development. What was your experience bringing your approach to leadership and coaching to China? Was it difficult or easy?

Jack: Well, both. When I first came to CEIBS, most of the marketing people and other professors advised me that Chinese executives would not accept the approach to leadership that I had developed. The reasons they gave were several: that it was too Western, too psychological, not practical enough, that the executives were coming to network and not really learn, and so on. It was essentially a cultural argument: that my approach to leadership didn't fit and wouldn't be accepted in China.

As we've seen, the psychological approach fits right into Chinese culture. Why? Because Chinese culture is very psychological. Confucianism, Taoism, Buddhism, and Communism are all philosophical and psychological approaches to life.

The traditional view of management is to plan, organize, control, and structure business processes. Many managers try to lead this way too, as if leadership were a rational and mechanical engineering process [10]. But this approach doesn't work any better with your employees at work than it does with your kids at home. Effective leadership has to integrate the rational and emotional elements that exist in all human systems: in organizations that are composed of groups and those rational and irrational elements in the individual human psychic and social structures.

Thinking psychologically for me has always meant working on at least two levels of understanding at the same time. The overt and the covert, the visible and the invisible, the conscious and the unconscious, the rational and the emotional, the formal and the informal, masculine and feminine, light and dark, yang and yin. Life appears to be a fluid balance and dialectic dialogue between two apparent polarities. [11]

When you are sitting in a meeting, and there is an agenda on the table, most of us become aware that there are several agendas under the table as well. The capacity to work on both levels competently is a psychological one. This kind of insight can be developed, but it's helpful to have an intuitive capacity to sense the implicit symbolic emotional meaning of things and not just stay on an explicitly concrete and rational level of understanding. To excel at coaching or any behavioral skill, you have to be able to read the written text on the paper and the unwritten subtext hidden beneath it.

Look at organizational charts. Chinese organizational charts look like German organizational charts, which look like American org charts, etc. That's the formal structure. They all look the same. But if you actually observe how, for example, an executive committee really works: where the relative influence resides, who talks, who gets listened to, and how the subgroups are arranged, you begin to see an informal structure emerge more clearly [12]. This informal structure is how decisions really get made. And it doesn't follow the lines of the formal organizational chart. Why? Because groups and organizations, like families, are organic—they're human systems. And the thing that moves them along—that inspires and motivates progress—is spirit and emotion!

Look, managers spend virtually all of their time working in a cognitive and rational way, while avoiding and suppressing uncomfortable emotions. The only emotions that really are accepted in management are anger and joy—the CEO pounds on the table or smiles broadly with a new acquisition. The other basic emotions, such as sadness, fear, and disgust, or more complex expressions of emotion like crying or "showing weakness," are suppressed. But strong emotions are a real part of life. At one point in the film *Saving Private Ryan,* Tom Hanks' character walks around to the other side of a German bunker, sits down alone, has a crying jag, pulls himself together into his role as a captain, then goes back to what's left of his platoon and continues to lead his men on their mission. I've witnessed a group of senior Air Force commanders in an unfolding combat situation acting like excited schoolboys. A commander of mine saw a two-star general groveling as if he were a butler and carrying the bags of an arrogant three-star general. These kinds of experiences give one pause to consider what leadership really is.

The same with coaching. When my behavioral professor colleagues come from an engineering background—and many of them do—their approach to leadership and coaching is to give advice. Like the former Big Five consultant. You're the expert. You tell people the right answer. It's a kind of engineering approach to leadership and coaching [13]. And that's what many managers think they want. But they don't really. This kind of engineering approach has its limitations. People are not machines. They are organisms. They have feelings and emotions. And they cannot be taught, much less led, to develop leadership mechanistically.

I did a study in 2008 while I led a coaching module every day in IMD's showcase program, Organizing Winning Performance (OWP). The coaching module got the highest rating of the program that year [14]. HR managers usually think that their executives want coaching to improve business performance. The study found, however, that only 22% in our survey selected increasing business competence. Moreover, the executives were also not particularly interested in advancing their careers or in expanding their network (15%).

"The top three coaching objectives, chosen by around two-thirds of the respondents, were life development (71%)—balancing personal and professional roles more effectively; leadership (66%)—interpersonal skill development: improving my skills in leading people [one on one] and leading teams; and self-awareness (63%)—becoming more aware of my shortcomings and growth opportunities as a leader, and understanding the origins and history of my behavior in work and its impact on others." [15]

Giving advice on life development, on leadership, and on self-awareness is not only ineffective; it's counterproductive. Giving advice is as useless as telling someone with an eating disorder that they simply have to change their habits and eat more—or eat less!

Frankly, for most people, their lives are more important to them than their jobs, although many live as if it were the reverse. And corporations perpetuate the fiction that your loyalty to your job is more important than your loyalty to your family. When that's true, the kids are in trouble. In order to do a competent job of developing executives, you need to address what they really desire as human beings. And you have to know how to design the architecture for the learning process that will help them arrive at their goal. Creating that framework is a bit of an art. You may help them clarify what they need, but then you need to be able to create a personal developmental experience in which their growth can take place.

Learning and changing are stressful. Developing one's leadership is stressful. It has to be. It's emotional! My PhD supervisor at Yale, David Berg, once remarked that if you want to learn, move toward the anxiety you feel. I've found that most people are willing to learn, even with the inevitable anxiety and discomfort. But they have to feel they are respected and relatively safe in order to open up and try different things so as to grow and develop. So I see my job as creating the conditions of relative psychological safety, for participants to have the opportunity to develop their capacity to exercise leadership responsibly.

Leadership Development Using Social Psychological Lenses

Katherine: Given our global experiences working with executives from different continents, countries, and cultures, we both agree that leadership development is most helpful when we focus not only on the rational, conscious, mechanistic aspect, but also on the irrational, emotional, and behavioral. Understanding psychological processes of leadership at both individual and group levels is an integral part of leadership development. The process is just as important as the results. I have not encountered a necessity to formulate a different approach or technique for leadership development in different cultures or countries. I think we both see the "universality" of leadership development and coaching processes through our experiences in different countries.

As China further develops its economy, talent and leadership development are key to its future growth and success. We've witnessed the increasing demand and importance that companies put on leadership development. Coaching, especially group coaching, has been increasingly accepted as a means of developing leaders. The demand for experienced coaching professionals is increasing, and I've noticed the demand for skilled leadership development coaches is gaining more attention, which also puts a high demand on the competency of professional leadership coaches.

Jack, any suggestions for developing leadership/behavioral coaches?

Jack: Giving people lectures and books to read doesn't really help. It's totally rational. And it doesn't change anything. Think of the last lecture or TED Talk you watched. You saw it and thought, this was really interesting. A week later you can't even remember what was said. People have to be put into situations where they experience life—and are then given the opportunity to make sense of that experience by offering them lenses through which they can see and make sense of that experience. This is what I call integral leadership—it fuses the experience with an emotion; it's an integration of their rational and emotional experiences. They become increasingly whole human beings who can apply the learning to new situations.

As a coach, you need to work with the here-and-now, including both the overt and covert realities of group dynamics. You need to attend to the behavior, thoughts, and feelings of everyone in the system (your group, the other groups, the staff group, the entire class, the school as a system)—each part gives you a different piece of the behavioral puzzle if you are patient enough, listen closely, and initiate effective learning events. You especially have to understand leadership as a group dynamic, not as an individual set of traits.

You need to know that your role as a behavioral leadership coach is to consult to the learning of your participant group, not to give advice or make them feel happy. This may require you to allow them to fail, to feel bad, and to learn from that failure in a non-judgmental way. To do that, you must be willing to have them be angry at you, be annoyed, be rebellious, and so on. All of that behavior is material for learning. Working with executives in groups requires a different capacity—the ability to work with invisible and unconscious phenomena that are not normally even seen in individual coaching.

In our leadership development designs, the coaching comes at the end of the program in a confidential one-on-one with each participant in one's group. The session is designed to access and integrate a participant's learning about how leadership works in groups, about themselves, about where their lives currently are, and the likely trajectory of their future—if they decide to change and grow or if they decide to stay in their comfort zone, or in their distressing yet familiar and reassuring discomfort zone.

All the material you bring to bear on their learning is confidential, of course, or they won't feel safe and secure to open up and grow. To aid in the process, you follow the participant's lead in the one-on-one interpersonal discussion. Listen to the subtext of what they are asking for, or avoiding addressing, in order to offer them an invitation to grow and develop both personally and professionally. This may include a required autobiography (a personal and professional identity narrative, PPIN), a non-judgmental MBTI personality inventory, and a group peer review—a report comparing self-rating and the ratings of the others in their group. Together with the unconscious focus, this material encompasses a different kind of learning than the typical cognitive coaching experience— you are providing different lenses to give them a more layered psychological approach to their entire social system(s).

Companies love to have lists of competencies. These provide HR a comparative "score" of who you are. Most 360° instruments attribute individual results to traits. But this is not true. Take a typical leadership competency, like "takes initiative." You can get a high "takes initiative" score in one group, and everyone thinks you have a high trait in this that you carry within you. But if you find yourself in another group—even in the same company—you will get a low "takes initiative" score. You haven't changed. But the two groups are two distinct social systems. In the one you are authorized; in the second you are de-authorized. So what HR thinks of as a competency is not a trait, but is rather a result of group dynamics. It's a function of the projections of the others in your group and the role they are trying to put you in.

To work in a competent manner with this understanding of leadership puts the work well beyond the scope of typical individual coaching, or counseling, or even therapy [17]. All these professions work in the psychological domain, but they do not work on the same task of integrating conscious, logical, and rational behavior with unconscious, emotional, and irrational behavior.

Katherine: What are some of the common mistakes traditionally trained coaches make in transitioning to a more holistic way of fostering leadership development?

Jack: Some common mistakes that new consultant/coaches make? Sometimes groups get discouraged, and they want to be cheered up. And coaches want to cheer them up. That's understandable but problematic. It's collusion: an unconscious agreement to keep a happy face and avoid learning.

Positivity can be toxic—it denies the reality of authentic emotions. "Coaching" a group to operate smoothly, to increase performance, or to feel satisfied with themselves inhibits learning. When your child trips and hurts their knee and starts to cry, they don't run to the parent who gives them medical advice: "It's OK. It's just a scratch. Here, I'll clean it with iodine and put on a band-aid. See. You're good as new. And stop crying. Be a big boy." They are not looking for medical advice, and medical advice doesn't address their feelings and emotional pain—it invalidates the feelings of the child. So the child naturally runs to the parent who picks them up and comforts them. It's a subtle difference, but it's clear how being rational and giving advice invalidates the experience of other people. Effective group leadership coaches must work with a group to understand the complex causes of their feelings, but it's even more important to understand the *purpose* of their feelings. Emotions arise in groups and in individuals so they can reorient themselves and chart a new task, direction or destination in life.

It's essential to understand that leadership is not an individual phenomenon—it's a social phenomenon. Virtually all coaching, counseling, and even therapy are oriented around individual and interpersonal dynamics—the relationship with one's boss, with one's assistant, with one's husband or wife, with one's child. But human life in general, and leadership in particular, are a function of the social systems in which you live. You are authorized—or deauthorized—by others to lead. Even your charisma is not your possession, but a social phenomenon consisting of, basically, the projected attributions of others. These may simply be illusions, or even delusions, that are divorced from any real quality you have as a human being or as a leader.

The skill set articulated above—the capacity for working with subtle psychological variables with a "systems perspective" (group, intergroup and organizational levels) and undertaking rigorous multi-level professional training and serious personal work—is far beyond the usual training of business school faculty, corporate consultants, self-employed coaches, individual counselors, or even individually-oriented psychotherapists. The coaching profession needs to deepen the way it works with groups and larger systems, or it will remain a relatively ineffective means for profound personal, professional or organizational growth and development.

End Notes

[1] Wood, J.D., 1996a, 196b).

[2] Wood, J.D., (2009).

[3] "Books, like conversations, rarely give us any precise ideas. Nothing is so common as to read and converse uselessly. We must repeat here what Locke has so strongly recommended, define the terms." Voltaire, from "Questions sur l'Encyclopédie par des Amateurs" (Geneva: 1774), vol. 1, "Abus des mots," p. 32; *Œuvres complètes de Voltaire* (2008), vol. 38, p. 76. Jack's translation. Original French: "Les livres, comme les conversations, nous donnent rarement des idées précises. Rien n'est si commun que de lire et de converser inutilement. Il faut répéter ici ce que Locke a tant recommandé, définissez les termes."

[4] http://www.etymonline.com/index.php?search=coach&search mode=none
Coach: 1556, "large kind of carriage," from Middle French *coche*, from German *kotsche*, from Hungarian *kocsi (szekér)* "(carriage) of Kocs," village where it was first made. In Hungary, the thing and the name for it date from the 15th century, and forms are found in most European languages. Applied to railway cars 1866, American English. Sense of "economy or tourist class" is from 1949. Meaning "instructor/trainer" is c.1830. Oxford University slang for a tutor who "carries" a student through an exam; athletic sense is from 1861.

[5] Wood, J. D. (1999).

[6] Personal communication with Geoff Church and Richard Hahlo, founders of London's Dramatic Resources, www.dramaticresources.co.uk. They base their data on the work of Albert Mehrabian, whose research has sometimes been misunderstood. The percentages are how much the three principal elements of a communication account for how much the receivers like the speaker. What isn't in dispute among scientific researchers (and ethologists who study animal behavior) is that the non-verbal elements in communication are significantly more important than simply the words used (verbal communication). We appear to pick up, interpret, and make judgments and decisions about others based mostly on the covert, non-verbal emotional subtext, not the overtly spoken or written text.

[7] Wood, J.D., Meister, A., Liu, H. (2021a).

[8] Lee Kuan Yew (2015).

[9] Wood, J.D., Liu, H. (2021b)

[10] Petriglieri, G., Wood J.D. (2005)

[11] Wood, J. D., Petriglieri, G. (2005b).

[12] Xin, K.R. & Pearce, J.L. (2020).

[13] Engineering and Clinical

[14] The highest rating happened even though it was the last elective to be offered, was not included in the first waves of advertising, and some of the participants got assigned to it because they couldn't get into one of their preferred modules.

[15] Wood, J.D., (2008), p. 223.

[16] Wood, J.D., Petriglieri, G. (2005a)

References

... Lee Kuan Yew: his most memorable quotes, The Telegraph, Reuters, 23 March 2015.

Petriglieri, G., & Wood J.D. (2005). Learning for leadership: The "engineering" and "clinical" approaches. In Strebel, P., & Keys, T. (Eds.), *Mastering Executive Education: How to Combine Content with Context and Emotion* (pp. 140-154). London: Financial Times-Prentice Hall.

Wood, J.D., Meister, A., & Liu, H. (2021a). Defining the good, the bad and the evil. In Örtenblad, A. (Ed.), *Debating Bad Leadership: Reasons and Remedies, Chapter 3,* (in press). New York: Palgrave Macmillan.

Wood, J.D., & Liu, H. (2021b). Failure in leadership: the deeper psycho-social currents. In Örtenblad, A. (Ed.), *Debating Bad Leadership: Reasons and Remedies, Chapter 10* (in press). New York: Palgrave Macmillan.

Wood, J.D., (2009). The Nature of Unconscious Processes [in Coaching]: Interview with Jack Denfeld Wood by William Bergquist and Michael Sanson, *International Journal of Coaching in Organizations* (ICJO) , 3, 6-3.

Wood, J.D, (2008). An effective coaching strategy—or, how do you keep Cinderella's coach from turning into a pumpkin? In Büchel, B., Read, S., Moncef, A., & Coughlin, S. (Eds.), *Riding the Waves of Global Change, Chapter 24*, (pp. 221-228). Lausanne, IMD.

Wood, J.D., & Petriglieri, G. (2005a). On coaches, counsellors, facilitators and behavioural consultants. In Strebel, P., & Keys, T. (Eds.), *Mastering Executive Education: How to Combine Content with Context and Emotion, The IMD Guide.* London: Financial Times-Prentice Hall.

Wood, J. D., & Petriglieri, G. (2005b). Transcending polarization: Beyond binary thinking. *Transactional Analysis Journal*, 35(1), 31–39.

Wood, J. D. (1999). Taking the irrational seriously. IMD *Perspectives for Managers,* 59(3).

Wood, J. D. (1996a). What makes a leader? *The London Financial Times Mastering Management Series, Part 14.* Reprinted as Wood, J. D. (1997). What makes a leader? In T. Dickson, & G. Bickerstaffe (Eds.), *Mastering management* (pp. 507–511). London: Pitman.

Wood, J. D. (1996b). The two sides of leadership. *The London Financial Times Mastering Management Series, Part 15.* Reprinted as Wood, J. D. (1997). The two sides of leadership. In T. Dickson, & G. Bickerstaffe (Eds.), *Mastering management* (pp. 511–515). London: Pitman.

Xin, K. R. & Pearce, J.L. (2020). Understanding power and politics in organizations. In Xin, K.R. & Pearce, J.L. (Eds.), *Understanding Organizational Behavior* (pp. 195-229). Beijing: China Machine Press.

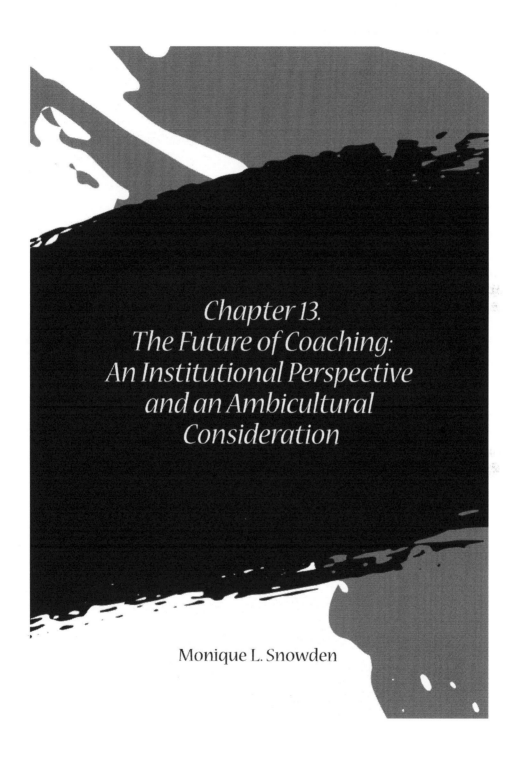

Chapter 13.
The Future of Coaching:
An Institutional Perspective
and an Ambicultural
Consideration

Monique L. Snowden

Abstract

The previous chapter discussed the value of increased learning and focus by the leadership coach on the psychological and systemic aspects of leadership development. In this chapter, the author introduces the influence of Eastern and Western philosophies on leadership coaching, using the lenses of coaching as a profession, practice and multidimensional process. The perspective taken provides a subject-object framing through each lens to ensure coaching discourse "provides stability and meaning to phenomena." An ambicultural approach describes a way to create balance and self-other perspectives, going beyond a dialectic approach to reflect the reality represented by words as they are known in different cultures, and to promote "striving toward expansiveness and inclusiveness."

Introduction

It is clear that the future of coaching is promising. This volume offers insight into the evolution of leadership coaching in China over the past decade. Collectively, the authors present coaching as an evolving *profession*, an institutionalized *practice*, and a multidimensional *process*. Coaching reflects and encapsulates each of the three conceptualizations, distinctively, and all together. In other words, coaching is an entangled and multifaceted phenomenon that escapes circumscription by a singular standpoint of its purpose, presence, and performance. The profession, practices, and processes are wholly a post-modern consideration of "Coaching in Wonderland" (Campone, 2020). American author E.B. White advises, "Always be on the lookout for the presence of wonder." Campone expresses a parallel sentiment:

> Curiosity is at the heart of all good coaching: curiosity about the [coachee], curiosity about the self as coach, curiosity about the processes and practices. When Alice tumbles down the rabbit hole...her reaction to this odd and unexpected experience is to cry out "Curiouser and curiouser!" (Carrol, 1865)....As thinking professionals, we have all found ourselves—like Alice—tumbling.... And like Alice, the best possible response is inquiry.... inquiry [is] a curiosity of head and heart, firmly grounded in theory and method. (2020, p.419)

The protagonist's exhalation suggests that every time she discovers something new, her surroundings become more unfamiliar. Strange encounters typically evoke a desire to know more, and emotions that lend to constructive and deleterious curiosity (Kashdan & Silva, 2009; Silva & Kashdan, 2009). The novel *Alice's Adventures in Wonderland* was at one time banned in China—and other countries—due to its *anthropomorphic* attribution of human behavioral characteristics and emotions to animals. Curiosity is an observable state in many species; however, its human enactment can be precarious at times. In Shakespeare's *Much Ado About Nothing*, Claudio chides Benedek, "What, courage man! What though care killed a cat, thou hast mettle enough in thee to kill care." Or, more plainly stated, "Curiosity killed the cat."

Keith To (2006) reflects, "In [China] (and many other Asian countries), parents taught us not to be curious. Curiosity is equivalent to danger and is deemed impolite" (BCW, 2006). Gong emphasizes that the "deeply rooted tradition of filial piety of Confucianism has a major influence on the values shared and behaviors exhibited between [Chinese] parents and children" (Chapter 11). Warner and Wang note, "Chinese millennials are not that different from their counterparts in Western countries," pointing out that the former are "equally curious" (Chapter 9). However, "unlike their counterparts in most Western countries, millennials in China face a number of uniquely Chinese pressures" (Warner & Wang).

The appropriateness and utility of curiosity, in this context, is dually paradoxical (neither/nor) and ambiguous (and/both). That is, one encounters an operative curious/incurious duality. In contrast to Western dualism, where the former is positively charged and the latter negatively charged, the ancient Chinese philosophy yin-yang connotes a harmonious interplay of ostensibly opposite or contrary forces toward complementarity, interconnectedness, and interdependence. Moreover, there is an intentional suspension of the East-West dichotomy that most often yields and reifies socially constructed divides and schisms, where lines are drawn and differences are problematized. Arguably, a more interesting and fruitful undertaking is holding East and West dissimilarities (real and perceived) in tension, within a liminal space between cultural and managerial philosophies.

Dialectical tensions of this nature can conceivably ground and figure nuanced understandings and thoughtful enactments of paradoxical leadership (Smith,

Tushman, & Lewis, 2016) in global organizations. This explicit call may be novel, but the noted practice has proven efficacious in business. Case in point, Stan Shih, founder and chairman emeritus of the Acer Group, interleaves Eastern and Western philosophies and methods to achieve high-performing organizational outcomes (Lin & Hou, 2010). The same can be said of his leadership, which has been lauded as "quite different from that of the typical Chinese business leader," and imbued with "distinctive Asian values" (Lin & Hou, p.7).

Shih evinces dialectical thinking and practice (Chin & Miller, 2010). Similarly, coaching with a sensibility to and a foci on dialectics has cultural utility (Potter, 2020). If indeed curiosity is at the heart of good coaching, then it seems plausible that curiosity may be conceived and enacted differently and similarly, in terms of coaching (for the coach and coachee) in the East vis-à-vis Western cultures. Furthermore, the concept of curiosity in coaching offers a point of introspection to explore an ambicultural approach to coaching that impels a dialectically actionable mindset.

To that end, the remainder of this chapter section is organized into three parts. First, coaching is presented as an evolving *profession* that is held strongly by coaching logics and rationalities. Second, coaching is presented as institutionalized practices that signify the profession-in-action. Third, coaching is presented as a collection of multidimensional *processes* that rationalize instrumental, appropriate, and orthodox coaching actions and discourse. Finally, ambicultural coaching is explicated, using curiosity in a dialectical frame as an exemplar.

Coaching as an Evolving Profession

This essay offers an institutional perspective of coaching as a developing profession globally, including in China. Leicht and Fennel (2008) point out that "the study of the professions, as they are defined in the developed world, has been deeply intertwined with institutional theory and topics central to institutional theory" (p.431). Two topics of particular salience to this discussion are (organizational) fields and (institutional) logics. Together, the concepts of fields and logics should impel field members to imagine broader and bolder future possibilities for the coaching profession.

Professions are epistemic cultures that hold, enact, promote, and diffuse specialized knowledge (Scott, 2008a). Knowledge is "about beliefs and commitment....a function of a particular stance, perspective, or intention....It is always knowledge 'to some end" (Nonaka & Takekuchi, 1995, p.58). Skills signify knowledge in action and context. And expertise connotes possessing, but also sharing, specialized knowledge to advance certain skills and generate new knowledge. Coaching knowledge is defined, legitimated, and institutionalized by way of broadly accepted ethical principles, rules of behavior, professional standards, core competency models, and skill assessment frameworks.

Professions are more than "promulgators and protectors" of professional norms and values (Kraatz & Moore, 2002, p. 121). Scott (2008b) asserts that "professions function as institutional agents—as definers, interpreters, and appliers of institutional elements" (p. 219). The collective beliefs and values of professionals emerge within an institutionalized field in the form of structured and persistent interactions between professionalized entities, such as professional organizations and associations. For example, the International Coaching Federation (ICF) is "dedicated to advancing the coaching profession by setting high standards, providing independent certification and building a worldwide network of trained coaching professionals."

Coaching is well beyond a watershed moment of being considered a profession, despite the absence of an exclusive domain of competence being delineated (Fietze, 2007). Notwithstanding the presence of a "professional collective self-obligation" (Fietze, p.5), coaching is a profession that has not yet fully developed into a durable institution, particularly in terms of regulative structures. However, the unequivocal existence of evidence-based practices and processes, accredited and recognized education programs, multiple types and levels of certifications, and sundry professional organizations render coaching as an evolving versus fledgling profession.

Coaching Field

Certified coaches, accredited coach training programs, coach certifying bodies, coach membership organizations, and assessment tools providers are some of the entities that comprise the organizational field (Scott, 1991) of coaching, in which a coaching constituent is embedded (hereto referred to as *coaching field*). The coaching field is embodied by professionals and professional communities of practice that establish, enact, and reify logics that emanate from coaching professions, practices, and processes.

Professional organizations, such as ICF, support and promote social exchanges constitutive of bona fide professionalized experiences, expressions, and understandings of coaching. They function as interest groups that aim for collective mobility (Macdonald, 1995). Moreover, coaching-related professional organizations and associations are conveners of discursive sites where coaching field members talk to and about themselves, regulating and legitimating a professional web of knowledge, competencies, and skills. These professional entities professionalize the coaching field by promoting institutionalized practices and normative processes.

Coaching Logics and Rationalities

The coaching field is comprised of constituents with fluid, overlapping, and evolving memberships and relationships that are shaped by convergent and divergent institutional logics (Scott, 1995). Institutional logics (hereto referred to as *coaching logics*) are collections of symbolic structures and material practices, which together encompass the principles that coaching constituents employ to gain power, influence, and recognition within the coaching field (Friedland & Alford, 1991; Scott, 2001). Friedland (2002) asserts:

> [Professions] have logics that both must be made material in order to signify and must signify in order to materialize…. logics constitute the cosmology within which means are meaningful, where means-ends couplets are thought appropriate and become the naturalized, unthought conditions of social action, performing the substances at stake within them. (p. 383)

Rationalities inform understandings of professionalized identities and practices. And intended outcomes for coaching constituents are necessarily rationalized. The constructs *logics* and *rationalities*, however, are not the same. Logics are antecedents to rationalities. Whereas logics structure actions, rationalities are invoked to explain and justify why particular actions have been or should be taken. Coaching rationalities contextualize coaching actions, which in turn render coaching logics visible and audible. Scott (1995) posits that logics are deeply-rooted regulative, normative, and cultural-cognitive structures mediated by rationalities that yield instrumental, appropriate, and orthodox actions respectively.

Professionalized fields have multiple and competing theoretical, formal, and practical rationalities that can simultaneously align and conflict with personal/ professional norms and values (Townley, 2002). The coaching field is therefore constitutive of value-laden and pluralistic rationalities. Contemplating extant coaching practices and the emergence of alternative practices, such as ambicultural coaching, is an exercise in identifying and explicating the principles and means-end actions—logics and rationalities respectively—that constitute, legitimate, and institutionalize the coaching field. Moreover, discovering coaching logics and rationalities necessitates unearthing and unpacking generally accepted coaching structures, practices, and processes.

Coaching as Institutionalized Practices

Coaching is a communication phenomenon, by which coaching logics are embedded in, represented by, and emerge from coaching discursive practices. Coaching knowledge, expertise, and logics are constitutive of discursive practices that are shaped by the interpretive schemes, norms, rules, and resources (allocative authoritative) that guide individual and collective coaching actions. Fairclough (1993) describes discursive practices as a domain of expertise and reflexivity (pp. 140-141), where reflexivity is the use of knowledge to organize and transform phenomena. Discursive coaching practices are reflected in core competencies. For example, Delgadillo (2015) summarizes ICF core communication competencies:

> [A] coach is not allowed to: use a direct, convincing communication strategy; tell a coachee what to do or how to do it; examine the past (particularly the emotional past); choose the topic/content of the conversation for the coachee; change the agenda without input from the coachee; be attached to any particular outcome or solution; substitute assessment for diagnosis; or simply teach a coachee.

Any set of communication core competencies is as multifaceted as the communication discipline and associated fields. Furthermore, while the social interaction between coaches and coachees might be illuminated by conversational analysis, coaching is more than a conversation or series of conversations. Schneiberg and Clemens (2006) emphasize that institutional actors generate discursive output, which reveals how they perceive problems and go about connecting (or not) concepts, objects, classification schemes and practices. In this regard, professionalized coaching is comprised of a constellation of models, methods, maps, plans, and scripts. Altogether, these institutional elements warrant an explication of discourse in general, and in the context of coaching specifically.

Coaching Discourse

Discourse is a lens or point of entry for seeing, learning about, and understanding a phenomenon (Putnam & Fairclough, 2001). Coaching discourses are transported in and by field members. Intraprofessional discourse between and among coaching field members advances certain types of expertise and knowledge as essential to coaching practices. Hall (2001) emphasizes that on one side, discourse "'rules in' certain ways of talking about a topic, defining an acceptable and intelligible way to talk, write or conduct oneself"; on the other side, discourse "'rules out,' limits and restricts other ways of talking or conducting ourselves in relation to the topic or constructing knowledge about it" (2001, p. 72). Coaching discourses promote and circumscribe how coaching fielding members make sense and give voice to coaching logics; prescribe meaning to coaching experiences; and produce, maintain, and reify institutionalized coaching practices and identities.

Reciprocally shared professional understandings (Greenwood, 2002) of coaching practices enable ordered exchanges of ideas and information through coaching discourse. In this regard, coaching discourse signifies a professional meeting of the minds that reveals presupposed and taken-for-granted conceptions (Taylor, Gurd, & Bardini, 1997) that inform disparate professional knowledge in the field. Conforming and appropriate intraprofessional discourse aims to reduce ambiguity and uncertainty for coaching field members and shapes fitting institutionalized coaching practices. Coercive, normative, and mimetic discursive discourses hold and structure coaching practices within the profession and field.

Coercive discourse promotes diligence and principles of reasonableness that "stem from influence or problems of legitimacy" (DiMaggio & Powell, 1991, p. 12). Coercive discourse reflects formal and informal pressures imposed in the profession mediated by cultural expectations. Normative discourse promotes professionalization by means of monitoring, sanctioning, and typifying coaching actions as more or less appropriate in the coaching profession. Normative discourse conveys dominant methods and heeds to extant power structures and relations shaped by coach training and the professional socialization of field members who enter into, persist within, swirl about, and exit from the coaching milieu. Mimetic discourse invokes "follow the leader" coaching actions. Whereas normative practices may be perceived as acceptable, mimetic ones are typified as good or best practices.

Coaching as Multidimensional Processes

Scott (2008b) conceptualizes a three-pillar framework that is a useful analytical scheme for locating, capturing, and representing coaching as an institutionalized field, professionalized phenomenon, and discursive practice. The framework is "comprised of regulative, normative, and cultural-cognitive elements that, together with associated activities and resources, provide stability and meaning to [phenomena]" (Scott, 2008b, p. 48). In the context of this essay, the pillars (Scott, pp.59-70) provide insight into coaching processes. The regulative pillar stresses both formal and informal rule-setting, monitoring, and sanctioning activities—dimensions that induce *instrumental* processes. The normative pillar introduces prescriptive, evaluative, and obligatory dimensions that promote *appropriate* processes. The cultural-cognitive pillar emphasizes the centrality of symbolic dimensions and the use of common schemas, frames, and other shared symbolic representations that guide *orthodox* processes.

Instrumental coaching processes are intensely rational. Coaching constituents involved in such processes may seek to understand and respond to the question: *What are my interests in this situation?* The underlying premise of regulative dimensions is that individuals engage in coaching processes they believe will advance their interests, and they will consequently exhibit conforming behaviors to secure attendant rewards (tangible and intangible) or to avoid associated sanctions (real and perceived). Conformity, however, is a contingent outcome that is not an all-or-nothing proposition. Additionally, instrumental processes do not necessarily yield repression and constraint. To the contrary, coaching processes within regulative dimensions can enable, empower, and benefit coaching constituents in materially objective and symbolically subjective ways. References in this volume that reflect the presence of instrumental processes, with respect to coaching in China, include self-regulation of motivation and emotions.

Appropriate coaching processes emphasize norms and values, and their stabilizing effect, in terms of being internalized and influencing others. Coaching constituents involved in such processes may seek to understand and respond to the question: *Given the situation, and my role within it, what are fitting behaviors to exhibit?* Normative dimensions manifest behaviors that can be prescriptive, evaluative, and mutually obligatory. In that regard, norms specify how things should be done, in terms of legitimate means to pursue valued ends. Toward reaching preferred or desirable states, values are wedded to standards of assessment. In addition to defining goals and objectives, coaching constituents decide on the most appropriate way to pursue and achieve intended outcomes. References in this volume that reflect the presence of appropriate processes, with respect to coaching in China, include coaching certification processes and programs, managerial behaviors and values, traditional and cultural values, and cultural norms.

Orthodox coaching processes involve common frameworks of meaning and action. Coaching constituents involved in such processes may defend traditionalism or justify modernism, asking the question: *Given the situation, and how familiar it is to me, what is the best course of action?* Perceived correctness and soundness of the principles and philosophies underlying repetitive action patterns can gradually become objectified and habitual. Cultural-cognitive dimensions invoke compliant behaviors where other types of behaviors may be viewed as inconceivable. Mimetic isomorphism reifies commonly accepted ways of doing things, as executed and adopted. Cognitive frames condition how coaching constituents form professional ideologies. Cultural notions and viewpoints often vary and may be relatedly contested. Also, divergent beliefs and contradictory sensibilities may yield conflicting and diverse coaching outcomes. References in this volume that reflect the presence of orthodox processes, with respect to coaching in China, include differences in managerial patterns of Chinese and Western managers, culturally acceptable interaction, speaking patterns, and language structure.

West Meets East: An Ambicultural Approach to Coaching
Language "is both locution (representation) and illocution (action, with practical consequences)" (Taylor & Van Every, 2000, p. 4). The functioning of language in thought and action, and its impact on knowledge formation and dissemination is essential to coaching within particular contexts. There is a delicate connection of words and facts, underlying the relationship between language and reality

(Hayakawa & Hayakawa, 1990). A universal epistemic questions is: How do we know what we know? Unpacking this question makes clear that knowledge, language, and culture are intrinsically connected:

> In Western thought, representations of reality are embedded in modern, low-context Western languages which cultivate categorical binary oppositions, with little or no emphasis upon 'fuzzy' shades of grey or paradoxes. Objective descriptions are embedded in language and language constitutes what counts as knowledge. (Lowe, Kainzbauer, & Tapachai, 2015, p.309)

In their explication of the knowledge conversion cycle, Nonaka & Takekuchi (1995) expound on the conceptual trilogy metaphor-analogy-model. The action sequence enables the circumvention and transcendence of barriers that are encountered in language processing—particularly with respect to creating representations of the self and others. Linguistic representations are abstractions of (inter)subjective experiences (Hayakawa & Hayakawa, 1990). Representation, by design, privileges the ideal and abstract over the contingent and specific. The act of representing engages the endemic tension between including the significant and excluding the decidedly insignificant (Star, 1995).

Representation is a cultural-cognitive process that delineates and influences coaching phenomena. Lowe, Kainzbauer, and Tapachai (2015) contrast a "Western mindset: I think therefore I am" with an "Eastern mindset: I am not separate," and in doing so illuminate the relationship of representation with knowledge, language, and culture. They write:

> The Western normative assumption is that knowledge, constituted through abstract representational language, should precede action.... The Western, cognitive self is therefore a construction that invents its existence through separation and the certainties provided by rational knowledge and knowledge awareness....The Eastern self is, by contrast with the Western individual and cognitive self, contingent upon affective relationships with much less emphasis upon the individual. (p.307)

Chen and Miller (2010) suggest bridging Eastern and Western cultural divides by way of an "emphasis on balance and self-other integration" (p.17)—shifting from a "West leads East" to a "West meets East" stance. While the authors' foci are on management and the development of global-minded executives, their conceptualization of the "enlightened citizen-businessperson" is apropos to coaching, coaches, and coachees. To that end, I place a clarion call, informed by research and scholarship (Chen, 2014; Chen & Miller, 2010; Lin & Hou, 2010; Lowe, Kainzbauer, & Tapachai, 2015), for coaching field members to embrace and advance an ambicultural approach to coaching.

Ambicultural

The root "ambi," meaning "both" and "around," conveys an active and persistent striving for "expansiveness and inclusiveness" (Chen, 2014). The parity between two ideas, forces, or characteristics—not necessarily in opposition—are reflected in the following terms:

Ambient: Moving around; surrounding on all sides
Ambiguity: Quality of uncertainty in meaning; multiple meanings
Ambidextrous: Ability to use both hands with equal proficiency
Ambicultural: Ability to functionally transport between cultures

Ming-Jer Chen, a leading and renowned authority in strategic management, coined the term *ambicultural,* in the course of conducting research on bridging Western and Chinese management practices. Chen (2015) also presents other ambicultural considerations for synthesizing (e.g., global-local, competition-cooperation, and professionalism-humanity). He aims to rise above opposites and realize integrations of cultural perspectives and actions. To that end, the term *ambicultural* has strong behavioral leanings and cognitive origins. Chen asserts that the action-oriented term may ultimately define the study of East-West management as a whole. He writes:

The idea of "ambiculturalism" advances the perspective that dichotomies can be integrated by separating the wheat from the chaff—extracting the best and culling the worst to produce a better, optimized, even enlightened result, be it product, service, management practice, or human behavior. The effect of an ambicultural approach to business, education, and life is a balance that can close the chasms separating former "opposites." (p.119)

The following lines of inquiry are informed by the 2011 Academy of Management Annual Meeting—"West Meets East: Enlightening, Balancing, and Transcending"—and additionally inspired by Chen (2015), who served as the meeting's program chair. Chen leveraged the meeting to further develop an ambicultural approach to management, which in this essay is applied to coaching:

1. How can coaching constituents gain insight from incongruent experiences?
2. How can coaching constituents achieve balance between opposing phenomena?
3. How can coaching constituents transcend opposition and draw strength from differences?
4. What can coaching constituents do realize the best, and circumvent the worst, from West meeting East philosophy and praxis?

Each question opens space to transcend and transform contrarian thinking from polarization, toward dialectical thinking and integration. According to Peng and Nesbitt (1999), "the Chinese have had an enduring reputation for being dialectical thinkers, reasoning in ways that are distinct from the formal logic paradigm dominating the Western tradition" (p.743). Eastern tradition typically views contradictions as constant, accepting that entities in opposition to one another are also connected. The optimal goal is to achieve balance, where two opposites harmoniously co-exist and are able to transmute into each other.

It is commonly perceived that the West focuses on the individual, and China places more emphasis on the collective. This sets up an individualism-collectivism dialectic. Holding the dyad in tension, avoiding problematizing or venerating either ideology, is an initial step toward ambicultural integration. A contingent and integrated reading of harmonious collectivism and individualism, respectively, connotes "a pride in the community and concern with one's reputation in the community" (Chen & Miller, 2010, p.20). The dialectical interplay intensifies the dyad, wholly, discovering and bringing forth a connection from the liminal space between the two ideologies.

Attaining an astute awareness and understanding of the individualism-collectivism dialectic is germane and applicable to ambicultural coaching, specifically with respect to how the coaching core competencies are enacted by coaches, received by coachees, and assessed in terms of coaching outcomes. For example, ICF core competency "Powerful Questioning" emphasizes that a competent coach should demonstrate the "ability to ask questions that reveal the information needed for maximum benefit to the coaching relationship and the [coachee]" (ICF, n.d.). Coaches' proficiency in questioning (Marlett & Benz, 2020) and "spirit of curiosity" (Norwood, 2020, p.351) are vital to practice. In the course of the coaching relationship, curiosity is inherently sparked for both the coach and coachee.

Curiosity

Exploring curiosity from an ambicultural lens has particular utility. Curiosity is core to coaching (Campone, 2020). The curious seek information and experiences through self-directed behavior (Kashdan, et. al, p.1). To (2016) writes, "Nearly every single book about coaching you can find in the bookstores will tell you to coach using curiosity and intuition. How about coaching someone who has very little curiosity or intuition?" There is both symmetry and asymmetry between the opposing states of being curious and incurious (To, 2006). Thus, curiosity is a nuanced phenomenon. Kashdan and colleagues (2020) synthesize decades of research to operationalize curiosity in multi-dimensional framework, with six dimensions:

1. Joyous Exploration – A pleasurable experience of finding the world intriguing (p.1)

2. Deprivation Sensitivity – The anxiety and frustration of being aware of information you do not know, want to know, and devote considerable effort to uncover (p.1)

3. Stress Tolerance – The dispositional tendency to handle the anxiety that arises when confronting the new (p.2)

4. Thrill Seeking – Arousal is not something to be reduced, but rather is part of what makes events intrinsically desirable (p.2)

5. Covert Curiosity – Defined by how details about other people are discovered in indirect, surreptitious, secretive ways (p.2)

6. Overt Curiosity – An interest in other people's behaviors, thoughts, and feelings (p.2)

Joyous Exploration

Joyous Exploration is explicated to illustrate how the aforementioned ICF core competency "Powerful Questioning" can be operationalized as dispositional curiosity. Kashdan and colleagues (2020) use the following statements to determine correlations with respect to work-related curiosity and psychological strengths:

• I view challenging situations as an opportunity to grow and learn.
• I seek out situations where it is likely that I will have to think in depth about something.
• I enjoy learning about subjects that are unfamiliar to me.
• I find it fascinating to learn new information.

> Joyous Exploration showed the strongest relations with open-mindedness, extraversion, the intellectual humility to revise one's viewpoints in conflicts, and valuing of self-direction. Joyous Exploration had the strongest relations of the curiosity dimensions to work-related curiosity, wisdom—specifically, the ability to consider others' perspectives and intellectual humility, innovation, a willingness to dissent from social norms and express contradictory opinions to supervisors and managers, a workplace promotion focus, and the valuing of self-direction and universalism. (p.6)

Viewed through an ambicultural lens, Joyous Exploration reveals the presence of a *universalism-particularism* dialectic. In universalistic cultures, generally, rules and obligations are given a high priority and more weight than relationships. Examples of cultures with this dimension include USA, Canada, Australia, the Netherlands, Scandinavia, New Zealand, Switzerland, Great Britain, and Germany. In particularistic cultures, rules' applicability and obligatory expectations depend on situations and relationships. Examples of cultures with this dimension include China, Russia and South America.

Engaging a universalism-particularism dialectic in the coaching context necessitates understanding how each side is connected to the other. That is, one exists because of the other's paradoxical presence and absence. Furthermore, it is neither obligatory nor necessarily desirable to accept either individually. Contemplating the compounded weight and circumstances of relationships is a process of discovering and placing value on contingencies while also accepting that there are an infinite number of possibilities, in terms of what is perceived and treated as obligatory (must do), permitted (acceptable to do, but not obligatory), discretionary (not obligatory, and not forbidden, but not necessarily permitted), and prohibited (must not do).

Overt Curiosity

Overt Curiosity is explicated to illustrate how the aforementioned ICF core competency "Powerful Questioning" can be operationalized as dispositional curiosity. Kashdan and colleagues (2020) use the following statements to determine correlations with respect to work-related curiosity and psychological strengths:

• I ask a lot of questions to figure out what interests other people.
• When talking to someone who is excited, I am curious to find out why.
• When talking to someone, I try to discover interesting details about them.
• I like finding out why people behave the way they do.

> Overt Social Curiosity showed the strongest relations with agreeableness, sociability, and the valuing of benevolence and universalism. Overt Social Curiosity had the strongest relations with wisdom—specifically, the search for compromise, adopting others' perspectives, and recognition of change—and the valuing of benevolence. (p.6)

Viewed through an ambicultural lens, Overt Curiosity reveals the presence of an *altruism-benevolence* dialectic. On one side, altruism is an individual's concern for the well-being of others, sans being largely motivated by one's own satisfaction. Examples of cultures with this dimension are USA, China, Brazil and Egypt. On the other side, benevolence is the sentiment of concern itself. Examples of cultures with this dimension are Mexico, South Africa, and Iran.

Engaging an altruism-benevolence dialectic in the coaching context necessitates understanding how each side renders a shadow on the other. Shadows depend on a light source, or awareness, for their presence. Shadow rendering, shadow boundaries, and shadow perspectives comprise a visibility set that illuminates the malleability of one state from another and to another. The altruistic acceptance and perhaps adoption of another's perspective is akin to making visible one's shadow self, while still maintaining a strong sense of self. Compromises may not be permanent, but they are no less essential to the good health and development of a benevolent relationship between self and others. Additionally, conflict avoidance may run counter to enhancing the welfare of others. Choosing pathways that have associated junctures of discord along the way can lead to fulfillment, because they are authentically traveled in light and with shadows.

The motivation, nature, and impact of curiosity in the coaching context is multifold. Taking an ambicultural approach to coaching is akin to looking through a cultural kaleidoscope at a coaching relationship where the coach and coachee are situated between dialectical flat plates and plane mirrors, turning and reflecting. Like the hued material that is constantly changing in the instrument (self and others), coaching engagements are an interplay that changes the position of the discursive bits of dialogue reflected in various patterns that can be disorienting, while also harmonious. In sum, there is beauty and utility in dialectical wonderment.

Conclusion

Contemplating the future of a profession is a laudable, but monumental, undertaking. Contextualizing that future from a global perspective, crossing geography and culture, is humbling to say the least. Nonetheless, the author of this essay comes to the task having experienced and reified the presence of ethnocentric Western thought that unconsciously drips into theory, research, and practice. Evaluating coaching through an ambicultural lens, identifying and grappling with taken-for-granted assumptions, constraints and caveats that are embedded in the constellation of coaching theories, models, methods, maps, plans, and scripts has utility for evolving the profession.

The authors in this volume call attention to the reinforcement of Confucianism and communism in the Chinese education system. Similarly, Christianity and capitalism rest at the core of U.S. education. The continuum between the two, where West meets East, proffers fertile space for advancing coaching as an evolving *profession*, as institutionalized *practices*, and as multidimensional *processes*. There is often considerable discomfort experienced by those who work from cores out to peripheries, traverse borders, and embrace the dialectical.

It is from that uneasiness, however, where many of the greatest opportunities for change and transformation emerge.

References

Blum, L. A. (2015). Altruism and benevolence. *Wiley Encyclopedia of Management,* 1-2.

Chen, M. J., & Miller, D. (2010). West meets East: Toward an ambicultural approach to management. *Academy of Management Perspectives,* 24(4), 17-24.

DiMaggio, P. J., & Powell, W.W. (1991) Introduction. In W.W. Powell & P.J. DiMaggio (Eds.), *The new institutionalism in organization analysis* (pp. 1-38). Chicago, IL: University of Chicago Press.

Fairclough, N. (1993). Critical discourse analysis and the marketization of public discourse: The Universities. *Discourse & Society,* 4, 133-168.

Fietze, B. (2017). Is Coaching on Its Way to Becoming a Profession? A Profession-Centric Sociological Assessment. In *The Professionalization of Coaching* (pp. 3-21). Springer, Wiesbaden.

Friedland, R. (2002) Money, sex, and God: The erotic logic of religious nationalism. *Sociological Theory,* 20, 381–425.

Friedland, R., & Alford, R. (1991). Bring society back in: Symbols, practices and institutional contradictions. In W. W. Powell & P. J. DiMaggio (Eds.), *The new institutionalism in organizational analysis* (pp. 232-263). Chicago, IL: University of Chicago Press.

Greenwood, R., Suddaby, R., & Hining, C. R. (2002). Theorizing change: The role of professional associations in the transformation of institutionalized fields. *Academy of Management Journal,* 45, 58-80.

Hall, S. (2001). Foucault: Power, knowledge and discourse. In M. Wetherell, S. Taylor, & S. Yates (Eds.), *Discourse theory and practice: A reader* (pp. 72-81). London: Sage.

Hayakawa, S. I., & Hayakawa, A. R. (1990). *Language in thought and action.* Houghton Mifflin Harcourt.

International Coaching Federation (ICF) (n.d.) Coaching core competencies. Accessed on December 1, 2020, from https://coachfederation.org/core-competencies.

Kashdan, T. B., Disabato, D. J., Goodman, F. R., & McKnight, P. E. (2020). The Five-Dimensional Curiosity Scale Revised (5DCR): Briefer subscales while separating overt and covert social curiosity. *Personality and Individual Differences, 157,* 109836.

Kraatz, M. S., & Moore, J. H. (2002). Executive migration and institutional change. *Academy of Management journal,* 45(1), 120-143.

Kashdan, T. B., & Silvia, P. J. (2009). Curiosity and interest: The benefits of thriving on novelty and challenge. In C. R. Snyder & S. J. Lopez (Eds.), *Handbook of positive psychology* (2nd ed., pp. 367–374). New York, NY: Oxford University Press.

Leicht, K. T., & Fennell, M. L. (2008). Institutionalism and the Professions. In R. Greenwood, C. Oliver, T.B. Lawrence, & R. E. Meyer (Eds.), The Sage handbook of organizational institutionalism (pp. 431-448). Chicago, IL: University of

Chicago Press.

Lin, H. C., & Hou, S. T. (2010). Managerial lessons from the East: An interview with Acer's Stan Shih. *Academy of management perspectives, 24*(4), 6-16.

Lowe, S., Kainzbauer, A., Tapachai, N., & Hwang, K. S. (2015). Ambicultural blending between Eastern and Western paradigms: Fresh perspectives for international management research. *Culture and Organization, 21*(4), 304-320.

Macdonald, K. M. (1995). *Sociology of the profession.* London: Sage.

Marlett, J., & Bentz, V. M. (2020). Embodied awareness: Transformative coaching through somatics and phenomenology. In T. H. Hildebrandt, F. Campone, K. Norwood, & E. J. Ostrowski (Eds.), *Innovations in coaching leadership: Research and practice* (pp. 224-250). Santa Barbara, CA: Fielding University Press.

Nonaka, I., & Takeuchi, H. (1995). *The knowledge-creating company: How Japanese companies create the dynamics of innovation.* New York, NY: Oxford Press.

Noordewier, M. K., & van Dijk, E. (2017). Curiosity and time: from not knowing to almost knowing. *Cognition and Emotion, 31*(3), 411-421.

Norwood, K. (2020). Beautiful form watcher: Coaching for equity in education. In T. H. Hildebrandt, F. Campone, K. Norwood, & E. J. Ostrowski (Eds.), *Innovations in coaching leadership: Research and practice* (pp. 346-371). Santa Barbara, CA: Fielding University Press.

Peng, K., & Nisbett, R. E. (1999). Culture, dialectics, and reasoning about contradiction. *American psychologist, 54*(9), 741.

Potter, P. (2020). Becoming a coach: Making sense of coaching students' transformative experiences. In T. H. Hildebrandt, F. Campone, K. Norwood, & E. J. Ostrowski (Eds.), *Innovations in coaching leadership: Research and practice* (pp. 371-394). Santa Barbara, CA: Fielding University Press.

Putnam, L. L., & Fairhurst, G. (2001). *Discourse analysis in organizations: Issues and concerns. In F. M. Jablin & L. L. Putnam (Eds.), The new handbook of organizational communication: Advances in theory, research and methods (pp. 235-268). Newbury Park, CA: Sage.*

Schneiberg, M., & Clemens, E. S. (2006). The typical tools for the job: Research strategies in institutional analysis. *Sociological Theory, 24,* 195-227.

Silvia, P. J., & Kashdan, T. B. (2009). Interesting things and curious people: Exploration and engagement as transient states and enduring strengths. Social and Personality Psychology Compass, 3(5), 785–797. Scott, R. W. (1991). Unpacking Institutional Arguments. In P. J. DiMaggio and W. W. Powell (Eds.), *The New Institutionalism in Organizational Analysis* (pp. 164–182). Chicago, IL: The University of Chicago Press.

Scott, R. W. (1995). *Institutions and organizations.* Thousand Oaks, CA: Sage.

Scott, R. W. (2001). *Institutions and organizations* (2nd Ed.). Thousand Oaks, CA: Sage.

Scott, R. W. (2008a). Lords of dance: Professionals as institutional agents. *Organization Studies, 28,* 219-238.

Scott, R. W. (2008b). *Institutions and organizations: Ideas and interests.* Thousand Oaks, CA: Sage.

Smith, W. K., Lewis, M. W., & Tushman, M. L. (2016). Both/and" leadership. *Harvard Business Review, 94*(5), 62-70.

Star, S. L. (1995). The Politics of Formal Representations: Wizards, Gurus, and Organizational Complexity. In Susan Leigh Star (Ed.), *Ecologies of Knowledge: Work and Politics in Science and Technology* (pp. 88-118). Albany, NY: SUNY.

Taylor, J. R., Gurd, G. & Bardini T. (1997). The worldviews of cooperative work. In G. Bowker, S. Star, W. Turner, & L. Gasser, (Eds.), *Social Science, technical systems and cooperative work: Beyond the great divide* (pp. 379-413). Hillsdale, NJ: Lawrence-Erlbaum.

Taylor, J. R., & Van Every, E. J. (2000). *The emergent organization: Communication as its site and service.* Mahwah: NJ: Lawrence Erlbaum Associates.

To, K. (Winter, 2006). Business coaching in mainland China and Hong Kong. Business Coaching Worldwide, 2(4). Accessed on December 1, 2020, from http://www.wabccoaches.com/bcw/2006_v2_i4/feature.html.

Townley, B. (2002). The role of competing rationalities in institutional change. *Academy of Management Journal,* 45, 163-179.

Section III.

Reflections on the Practice of Coaching in China

Karen Zong

Chapter 14.
Journeys to Transformation:
Finding Meaning
Through Adversity

"Since you cannot do good to all, you are to pay special regard to those who, by the accidents of time, or place, or circumstance, are brought into closer connection with you."

- Saint Augustine

For Bill, who taught me optimism.

As the daughter of oceanographer parents, I spent my childhood in Qingdao, a beautiful coastal city in the northeastern province of Shandong. We lived in a dormitory behind the China Oceanology Institute, and my parents worked in the research buildings in the front. Right outside the institute is the big blue sea, part of Bohai Bay, which eventually leads to the Pacific Ocean. As a little girl, I remembered often staring at the vast, endless ocean, wondering if there was another world lying beyond, and what it would look like.

My parents were the last batch of college graduates before the "Cultural Revolution" started, upon which almost all school education came to a halt. When I started school, they often reminded me how fortunate I was to be able to study. They set high standards for me, both academically and as an elder sister. I started learning how to cook at age 6, when I was barely tall enough to see inside the cooking pan. In addition, I was put in charge of making sure that all homework, for myself and my younger brother, was done properly.

There were times that I complained about unfairness: "Why do I have to do so much more just because I'm 2 years older?" My dad was too busy to respond, and mom would simply say, "It's good for you." Soon I realized that there was no time for complaining. I remember looking at the clock and realizing that I had less than an hour to finish cooking and to check my brother's homework before my parents arrived home from work. This regimen taught me independence, time management, and care for others. Most importantly, it taught me how much potential a child has to offer when given the space and responsibility.

Little did I know what a blessing it was to be able to grow up near the beach. My brother and I used to run back home from the beach every day after school, and we went swimming every day in the summer. We both grew very tall. I was on the track, basketball, and volleyball teams throughout school, which helped me to build friendships and a sense of belonging, when I lived in LA, Dallas, San

Francisco, Hong Kong, and Beijing. Years later, when I was doing one-on-one coaching and counseling, I observed that people who were able to calm down quickly, and take meaningful action in the midst of adversity, were often those who practiced regular physical exercise. An active mind can only be hosted in an active body. Positive emotions generated from exercise enabling positive action.

A few months ago, I met a senior leader who, during 1-1 coaching, told me how tired he was every day from his hectic schedule, and how he worried that this would take a toll on his health. When I suggested exercising 3 to 4 times a week, his immediate response was, "I have no energy left." I smiled and said, "That's exactly why you need it." A month later, when we met again, he gave me a big grin. "I had a good run this morning," he said; "It feels really good whenever I do it."

While going through graduate school, I met Bill Mobley, who was the advisor for my independent research project. Like other professors, Bill was intense, focused, and analytical when it came to work. Yet, at the end of every conversation with him, you remembered his encouraging smile and hearty laughter, and you believed in the possibilities even when things were challenging. Our project, "The Attraction and Retention Factors of Chinese Young Professionals," involving Motorola, P&G, PPG, and graduating students from Beijing University, won the top research award that year. In a way, Bill was my first coach. Unlike the authoritarian leadership style I was used to, Bill showed me that a leader could focus on results *and* care for the person at the same time.

In 1999, I joined the Dallas office of Personnel Decisions International (PDI), an international leadership assessment, coaching, and talent development firm; at the time, Bill was heading PDI's operation in Hong Kong. The PDI years constituted an accelerated professional developmental experience for me, a period during which I had the opportunity to work on leadership assessment, workshop facilitation, and 1-1 coaching with leading multinational corporations such as HP, Dell, Compaq, Shell, PG&E, and Coca-Cola.

Two aspects of this developmental experience were fascinating for me: learning the art of coaching through provocative questioning, and observing the transformation of both coach and coachee. I remember working with a young lady, newly-promoted to the role of director, who wanted to enhance her executive presence and assertiveness. Young as I was, and unsure of what to offer her, I didn't feel comfortable taking on this assignment. So I decided to share with her, in our first meeting, my uncertainty and (of course) my commitment to learning together with her. For the next 9 months, coach and coachee explored new territories together. As a result, we formed a strong partnership and remained friends for years. During this coaching process, I learned the importance of humility, out of which commitment to learning and change became possible.

On September 11th, 2001, I watched the TV news in disbelief and dialed Bill's number. "Why is this happening, Bill?" To which Bill answered, "I don't know, Karen. I really don't know. But there must be a meaning somewhere…."

In the aftermath of 9/11, I made a personal decision to be closer to my family, and I moved from San Francisco to Hong Kong. Reporting to Bill, I took on the responsibility of expanding PDI's business in China. This meant a lot of trips to Shanghai and Beijing. There was also a lot of learning —how to recruit, train and retain team members, and how to develop business and manage coachee relationships. During this time, I continued to learn from Bill the true essence of coaching: humility, trust, encouragement, and role-modeling.

Once we had to present the final project summary to a group of "quite picky" senior HR leaders from a British firm. I was nervous, worked hard on the presentation, and sent it to Bill for review the day before the meeting. I didn't hear back from Bill, so I went to ask him for feedback early the next morning. Bill looked up from his desk, gave me his usual big smile and said, "Relax, Karen. I know it's in good hands. It will go well." And it did.

Years later, as I started to manage a sizable HR team at Wal-Mart, I tried to follow Bill's way, delegating, empowering, and trusting. There was a young girl who was smart, a quick learner, but who couldn't maintain accuracy when consolidating data from the system. One afternoon, she came into my office, frustrated and with tears in her eyes: "I've been told not to make mistakes again like I have in the past two months. I need to submit the new report tomorrow morning, and I'm just not sure I've got it right." At that moment I could see Bill sitting right in front of me, so I said, "Relax, Lillian, I know it's in good hands. It will go well." She nodded and went back to check again.

Trust is one of the highest forms of motivation. It brings out the best in others.

After years spent consulting with different client organizations, I started to wonder what it would be like to work inside a company. So in 2003 I joined Wal-Mart Global Procurement, the direct import procurement division of Wal-

Mart U.S. I initially managed the Organization Development team, and later took on the role of HR director, overseeing the entire HR function for Overseas Operations. Wal-Mart has a deep-rooted, people-oriented culture. Working in the HR function of a people-driven company provided a significant platform to create, contribute, and learn. The HR team at the overseas headquarters in Shenzhen provided support on recruitment, C&B, L&D, and employee relations to over twenty overseas offices in China, EMEA, South-East Asia and Latin America.

As the youngest member of the leadership team, and its only female member, it wasn't easy for this "hot-shot ex-consultant" to gain trust and build partnerships with the internal stakeholders. I started to wear dark suits and glasses, and intentionally speak up at meetings. I quickly learned that it didn't matter very much how articulate I was, how professional I looked, or how sleek my PowerPoints looked. What to do?

We launched a 360-based leadership development project. I remember the guarded looks and cautious eyes during the conversation about the stakeholders' key development needs. So I went back to one of the basics of coaching: active listening. Through observation, open-ended questions, paraphrasing, and being present with the stakeholders when things got tough, I began to understand the *context* of their work. People then started opening up about their challenges and frustrations, and we were able to partner and get through the challenges together. As Bill said, "there is always a meaning in every challenge."

I entered my thirties at this time, and the key personal challenge I was facing was common to many Chinese women at this stage of life: managing the family anxiety of still being single. I dreaded the many calls received from family members and relatives every Chinese New Year, showing their concern and sharing loads of advice. I don't even remember how many conversations I had with my parents on this topic, but eventually they seemed to come to terms with my belief: true love is worth waiting for.

In 2003, I met "L" from Philadelphia, who was also working in Hong Kong. We shared the same hobbies of running and basketball. We were two busy professionals who found time to slowly develop our relationship, becoming engaged during the Chinese New Year of 2005. Needless to say, my parents were very excited.

One month later, in the middle of our annual global HR conference in

Shenzhen, I received a call from a doctor in Hong Kong: "Please come to the hospital ASAP; L is in very serious condition." He was diagnosed with late-stage lung cancer. We were both in a daze, unsure how a non-smoking sports fanatic could be diagnosed with this. Two days later, I accompanied L back to Philadelphia, where he started intense treatment. For the next eight and half months, I commuted back and forth from Hong Kong to Philadelphia.

The most difficult were the initial days. I did not know the right things to do, or the right people to talk to. I called Bill, in tears. He said, in the same caring voice, "Oh Karen, I don't know why this has happened. It will be okay. He is very lucky to have you. There must be a meaning somewhere…."

I read over 30 books on cancer, integrated medicine, the healing of body, mind and soul, and on death and dying. As I accompanied L through various treatments, I learned to practice self-coaching: self-awareness, self-acceptance, and self-care. Yoga and journaling were my two best friends during this period. I discovered that the best gift you can offer someone who is approaching the end of life is your peace, acceptance, and positive faith. And of course, your smile and presence.

It was the first death I had witnessed. I thought it would be scary and troubling; instead, it was very sacred, intimate, and profound. We had peaceful dialogue at the end—not many words, but enough to show that there was hope at the end of life. "It will be okay," I knew.

It was during this period of regular visits to Philadelphia that I discovered that the University of Pennsylvania was offering a master's degree program in applied positive psychology (MAPP), a program led by Dr. Martin Seligman, the founder of positive psychology. I was immediately attracted by the notion of positive interventions and development, decided to apply for the MAPP program, and became the first Chinese student to be enrolled in it.

In the program, I learned the essence of positive psychology—positive human functioning, flourishing in life, factors contributing to a well-lived and fulfilling life, resilience, and growth through adversity. I realized that there was indeed deep meaning in going through adversity: *adversarial growth, finding and leveraging strengths, learned optimism, mindfulness, self-efficacy and positive beliefs, humility, and the continuous journey of learning and transformation...*

In 2007, I was ready for a new challenge, professionally. Deep down, I was looking for a place where I could test the learning from U Penn. I subsequently joined Microsoft as Director of People and Organization Capability, overseeing the organizational development, leadership development, and learning and talent management functions for the Greater China region.

Microsoft has a distinctively different culture from that of Wal-Mart. In addition to the differences between retail and hi-tech, there were many individuals who were not only highly intelligent, but also critical and demanding, with shorter attention spans. Many silos, multiple communication channels with headquarters, and different business units and functions definitely brought a new set of challenges.

I started to wonder how these smart, critical people would react to a strengths-based approach to leadership. So I tried. I asked the leader who was complaining to one of his team members: what was one strength of this individual that could help him at this moment? I also suggested a team exercise called "treasure-hunt," during which the members of a team would offer positive encouragement and suggestions to each other. People reacted with thoughtful, smiling eyes and, often, red faces.

As well, I started to deliver a series of "Happiness Seminars" during lunch breaks, initially for a small group of people interested in positive psychology. Then the small group became bigger. People began coming to the sessions to share their personal experiences, reflections, and practices, and how exercises of gratitude, self-efficacy, learned optimism, etc., had changed them and their teams.

I realized that it was the pursuit of happiness, as well as the desire for sustained meaning in life, that was driving their learning and practice. It meant that there was a real opportunity to promote ways of unleashing potential and flourishing lives in China.

Working with Microsoft brought another breakthrough. I had known "C," a fellow Church member, for a long time. He knew me well, and was there for me as I went through the toughest moments. We were different in so many ways: one from Spain and one from China, a banker and a psychologist, one outgoing and one reserved, one organized and one spontaneous. Yet we shared a lot in common: faith, yoga, traveling, and a love of reading.

We married in 2007. I wrote in my diary: "On the journey of finding love, you searched and searched and were so tired that you wanted to give up. This is an internal battle. When you have won over the suspicion, frustration, and disappointment in your heart, when you decide to keep faith in love, just as you keep faith in life, then love happens at the most unexpected place. There is true meaning in every adversity."

I became a mother at the end of 2011. With the arrival of Anna, life offered a new direction. One area of focus in applied positive psychology is positive education, integrating education with well-being through the development of positive character traits. There is indeed a significant opportunity for character development with the young Chinese generation.

It was not easy to say farewell to Microsoft, and many of the colleagues are still my friends to this day. In 2011, I took a leap and started the Integrated Development Group (IDG), opening its first office in Beijing and the second, later, in Shanghai where I am now based.

IDG was one of the first firms in China to focus on the application of positive psychology. Over the past ten years, we have built delivery teams focusing on positive organizations, positive education, and positive individuals. In addition to supporting kids and their families, we support corporate clients—Chinese and multinational firms and, increasingly, local start-ups.

Becoming an entrepreneur presented a whole new set of challenges: hiring the right people, motivating them, being strategic while also able to drive execution, balancing delegation with attending to details, forging strategic partnerships with others, learning to say no to stay focused on the right priorities, and taking care of myself for the long haul. I continue to benefit from coaching, from my daughter, my husband, my team members and, often, clients going through similar journeys as I did.

I remember coaching a lady who was the newly-promoted general manager of the China subsidiary of a French company. Her manager in France put the coaching goal very simply: help her to transition smoothly to the new leadership role. The GM encountered one challenge after another: leadership team turnover, supply chain problems, headquarters restructuring, a change of boss, a huge budget cut-back, and others! It felt like the situation, years ago, when, as a new coach, I didn't know what to do. So we explored and internalized together. We celebrated small successes, and kept reminding each other that there would be positive meaning arising from these challenges. Not only did she rise to be the star of the year, company-wide, but she also learned to be a better leader, and a better mother, during the process. Again, I learned the power of humility and commitment to learning and change.

Along the way, I kept the habit of journaling. "Life is not easy. You grow when you try something which isn't easy. You are bound to find meaning as you face and deal with adversity."

Our Mandarin program, "The Secret to Positive Psychology," began live streaming in China in June 2017. The program, which consolidated research findings and wisdom from positive psychology over the past decade (including case examples, self-assessments, and application methodology), was well-received, reaching over 800,000 times/listeners within six months.

I am spending more time, now, partnering with educators and teachers to integrate positive education into development programs for children and youth. In an era when depression is spreading among our kids like flu, I hope more and more people will have access to these sets of wonderful tools and methodologies.

I care deeply about the well-being of Chinese people, including the wellbeing of children, their parents and grandparents, and those who struggle with work demands and career progression. Positive psychology can be applied to foster meaning and happiness for all of us, especially at a time of great and rapid economic and social change.

I have witnessed the positive transformation of so many lives, including my own. It is indeed a privilege to be doing this work.

More than anything, I want to do my best to be a caring mother and wife. These days, I cook dinner for the family wherever possible. Nothing is more fulfilling than the joyful sharing at the family dinner table.

I think, sometimes, about the little girl from Qingdao, staring at the ocean. I also see her face, as a young woman, standing on the stage, face tense, ready for her first workshop. And I remember Bill's voice saying, "There must be a meaning somewhere."

Life is magical when you believe in it.

Thank you, Bill Mobley, for showing me the magic of transformation.

Alex Eunkyeong Yu

Chapter 15.
Accessing and Developing
One's Potential

"The only person you are destined to become is the person you decide to be."
 – Ralph Waldo Emerson

I call myself an "accidental practitioner of coaching." I never thought about being a professional, nor was I ever encouraged to be one. It was not until my mid-30s that I even considered it, when a friend called to ask if I would be interested in working for an interior design firm, in Seoul, taking care of the firm's English communication. Born and raised in Busan, one of the most conservative cities in Korea, I thought that my life would just evolve as a good daughter, good student, then a good wife and mother. There was a choice of continuing on to a PhD program after I finished my first master's degree but, frankly, I didn't consider myself to be "PhD material." Instead, I got married, soon had a daughter, and filled some of my spare time translating English novels, and literary or art theories, into Korean. One of my projects involved translating feminist theories for a feminist magazine. Interestingly, I never spotted the gap between the content of the translated articles and my own life as a full-time wife and mother.

When I got the call to enter a "profession," it was less of a clear decision to get into professional life and more about exploring something "new" that made me accept the offer. Fifteen minutes into the interview, I was offered a manager's position, as my age matched that role in the firm. The interior design firm proved an ideal environment for me to discover what was happening in the business world. As the firm primarily catered to major global companies, I had to understand how client businesses functioned in order to understand their floor plans. As a quick learner with excellent organization and coordination skills, I grew into the role of project manager, and within a year, I was handling a USD 2 million project for a global tech giant's 12-story office fit-out.

I became serious about having a professional career after a year of working at the firm and decided to go to business school in the U.S. I simply felt the need to learn more about business if I was to continue. Receiving a scholarship from the Thunderbird School of Global Management made my choice of school easy, and it led to increased opportunities for expanding my global knowledge and contacts. Being in an environment where 75% of the student body was from all over the world naturally exposed me to additional opportunities for international collaboration.

I came back to the interior design firm after Thunderbird, half out of loyalty and half because I could not find a better opportunity elsewhere. I became a restructuring consultant, focusing on operational efficiency, and subsequently took charge of the International Division. However, soon afterwards, as I felt that my learning from business school was not being fully leveraged, I decided to leave the firm, even with the uncertainty of not knowing what could be next.

Wanting to show respect to my former boss, who had hired me when I had no standing in the business world, I did not just jump into a new position. Rather, I spent the next 6 months deep in soul-searching, deliberating about what I really wanted from life, wanting to reorient my life from the ground up. Did I really want to work in the business world? If so, doing what? It was almost at the end of 6 months that I picked up a book by Dr. Geert Hofstede about intercultural management. The book made sense of all my experiences working with foreign clients, and I felt that I had found a topic for which I felt excitement and enthusiasm. I contacted the Dutch consulting company mentioned in Hofstede's book and began representing them in Korea. I set up my own, one-person consulting firm and became an intercultural management consultant. Looking back, this was the second project I initiated, after deciding to go to business school in the US, in which I made my own conscious choice about the direction of my life.

The timing of this second decision was good, as 2004 was the year Korean conglomerates started to grow into global companies. I worked with Korean expatriate managers overseas, with foreign leaders working with Koreans, and with leaders from the C-suite on down, at various organizations. Apart from interacting with Chinese students at Thunderbird, this was the first time I gained substantial business experience with Chinese culture and leaders. After observing that nuanced cultural differences among East Asian countries sometimes caused unexpected conflicts, I decided to write a cultural training book, Cultural Detective East Asia, comparing cultural similarities and differences among Chinese, Japanese, and Koreans.

It was in 2008 when one of the Korean conglomerates approached me to be a coach for their country heads in foreign subsidiaries. When the person asked whether I had a coaching credential, I remember thinking, "Why on earth do I need a certificate to be a coach, when I already do lots of 1:1 consulting?" I had heard of coaching as a field but had no clue what the process really entailed. I thought it was simply a fancy name for a 1:1 interaction in management consulting. Regardless, to comply with the client's request, I searched for a coaching certificate program and found Fielding Graduate University's Evidence-Based Coaching program. I recalled that Dr. Adair Nagata, a Fielding graduate, had earlier recommended the PhD program as her best learning experience, so I had researched it. At the time, it all seemed "Greek" to me, and once again I thought of myself as "not PhD material." When I discovered Fielding's year-long coaching certificate program, I thought that it could be a trial for their PhD program.

Fielding's Evidence-Based Coaching (EBC) was an eye opener for me. Coaching is neither 1:1 consulting, nor is it a nice dialogue. It is a discipline dedicated to bringing out the best version of a person, and the process of change and transformation through collaborative enquiry is now evidenced by rigorous research and science. What fascinated me most were systems theory and organizational change theory. Those theories were "nudges" for me to see and go beyond individuals; in a word, they were an invitation into big-picture thinking. The EBC program was not just about the science of coaching, but also about the art of coaching. The art part of coaching is mostly defined by who you are and how you show up as a coach. The journey of becoming a coach in the EBC program turned out to be more than training culminating in a certificate; it became a transformational journey for life that opened more possibilities for me.

At the core of the transformational journey was the Fielding EBC community, which was so supportive of learning and development. At the end of the EBC program, it felt natural for me to apply for the PhD program in Human and Organizational Systems. Looking back, the EBC program was the first time I was exposed to theories of human and organizational development in a systemic way, and it stimulated me to reflect upon the meaning of supporting others' developmental process, and how privileged it is to be a companion on that journey. My curiosity was definitely tantalized, and I wanted to learn more about the subject. Being or not being "PhD material" was not even a question this time, as I embarked on the journey of becoming a PhD.

It was in my first year of the PhD program that I became acquainted with Dr. Marjorie Woo, and through her, Dr. William Mobley. What impressed me from the beginning was their gentle inclusiveness, and their generosity in offering opportunities for growth. They put trust in me from the beginning and opened the door for me to work with leaders in China and the broader Asia Pacific Region, through offering an opportunity to work with Dr. Mobley's consulting firm in Shanghai. Frankly, I was not sure, initially, whether I was worthy of their trust. When Bill suggested the opportunity to lead a leadership development program in China for a global food and beverage company, I did not feel that I quite "clicked" with the project's focus, and declined. Bill did not push me, but gently smiled and said, "Well, let's look for another opportunity, then." I also declined Bill's second suggestion, with a different excuse. Looking back, it was not that I didn't like the topic or the industry, rather that I was not yet ready to stretch my comfort zone through marching into unknown territory. I thought that Bill would never come back to me with another offer but, luckily for me, he did. The next suggestion was partnering with him, so that I could learn from his role-modeling. He never gave up believing in people. Instead, he kept changing his strategy until the other ran out of excuses. He was patient and made it safe for me, one who initially resisted plunging in to learn how to swim in the vast sea of China.

The Chinese leaders I met were like sponges, seeking to absorb all the learning they could find. That was understandable, as most Chinese leaders were working, at the time, in a rapidly developing economic system, one operating beyond their level of development in terms of its size and level of complexity. Harvard Professor Robert Kegan described this mismatch between a leader's developmental level and the complexity of her/his context in his book *In Over Our Heads*. However, the ripple effects of the positive impacts they could create when they could match their level of maturity to the system were immense.

In one case, I coached a Chinese VP at a global financial institution on the topic of better managing her global stakeholders. The VP initially thought the work would mostly involve upgrading her skills in interaction and communication. She did adapt her approach according to the stakeholders' differing backgrounds and preferences, but the really exciting change started to happen when she reformulated the coaching question: "How might we use coaching dialogue to co-create meaningful outcomes that serve the bigger organizational system?" The client realized that while her initial approach to communicating might well support her next promotion, her reframed question positioned her as a global player, and opened up more possibilities to interact with stakeholders based on mutual respect and responsibility. This reframing also enabled her to enjoy her interactions with counterparts in the region and at Global Headquarters.

Chinese leaders could easily stay focused solely on career achievements. Who wouldn't, in an environment of ample opportunities for higher and faster achievement? In my observation, it was when clients shifted their attention to listening to their inner voices, and changing their perspectives, that transformation happened. This may be the exact reason why China needs more transformational coaches; coaches can be partners in the success of Chinese leaders. More than that, this partnership on the journey will help create positive influences on those surrounding these leaders.

I could see the transformational power of coaching easily when I worked with fellow coaches in China. Many of those in Keystone's EBC program in China have been touched by coaching in a positive way. They felt more empowered; their lives got bigger through coaching. What brought them to the journey of becoming (or being) a coach was a desire to expand the ripple effects of possibility, and to support transformational opportunities for others. Coaching is all about expanding possibilities, and coaches need to embrace those possibilities themselves first.

I remember a young management consultant who was sent to a coaching program by her firm. Initially, she thought coaching was a nice addition to her profile. Being smart and ambitious, she started a promising career as a consultant, but her approach to her profession and her clients was overly-transactional. As she was exposed to what coaching is really about, she created a different professional identity, one based on the larger purpose of creating a more positive society through the transformational coaching of leaders. Another coaching student was the office director of an architecture firm. She had lost enthusiasm for her work and was encountering a crisis in her private life. She then had a chance to work with a coach and felt the power of coaching. Coaching helped her to overcome the crisis and become centered again in her work and broader life. This positive experience made her pursue a new career as a coach, as she wanted to be the one who helps empower other female professionals, just like her coach had helped her.

Looking back, lessons I derived from my coaching journey include, first, to make a conscious choice of how to construct your life. Create a situation rather than wait for a situation to happen for you . I remember, growing up, my family motto was "Do not initiate things unless you have to (especially women)." However, starting with making the decision to go to a U.S. business school, when I made a conscious choice of my next steps life opened doors for me.

Second, life always opens doors for you when you listen attentively with open curiosity. Say "Yes, and . . ." to what is happening. It takes the same energy as resisting what is happening.

Last, be the one who believes in people and fosters an environment wherein they can bring their best versions of themselves. There were many coaches and mentors who guided my developmental journey, Dr. William Mobley being one of the most notable. I intend to pay forward his and their generosity for the benefit of the larger community of coaches.

Becoming a coach is an ever-humbling process, a lifelong learning journey, as well as an opportunity to contribute to the bigger system by supporting more leaders to create positive impact in each of their organizations. Going forward, offering coaching supervision will enable me to contribute further to the coaching field. Through collaborative inquiry with fellow coaches, I hope to support the growth and development of coaches' capacities to work more deeply so as to better serve their current and future clients and all of the ecological systems involved in their coaching work. Coaching supervision is both challenging and enjoyable as it aims to keep both parties at their learning edges. Why not use this learning platform to keep ourselves living on the edge of discovery continuously!

Chapter 16.
A Personal Story:
Becoming a Leadership
Coach – Many Firsts

Yimin Wang

"Follow what inspires me, release what diminishes me."
  –Diane Dreher

I am Yimin Wang, an early graduate of Keystone Group's EBC program. During and after my journey to becoming a coach, I took to heart and applied the principles of coaching, including self-reflection, to changing my own career path. I learned to focus on the needs of coachees from a broad array of MNC and Chinese companies by applying effective coaching skills and foundational theories to coachees. I also extended the application of these principles to the broader Chinese community, by helping a number of charitable organizations in China to grow and meet the needs of their constituents. This is my story of some of my "firsts" during this journey.

My first encounter with leadership coaching was during a corporate training program in 2008. 2020 marks the 10th year of my first structured coaching training with evidenced-based coaching (EBC). Looking back on the last 10 years, what are some memorable moments? What role has coaching played in my work, life, community-building, and beyond? When I lay my head down, close my eyes, some of these moments surface naturally.

First homework –

During the Spring Festival of 2011, I was working on my first homework assignment from the EBC program. I can still feel my excitement, curiosity, and enthusiasm for the program, a 10-week online course from Fielding Graduate University. I checked the online learning system every day and read every single response of my 11 classmates and of our professors.

The program opened a new horizon for me. It provided a solid structure for me to learn a new subject, to explore a different way of communicating, to gain a new perspective. What was more, the program planted a seed for my transition to becoming a leadership coach. Within 12 months of completing the program, I decided to focus on coaching and talent development.

First internship –

I was offered pro-bono coaching internship programs with some business schools. One of these was a mentor-mentee program with Shanghai International Studies University (SISU). I participated in that program in 2011 and coached four MBA students. I still stay in touch with those four students. I recently asked one of them, "What do you remember about our coaching partnership?" The answer was, "You made me think, you helped me understand myself better, and I changed one behavior."

This kind of internship program has become a common element for many coaching institutions in China. It offers benefits to each of the three parties involved. For junior coaches, it is a safe stepping-stone that helps them hone their coaching skills, build credibility, and increase their confidence.

First paid coaching work –

During the EBC program, I made an effort to mention to my contacts that I had started to do leadership coaching. Pretty soon, I got my first paid coaching work, from a former colleague who wanted to give her husband Matt a special birthday gift. I was so fortunate to have such a great coachee who was mature, highly-conscious, and up-and-coming. I was very careful and diligent in every aspect of our coaching process. One learning from that engagement: I tended to explain too much.

I later asked for Matt's endorsement, and he wrote, "It is very lucky for me to have Yimin as my coach. He helped transform the coaching sessions from 'symptom' talks to a soul-searching process. His professionalism, accountability and passion to make an impact enabled me to think bigger and deeper about both my professional life and my personal life. On top of that, he also helped me conceive proper action plans and make things happen."

What have I learned? First, that there is no perfect time to announce that you are a coach, or whatever new endeavor you have started. There is no point to wait until you get a certificate or graduate. Second, business usually comes from someone who trusts you. Third, a great coachee has the qualities of being highly-committed and willing to change; these are a recipe for success.

First coaching platform endeavor –

While I enjoyed learning and networking in my new capacity as a coach, I started to realize that many of my peers were not utilizing their talents and experiences, which I found a pity. I started a coaching platform, Sense Mentoring, in 2012. I hoped to fill a market need by utilizing those coaches' experiences and passion. The platform offers 1:1 career coaching and mentoring to young professionals seeking personal growth. I worked out the business model with my business partner, Stephen, but we soon realized that, without a large investment, it was not possible to make the program into a viable business. So we changed its operation to part-time.

Thanks to many volunteers, including both coaches and coachees, we were able to operate for almost four years. During that time, we wrote articles on our WeChat account and organized regular workshops to promote the concept of coaching, demonstrate its impact, and attract coachees who believed in us. I have many fond memories of organizing mentor meetings, handling inquiries from potential coachees, and matching coachees with coaches.

It was with some pity that I decided to stop operating Sense Mentoring. It was, however, a great learning experience for me, as I went on to build several communities over the years. I am now more experienced and focused on building communities.

First action in charity –

While I was coaching corporate leaders, I would sometimes challenge myself, "Your past is history; what about now? Can you walk the talk?" I imagined that my coachees probably had the same thought. An interesting opportunity presented itself in 2013. It was a fundraiser, in the form of a walkathon, where participants had to finish a 50 km walk in one day. The goal of the participants was to raise as much money as possible through their networks. I signed up for it without hesitation and formed a team of six within a matter of days. I then organized several meetings, during which we decided our team name and slogan. I also organized many training sessions to ensure that all my team members got enough practice. It turned out that all except one completed the entire 50 km. Our team raised more than 10,000 USD.

Guess what my personal slogan was? Walk the talk! I was proud to tell my coachees that I am a man of my word and that I wanted to hold them accountable for their actions, too. I also became more and more involved in charity work.

First leadership coaching assignment –

My first leadership coaching assignment came quickly and easily. In 2012, a coach referred me to her coachee, the Greater China CEO of a US company, who was looking for a coach for one of his team members. I met the CEO, the HRVP, then my coachee. Then, I got the job.

I worked with my coachee for approximately eight months. The feedback from the CEO and other key stakeholders was so positive that the company decided to promote my coachee ahead of their original plan. Over the next three years, the scope of her responsibilities grew from 100 million USD to 500 million

USD, and she got two more promotions.

What did I learn? That networking and business referrals are critical. If our work is good, or perceived to be good, others will feel comfortable referring new coachees to us. Also, that coaching is a two-way street, so it is critical that our coachee be committed to making a change and that we are able to support that. In my experience, my coachee had a tremendous transformation, and I was proud to be the catalyst for it.

First personal branding statement –

When my coaching practice took off, I tried to establish a unique reputation. One of the things that I thought long and hard about was my personal branding. So I came up with my first branding statement, ACE, an acronym that means Aware, Change, and Excel. This explains my coaching philosophy and my coaching approach. I put the three keywords on my name card and called myself Coach ACE.

I am of the view that every coach (especially freelance coaches) needs to have a unique branding statement. Of course, our brands keep transforming as we mature. I am no longer Coach ACE. I keep asking myself, however, "What sets you apart? What do you stand for? How do you deliver your unique value?" I then update my branding statements periodically.

First seemingly-impulsive business decision –

I have always been quite cautious and deliberate in my decision-making. But that pattern made a huge shift in February 2015. I went to Hong Kong to get certified in a new assessment tool I would use in a leadership development program that I was about to deliver. The learning experience was so gratifying that I started to scribble in my notebook that very same evening in my hotel room about a China-focused business roadmap for the use of this new tool. My thinking and scribbling lasted for quite some time, and I was still awake at midnight. I thought it was a signal, because I seldom have trouble falling asleep, even when faced with highly-challenging situations. So the next day, I asked the trainer to introduce me to the founder and CEO of the company offering the tool, Dr. Stewart Desson. I then proposed to Stewart that I run his China business. We had some discussions and negotiations, and I became their exclusive distributor in China in March 2015.

Looking back at my seemingly impulsive decision of five years ago, it actually had quite a lot to do with coaching. Never before had I encountered an assessment that was so aligned with my coaching philosophy—that everyone is complicated and unique, everyone has potential, and that we can create better results by understanding each other and embracing diversity.

The decision led me to take on a new challenging venture, to build another engaging community, and to continue to expand my business scope. Our community has attracted many leading consultants and coaches, and we are known for our openness, compassion, and humility.

First community level pro bono service –

2020 is the 10-year anniversary of the fund-raising walkathon. When I read the 10-year anniversary brochure, a thought came up—why don't I initiate a pro bono service agreement with the Shanghai United Foundation? So, I did. I have already assembled a team of volunteers from our coach practitioners. We offer pro bono coaching, facilitation, and consulting services to Shanghai United Foundation and its key stakeholders, including members of its Donor-Advised Fund (DAF) and other major donors.

In September 2020, three influential, female-led DAFs, Unlimited Her, San He Yi, and 250 Love, came together for social networking, storytelling, and best-practice sharing. I had the honor to co-design and co-facilitate the party.

Final thoughts –

Are there any patterns? Can I connect the dots? I can name a few—my desire to fully utilize people's talents, my passion to build a collaborative community, and my drive to serve more people and make more of an impact. Coaching has definitely influenced my way of thinking and being, my business decisions, and my life journey.

About the Authors

Dedication

Allen L. Parchem, PhD is the retired chairman and CEO of RHR International. During his tenure, the firm renewed its commitment to serving clients around the world and providing support to the development of consulting psychology. He initiated strategic equity interests in Talent Intelligence (Australia, U.K.) and Mobley Group Pacific (Shanghai, Hong Kong). Previously, as COO of RHR, he oversaw operations in North America (Canada and U.S.) and Europe (London, Brussels, Cologne, and Moscow). In his 40-year consulting career, he has consulted with senior executives at major national and international corporations. Dr. Parchem assisted clients in the following areas: succession planning, executive assessment, senior leader development, high potential identification, new leader integration, and organizational change implementation. Dr. Parchem was awarded the Distinguished Psychologist in Management Award from the Society of Psychologists in Management (SPIM). He is also a fellow of the American Psychological Association, Division 13. Allen can be reached through aparchem@alpendeavors.com.

Foreword

Marcia Reynolds, PsyD, MCC has delivered programs in 41 countries and reached hundreds of thousands more online on leadership topics and mastery in coaching. She is a past global president of the International Coaching Federation (ICF) and recently inducted into the ICF Circle of Distinction. Currently, She is the training director for the Healthcare Coaching Institute in North Carolina and on faculty for coaching schools in China, Russia, and the Philippines. Global Gurus recognizes her as one of the top 5 coaches in the world. She has authored four books, including her latest international bestseller, Coach the Person, Not the Problem. Read more at www.Covisioning.com. Marcia can be reached through marcia@outsmartyourbrain.com

Preface and Introduction

Marjorie Woo, PhD, MCC is founder and a member of the Board of Directors of Keystone Group Shanghai, Inc., a coaching service enhancer dedicated to the development of coaches and the coaching profession in China and Asia. During her more than 30 years of executive leadership, Dr. Woo worked as a managing executive of the Xerox Corporation, founded Keystone Group Shanghai, Inc., and founded Leadership Management International China Ltd. As an executive coach for 32 years, she set an example of excellence, coaching executives in China and other Asia Pacific countries. Since 1998, Dr Woo and her cohort have coached over 2,000 managers and senior-level executives per year, and a total of over 30,000 mid-level managers in China in companies such as General Electric, IBM, Microsoft, Hewlett-Packard, BASF, AXA, Schindler and Texas Instruments, among many others. She holds a doctorate in Human and Organizational Development Systems from Fielding Graduate University in Santa Barbara, California. She is a master certified coach (MCC), and on the board of the International Coaching Federation, supporting programs for the Credentialed Professional Coaches Certification Program. Marjorie can be reached through woomarjorie@gmail.com

Sabine Menon, PhD, a French citizen, has been an expatriate for over 20 years. She has lived and worked in the UK, Germany, the USA, and Argentina. After working at the London Business School, Sabine relocated to Shanghai, China in 2009 and founded Reflections, which has now over 20 associates worldwide. She is the only China-based INSEAD coach and is a supervisor in the Executive Master in Consulting and Coaching for Change (EMCCC). Sabine coaches individuals at senior levels and C-suite as well as working with global leadership team—mostly expatriates but also local Chinese working for MNCs in Asia. She helps individuals optimize their performance by increasing their awareness of self and behaviors. Sabine brings a unique set of neuro-psychology, business, and cross-cultural background; her technique blends academic rigor with pragmatic solutions grounded in the business context. She is also a fully accredited mindfulness teacher. Sabine can be reached through sabinemenon@me.com.

Yi Wang, ACC was among the first batch of US returnees who went back to China and joined the HR profession in the mid-1990s after a few years of business consulting in the US. Her career coincides with a period of robust growth for multinational companies in China. Yi's HR work spans across China, US, and Hong Kong in telecom, financial services, and pharmaceutical industries. Her career is not short of historical moments such as Motorola's decline, the 2008 financial crisis, and the GSK crisis in China. These experiences taught Yi where and how to contribute to both enterprises and people. Yi got her ACTP in 2009 and is now an ICF ACC. She was a GSK certified internal coach and is also certified by Hogan. Coaching is a life-long passion for Yi as she is grateful to work with clients and help them in whatever way they need. Besides coaching, Yi advises fast-growing Chinese companies on organization and talent strategies. Yi can be reached through yiwang9208@outlook.com.

Frank Rexach, MS brings a broad range of international executive experience to his career portfolio, spending more than two decades of living and working across Asia culminating with the position of Vice President Asia Pacific at WeWork in Shanghai during its start-up phase in China. Frank also held senior leadership regional roles across multiple industries including property management, technology, furniture, and office products. In addition to China, Frank was based in Australia, Hong Kong, and France. Among other acknowledgements, he was awarded by the Shanghai government the Magnolia Award in recognition of his contribution to the city's development. He earned a Bachelor of Science from the University of Southern California and a master's in international management from the Thunderbird School of Global Management at Arizona State University. Frank can be reached through rexachf@yahoo.com.

Jason Ramey, CPA, is an accomplished global executive who has served on the Global Leadership Team of Grant Thornton. He is responsible for leading service lines, driving strategic growth, and developing capabilities. Jason was previously US National Managing Partner of International Client Services. Jason has been working with clients with operations in China for almost two decades, and he completed an assignment in China from 2007 to 2011 where he served in senior leadership roles, executed global strategy, and led efforts to develop leadership talent and significantly grow and scale the China business. Jason held previous roles at TL & Co, Arthur Andersen, and PwC. Jason has a BBA–Accounting degree from Texas A&M University and completed the International Senior Leadership Program at University of Oxford. He serves as board chair of the Global Food banking Network and he serves on the Board of the Chinese Fine Arts Society of Chicago. Jason can be reached through jason@ jasondramey.com.

James C. Warner, PhD, is the CEO of Keystone Group and president of the Keystone Coaching Academy. Keystone Group is one of the first coaching training organizations in China to be accredited by ICF at the ACTP level and has produced a large number of China's PCC-level coaches. His previous leadership experience includes managing director and senior partner of Korn Ferry Leadership and Talent Consulting – China, founder of his own leadership development and coaching consultancy in 1986, and other senior executive roles with technology companies in the US. James has served as adjunct faculty at Beijing Normal University, Concordia University, and the University of Minnesota. He holds a PhD in the Psychology of Human Development from the University of Minnesota. James has lived in Shanghai since 2010. James can be reached through jamescwarner@msn.com

Amanda Shang, MSC is chairman of Keystone Group and also a licensee in LMI China. In 2012, she began to work as a leadership coach in China. She has trained and coached more than 200 students. She graduated from Sheffield Hallam University in the U.K., earning a Master of Science in International Marketing. Amanda can be reached through Amanda.Shang@keystonegroup. cn.

Jeff Hasenfratz, JD is managing director of Mindsight Executive Development Services, a Shanghai-based consulting firm focused on helping senior leaders improve their team and organizational effectiveness through more valuable collaboration. Jeff, an executive team coach, coaching supervisor, dialogue facilitator, and Mandarin speaker, also holds the degree of Juris Doctor. He has lived in Asia for nearly 30 years. Jeff has supported clients in the technology, manufacturing, pharmaceutical, and financial services industries, and was previously associated with Hewlett Packard, Russell Reynolds Associates, and Cincinnati Bell. In his free time, Jeff enjoys deep conversations, travelling, reading, and practicing Chen-style tai chi. Jeff can be reached through jeff@ mindsightasia.com.

Andrew P. Newmark is a Human Resources business partner who has been with Marriott International for 27 years. His multi-market experience crosses over generalist HR operations, L&D, and talent management. With Marriott's significant growth in Asia Pacific, Andrew has played a significant role in the design, development, and delivery of leadership development programs to support the growth of leaders across the region. In 2016, and with Marriott's acquisition of Starwood, Andrew held additional responsibilities for change management and integration efforts of the two companies, with a critical focus on talent and culture. His current role oversees the HR function for 23 countries and 450 operating hotels. Andrew is currently completing his master's degree in change management with the Australian Graduate School of Management. Andrew can be reached through andrew.newmark@marriot.com.

Tom Payne, MS has a Master of Science in I/O Psychology from the University of Wisconsin with an emphasis on the contribution of psychometric assessments in the selection process. He has published articles and presented at the International Association of Applied Psychology (IAAP) and the Society of Industrial/ Organizational Psychology (SIOP) in the US. He is trained and certified in a number of psychometric assessments, and in recent years, he has been heavily involved in the creation and testing of psychometric assessments. Tom was director of Kimberly Clark Human Resources in Asia and VP of HR International for Hanesbrands, stationed in Asia from 1994 through 2012. He was heavily involved in M&A activities for both Kimberly-Clark and Hanesbrands. He has extensive experience in reorganization, right-sizing, and talent management. He set up selection and talent management processes and introduced psychometric assessment to support both processes. He was global head of Customer Development at Assessment Associates International. He is currently co-founder of Talent Assessments International, publisher of the Management Alignment Questionnaire (MAQ), the Talent Alignment Questionnaire (TAQ), Sales Alignment Questionnaire (SAQ), the Professional Alignment Questionnaire

(PAQ), the Applicant Alignment Questionnaire (AAQ), the TAI Job Analysis Questionnaire (JAQ), the TAI 360 Survey for Managers and Executives, and the Cognitive Ability Questionnaire (CAQ). Tom can be reached through tompayne031@gmail.com.

Nancy Zhang, MBA is the founder and CEO of Empower Leaders Consulting, which focuses on supporting leaders and teams through coaching and facilitation. Before she established ELC in 2015, she was the founding partner for Mobley Group Pacific for 11 years, which is one of the leading consulting firms in East Asia for leadership development, talent assessments, and organizational culture. Over the past 16 years, she has built two successful consulting practices, supported over 400 organizations (50% MNC, 40% China local, 10% SOE), coached over 150 senior leaders (primarily CEOs, GMs, VPs and SVPs), and facilitated over 100 top management teams. She has extensive experience in the assessments area and especially in leveraging personality assessments in coaching and other development work. Nancy received her bachelor's degree with a computer science major in 1999, and completed her MBA study at China Europe International Business School (top 5 MBA program by Financial Times 2019). Nancy is passionate about coaching and has been advocating the use of coaching to support people development. Her motto is after the legendary Japanese entrepreneur Kazuo Inamori, "Leveraging oneself to support others to arrive where they'd like to arrive, and they themselves would eventually arrive also." Nancy can be reached through nancyzh@empower-leaders.com.

Axel Kuhlmann started his coaching & development career in 2010 with his education and certification. Moving to Shanghai 2013, he started his own company "akcc", with operations in Shanghai and Hong Kong. Axel served as President of the Shanghai Coaching Circle (TSCC) 2015-2017, arranged gatherings with such world-leading coaches as Marcia Reynolds and Philippe Rosinski. Under his leadership TSCC grew substantially, a fact noted in 2017 with its designation by the ICF Shanghai as the "Most Glocal (Coaching) Community". Axel has lectured at the Shanghai University for Science and Technology and at the African Leadership Academy/Johannesburg. He is also a Co-Founder of Code of Africa, an IT service with the vision to create work and to support education in East Africa. Axel currently works in and from Germany, focusing on systemic changes in organizations. Axel can be reached through axel@akcc.de.

Alan Babington-Smith is a career British international banker who turned to coaching in China. From 2003-2019, he was a founding member of a team of eventually 70 LMI -China coaches who delivered whole-person development programs to teams and individuals, both Chinese and foreign, across the full range of seniority, business scale, and type. As foundations of his coaching, he combined a structured process with his 35 years' multinational and multicultural business experience. He also is a graduate of the Fielding Graduate University Human and Organisational Systems Program. Alan can be reached through alanbs100@outlook.com.

Daniel Denison, PhD is a Professor Emeritus of Management and Organization at IMD. His work on organizational culture and business performance is well known around the world. Prior to joining IMD in 1999, Denison was an Associate Professor of Organizational Behavior and Human Resource Management at the University of Michigan Business School, teaching in MBA, PhD, and Executive Education programs. Professor Denison has taught and lived in Asia, Europe, Latin America, and the Middle East. He received his Bachelor's degree from Albion College in Psychology, Sociology, and Anthropology and his PhD from the University of Michigan in Organizational Psychology. He has authored four books and numerous articles on the importance of organizational culture. Daniel can be reached through dan.denison@imd.org.

Bryan Adkins, EdD is the CEO of Denison Consulting, a global research, diagnostic and organizational development firm known for linking organizational culture and leadership practices to business performance. He works with Fortune 500 organizations from across the globe to build high-performance organizations and leaders. Bryan's work has been published widely in journals and books including *The Journal of Organizational Behavior, Advances in Global Leadership* and *From Promise to Payoff: The Art and Science of Creating a Learning Organization.* His professional background includes leadership positions within the manufacturing, professional, and not-for-profit sectors. Bryan holds a master's degree in business management from Pennsylvania State University and received his doctorate in human and organizational studies from The George Washington University. When he is not traveling the globe in support of clients, he resides on the Monterey Peninsula, California. Bryan can be reached through badkins@denisonculture.com.

Tianran Yin, PhD is an expert in cross-culture management and change management, areas in which she teaches at the graduate level in China and also serves as EMBA and DBA thesis supervisor. She received her PhD in management at the French National Centre for Scientific Research (CNRS), and is recipient of the French National Eiffel Excellence Scholarship. She has spent more than 15 years working with leaders to apply management theories in Fortune 500 companies and large Chinese local firms, including companies like Dell Computer (China) Co. Ltd, Mars Group, Safran Group, Meituan, and HUAFA Group. She was assistant director of Programs in the French business school, EMLYON, and worked to develop international collaboration with top Chinese universities. She has a strong interest in innovation and entrepreneurship, and currently works for HCD Learning as partner. She was also nominated by Chinese Education Department as entrepreneurship tutor. Her case-studies have been published in the *Harvard Business Review* (Asia-Pacific version) and ECCH. She is co-translator of *Immunity to Change,* Chinese version. Tianran can be reached through yintianran333@hotmail.com.

Cindy J.W. Su, PCC has been helping leaders define and reach their goals for or more than sixteen years. She has a Bachelor of Arts from Peking University, China, an IT Management Postgraduate Diploma from DeVry College, Canada, and Evidence-Based Coaching Program certificate from Fielding Graduate University, USA. She is an accredited, certified coach with the International Coaching Federation. She is also a leadership coach and an organization development consultant specializing in organization effectiveness, vertical leadership development, developing emotional and authentic leadership, and supporting executives in transition and change. Cindy has coached leaders in the high-tech, IT, automobile, retail, hospitality, food, and banking industries as well as nonprofits and academia. Cindy Su's coaching case was awarded the trophy of the "ABP Award Finalist" by The Association of Business Psychology, England in 2016. Cindy can be reached through 1956761960@qq.com.

Joey W.K. Chan has been working as an OD consultant for more than 20 years. He lives in Hong Kong with his wife and two sons. Joey strongly believes working leaders can grow, and he also believes it's not always easy. If we can master both the theory and practice of the adult development, we'll have a better chance. In the current theories and practices, Joey finds the work of Jennifer Garvey Berger and her colleagues' "Growth Edge Interview (GEI)" to be the most robust of all. Joey is committed to bringing Growth Edge ideas to the wider public, especially in the Greater China region. He has translated Jennifer's *Changing on the Job: Developing Leaders for a Complex World,* and it became a rare best-seller in this genre. He also co-translated Robert Kegan's *An Everyone Culture* and Frederic Laloux's *Reinventing Organizations* (illustrated version). Joey has been an independent OD consultant to Alibaba and Ant Financial since 2016. Joey can be reached through joey@birdview.com.hk.

Gary Wang is CEO of MindSpan, an ICF accredited coaching training company which he founded in 2006 and which serves over 450 global and local clients, including 133 global Fortune 500 companies. Headquartered in Shanghai, MindSpan serves clients in 18 countries including Greater China, Japan, Korea, Thailand, Singapore, Vietnam, Indonesia, India, Australia, and South Africa. During his career, Gary has extensive leadership experience with MNCs including Greater China country general manager for a division of Dupont and held other senior functional and business leadership positions in Sony, Dell, and Agroloimen. He is an avid marathon runner competing in a number of marathons each year. Gary is committed to being a catalyst to help leaders reach their full potential. Gary can be reached through gary.wang@mindspan.cn.

Pam Van Dyke, PhD, PCC has been helping individuals, teams, groups, and organizations define and reach their goals for more than 25 years. Using evidence-based methodologies, she works across multiple industries and at all levels, though most of her practice is with executives at all different levels within organizations; she does so both face to face and virtually. Pam's diverse background in behavioral health, Fortune 500 companies, and academia provides her with a unique and rich blend to understand the complexities and dynamics of organizational life. In addition to providing consulting and coaching services, Pam is the founder and CEO of Team and Group Coach

Academy, which launched February 2017 to provide ICF continuing education and certification for those interested in team and group coaching. A life-long learner, Pam has obtained multiple certifications and 6 degrees, including a bachelor's degree in sociology and master's degrees in counseling psychology, education, management and organizational development. Her Ph.D. is in human and organizational systems from Fielding Graduate University. Pam is a member of, and holds a coaching credential from International Coaching Federation and has served on the board of the North Texas Chapter. Pam is the author of *Virtual Group Coaching: A Research Study* and she is a contributing author to *The Practitioners Handbook of Team Coaching*. Pam can be reached through drpam@teamandgroupcoachacademy.com.

Joseph Chan, PCC started his international work with Schindler Elevator in 1997, where he served as CIO, AsiaPac and China, HR director. In these roles, he experienced the complex relationship and power dynamics that occur when an organization transforms from a joint venture to wholly-owned foreign enterprise (WOFE). He also led large transformational initiatives in new factory setups and country and regional team reorganization. He was CEO of Keystone Group (Shanghai) and founded his own consulting firm Nuomingda Consulting. He continues to work mostly with MNC clients, such as Grundfos and Dupont. Joseph sees people as the most critical organization success assets and continues to contribute to developing leadership coaches in China as faculty for Keystone Group's EBC program. Even before he began coaching professionally in 2015, he advocated a coaching culture and leader-as-coach practice and saw the benefits in people development readiness, team collaboration, and sustained high performance. As an experienced PCC coach and former vice president of the Shanghai ICF Chapter, he brought the International Coaching Week (ICW) initiative to China to further promote coaching to the public. Joseph holds a Bachelor of Arts in Economics from the University of Winnipeg and a graduate diploma from Finsia. Joseph can be reached through pangchan99@sina.com.

Joyce Yuan Gong, EdD is a Senior Client Partner with Industrial & Financial Service Practice of Korn Ferry International, based in Shanghai. She is also heading China Education Practice, leading to promote Korn Ferry's total talent solutions in China. Ms. Gong has over twenty-five years of experience in human resources consulting in China, and twenty years in the executive search business. Ms. Gong successfully led to build HR functional practice in China, developing "on-boarding process" for senior leaders in China. Ms. Gong holds her Doctor of Education from Rossier School of Education at University of Southern California, a Master in Business Administration from Marshall School of Business at University of Southern California, and a bachelor's degree in Scientific English from Shanghai University. She also completed a master program in Human Resources Management from China Peoples' University. Ms. Gong is a certified coach of International Coach Federation. Joyce can be reached through joyce.gong@kornferry.com.

Katherine Xin, PhD is professor of Management, Bayer chair in Leadership, Director of Leadership Development & Coaching Centre, and Associate Dean (Europe) at the China Europe International Business School (CEIBS) in Shanghai, China. She holds a PhD from the University of California, Irvine, and she was previously on the faculty of the University of Southern California, Hong Kong University of Science and Technology, and IMD, Lausanne, Switzerland. A native of the Chinese mainland, Prof. Xin has extensive teaching, research, and consulting experience around the world. She specializes in the areas of leadership development, organizational culture, and change management. Her research work has appeared in leading international management journals such as the *Academy of Management Journal, Administrative Science Quarterly, Strategic Management Journal, Organization Studies, Leadership Quarterly, Harvard Business Review, etc.* Her most recent books *The Platform Organizations* (2019) and *Understanding Organizational Behavior* (2020) received broad attention from academics and executives alike. Katherine can be reached through katherinexin@ceibs.edu.

Jack Denfeld Wood, PhD is Professor of Management Practice, China Europe International Business School, Shanghai; Visiting Leadership Professor, Moscow School of Management; and Emeritus Leadership Professor Leadership IMD, Switzerland. Academic and practitioner publications include co-authored articles in *ASQ* (2018); *AMLE* (2012: Best Paper in Graduate Management Education Award); *Transactional Analysis Journal* (TAJ); *Financial Times; Forbes;* and numerous book chapters. Interests include leadership, ideology, and group and system dynamics. He's a member of the American Psychological Association, International Association for Analytical Psychology, American Academy of Management, and the International Transactional Analysis Association. He's a former USAF and Air National Guard fighter pilot and FAA instructor pilot. He earned a Master of Arts in Social Psychology from Syracuse University, M.A., M.Phil., and Ph.D. degrees from Yale University, and a diploma from the C.G. Jung Institute, Zürich. He's a practicing analyst, has Swiss and American nationality, and is married with four children.

Monique L. Snowden, PhD is Provost and Senior Vice President at Fielding Graduate University. Dr. Snowden began her professional career as a business consultant and software developer for a global technology solutions and services firm, working as an expatriate project lead for one of the oldest and largest insurers in Japan. She has more than 25 years of higher education leadership experience, with particular expertise in strategic enrollment management, institutional and educational effectiveness, and enhancing data and analytics for equity outcomes. Dr. Snowden is teaching faculty for the University of Southern California Equity Institutes, 2015 - 2016 American Council on Education Fellow, and elected commissioner on the WASC Senior College and University Commission. She earned a BBA in business analysis; MS in management information systems; and PhD in organizational communication from Texas A&M University. Dr. Snowden holds a certified Project Management Professional designation from the Project Management Institute. Monique can be reached through msnowden@ fielding.edu.

Karen Zong, MBA, MAPP is the founder and CEO of Integrated Development Group (IDG), with offices in Shanghai and Beijing. For the past 10 years, IDG has been a champion in applying positive psychology in the development of leaders, teams, individuals, families, and kids. Its mission: to enhance the well-being of Chinese people through the application of the most state-of-the-art findings of positive psychology. Karen can be reached through kzong@idg-asia.com.

Alex Eunkyeong Yu, PhD, PCC is an executive coach and organizational development consultant with primary areas of focus on global leadership, executive team development, culture change and transition, and other subjects related with organizational effectiveness. Consulting, coaching, and facilitating since 2004, she has worked with C-suite/senior level executives across a wide range of sectors, including consumer products, luxury, hospitality, financial services, pharmaceuticals, and IT. Most recently, she has been representing a Finnish consulting firm in Korea. Prior, she was a senior consultant at a Shanghai-based consulting firm. As a certified coaching supervisor, she serves as faculty for coaching education programs at a Shanghai-based coaching firm and a Seoul-based coaching firm. Alex holds both a PhD and an MA in human and organizational systems from Fielding Graduate University. She also holds an MBA in international management from Thunderbird School of Global Management with the honors of Beta Gamma Sigma and Phi Sigma Iota. Alex can be reached through eyu@email.fielding.edu.

Yimin Wang, EMBA is the founder and CEO of Sense Consulting, a boutique consultancy. He is also the China partner of Lumina Learning, a U.K.-based international selection and development company, which he introduced to China in 2015. Yimin has been in talent development and talent recruitment since 2002. He has extensive experience in the fields of coaching, facilitation, and psychometric assessments. He has worked for the global leading executive search firms Spencer Stuart Associates and Russell Reynolds Associates. Yimin is also an adjunct associate professor at Fudan University, teaching in SKEMA's EMBA program. Yimin can be reached through yiminwang@luminalearning.com.

Made in the USA
Middletown, DE
21 March 2021

35952550R00184